Women on the Frontlines

Convergence of Fact and Fiction in Martha Gellhorn's Works

Women on the Frontlines
Convergence of Fact and Fiction in Martha Gellhorn's Works

Rituparna Moharana
Gurudev Meher

BLACK EAGLE BOOKS
Dublin, USA | Bhubaneswar, India

Black Eagle Books
USA address:
7464 Wisdom Lane
Dublin, OH 43016

India address:
E/312, Trident Galaxy, Kalinga Nagar,
Bhubaneswar-751003, Odisha, India

E-mail: info@blackeaglebooks.org
Website: www.blackeaglebooks.org

First International Edition Published by
Black Eagle Books, 2024

WOMEN ON THE FRONTLINES
Convergence of Fact and Fiction in Martha Gellhorn's Works
by **Rituparna Moharana**
Gurudev Meher

Copyright © Rituparna Moharana, Gurudev Meher

All rights reserved. No part of this publication may be reproduced, stored in a retrieval system, or transmitted, in any form or by any means, electronic, mechanical, photocopying, recording or otherwise without the prior permission of the publisher.

Cover & Interior Design: Ezy's Publication

ISBN- 978-1-64560-539-3 (Paperback)
Library of Congress Control Number: 2024935146

Printed in the United States of America

CONTENTS

Preface 07

Chapter I
Introduction: Martha Gellhorn and Literary Journalism 11

Chapter II
Reporting as a Journalist: Gender and War 42

Chapter III
Frontline Female Reporters: A Study of Gellhorn's
Non-Fictional Writings 87

Chapter IV
Women and War Work: A Study through Gellhorn's
Short Stories and Novellas 121

Chapter V
Conclusion 211

Works Cited 262

Preface

As one of the first female wartime correspondents, Martha Gellhorn witnessed and covered many pivotal moments of World War II and the rest of the twentieth century. While she is mostly remembered as the third wife of fellow journalist and literary giant Ernest Hemingway over her 50-year career as a war correspondent, she experienced and documented many critical episodes of World War II and later conflicts.

Literary journalism is a type of creative nonfiction that is closely tied to journalism in newspapers and magazines. It is sometimes known as immersion journalism since the author must get physically near to the issue and the people he or she studies. It is anticipated that they would provide readers with vital knowledge and insight. Literary journalism, often known as narrative journalism, presents true stories as if they were fiction. Through storytelling, journalism becomes more engaging and personal. Literary journalism focuses on the intersection between fact and fiction and merges literature and journalism. Literary journalism is a type of writing for newspapers and magazines that stands in contrast to factually accurate and objective journalism. It depicts historical events rather than offering answers to factual queries such as who, what, when, and where. It has also avoided the conventional and formulaic pattern of newspaper feature writing. Instead, it chooses to depict everyday life through the lens of realistic fiction. Literary journalism, a genre of nonfiction, combines factual reporting with some of the narrative and stylistic tropes found in fiction. It is also known as narrative reporting. Whereas traditional journalism constructs its arcs around the building block of chronological events, literary journalism constructs its arcs around the building block of a scene, a structure particularly, meticulously constructed by the author and at first glance not necessarily relevant. The distinction is in how the narrative is told: Literary journalists, as opposed to traditional news media, use an engaging writing style to generate memorable tales. When it comes to the use of subjectivity vs objectivity, literary journalism frequently clashes with regular journalism. Literary journalists tread a perilous line between objectivity and subjectivity, telling and showing. Although there are necessary drawbacks to immersion journalism due to inherent subjectivity, well-executed examples of literary or immersion journalism can also serve to add depth to the stories and allow the stories to reach a level of personal connection that traditional journalism cannot. The effect of outstanding immersion journalism is greatly influenced by the author's use of structure, how much of themselves the authors include, and why they include themselves. Though literary journalism is more commonly regarded as a type of creative nonfiction, the phrases literary journalism and creative nonfiction are sometimes used interchangeably. Literary journalists in the United States include John McPhee, Jane Kramer, Mark Singer, and Richard Rhodes. Famous literary journalists from the last century include Tom Wolfe, Jack London, George Orwell, and Stephen

Crane. It evolved from the objective, factual reporting provided in newspapers and periodicals. Furthermore, newspaper feature clichés are avoided in Literary Journalism. Instead, it gives details in the style of realistic fiction that is representative of everyday life.

This book blends journalism and literature to provide readers with the most complete and nuanced picture of modern society. This replaces traditional reporting's objectivity, clear language, and inverted pyramid shape with narrative storytelling and literary methods. This tendency has been labelled as intimate journalism, literary nonfiction, new journalism, and creative nonfiction. Writing in the style of a report, these journalists creatively craft their facts, making the unfamiliar familiar to us, so that it seems more like a work of fiction than reality. It evolves into a type of nonfiction that blends traditional journalism with fictional storytelling approaches. This evolves into a hybrid of two genres, blending fiction and nonfiction. Literature tends to distort the truth, whereas journalism is concerned with reporting the facts. Many people regard journalism as little more than a factual record, assuming it lacks the richness and complexity of literary works. However, Martha Gellhorn's writing illustrates the same while depicting the facts as any novel. Through an examination of some of Gellhorn's works, this book will demonstrate how her writing transcends journalistic conventions and enters the realm of literature.

Gellhorn's journalism is defined by her commitment to accuracy and her function as an objective witness to historical events. During World War II, she reported on war crimes from the front lines in Spain, China and across Europe. Her writing is noted for its direct, unapologetic tone. Gellhorn's art, on the other hand, demonstrates her compassion for the victims of these disasters, as well as her attention to the minute intricacies of human experience that bring these stories to life. Gellhorn's use of language plays a crucial role in lifting her journalism to the level of literature. Her writing appears to be outstanding because of her ability to choose the right words to describe the mood of a scenario. Gellhorn's work has depth and complexity that goes beyond a simple narration of what she observes. She was, indeed, more than accomplished in her own right, having covered practically every major global conflict from the Spanish Civil War to Vietnam. During her career, she covered nearly every major world battle. She gave a human face to the devastation inflicted by conflict. Her interests as a journalist were to expose the lies stated by those in authority that led to wars in the first place, and to be an eyewitness, revealing the tales of ordinary people caught up in violent conflicts.

Gurudev Meher

CHAPTER I

Introduction: Martha Gellhorn and Literary Journalism

This book investigates Martha Gellhorn, a female reporter whose character has developed throughout contemporary American literature and culture. Here, the researcher tries to investigate the beginnings of Martha Ellis Gellhorn's career as a writer and as a journalist by analyzing some of her works from the front-line journalism written during World War I, the Spanish Civil War, World War II and the Vietnam War. For a good deal of time, literary critics and academics have argued over whether or not journalism can be considered literature. Some believe that journalism is fundamentally different from literature as a form of storytelling but others believe that it is a valid art form with the potential to be just as artistic and expressive as any novel or poem. This book investigates how acclaimed journalist and writer as well as war correspondent Martha Gellhorn's work breaks the boundaries between the two genres of writing. This book examines some of Gellhorn's writings in depth, arguing that her journalism is a remarkable example of literature in its own right.

Literary journalism, a form of creative nonfiction, closely related to journalism in both newspapers and magazines, is also known as immersion journalism due to the necessity of the author's physical proximity to the topic and the people he or she investigates. It is hoped that readers will gain knowledge and insight from them. Literary journalism, also referred to as narrative journalism, tells true stories as though they were fiction. Journalism becomes engaging and intimate through storytelling. Literary Journalism primarily deals with the convergence of fact and fiction and combines literature and journalism. As a journalist, Martha Gellhorn covered several conflicts. She details almost all major encounters in her books. As a counter to factually accurate and impartial journalism, literary journalism is a genre of writing for newspapers and magazines. It illustrates moments in time rather than providing answers to factual questions such as who, what, when, or where. Additionally, it has avoided the predictable and cliched newspaper feature writing pattern. Instead, it chooses to depict normal life using the approaches of realistic fiction. Literary journalism, which is known as a type of nonfiction, mixes factual reporting with some of the narrative devices and stylistic devices usually seen in fiction. It is also referred to as narrative reporting. Whereas traditional journalism builds its arcs around the building block of chronological events, literary journalism builds its arcs around the building block of scene, a structure specifically, meticulously built by the author, and at first glance not necessarily significant. The difference is in the way the story is presented: Unlike typical news media, which can be very dry, literary journalists use an engaging writing style to craft memorable stories. Literary journalism often butts heads with traditional journalism when debates arise around the use of subjectivity versus objectivity. Literary journalism, specifically immersion journalism, in which the author is present for the story and may even play a part in it, is a window providing readers with a unique view of the world, a way of life, and a subculture. It is most importantly; however, a mirror, providing readers with experiences that make them reflect upon their own lives and the human condition. Literary journalists walk the dangerous line of objectivity versus subjectivity, of telling versus showing. Although there are necessary detractions to immersion journalism due to inherent subjectivity, the subjectivity that is present in well-executed examples of literary or immersion journalism can also serve to add depth to the stories and allow the stories to reach a level of personal connection that traditional journalism cannot. The effect of great immersion journalism is incredibly shaped by the author's use of structure, how much of themselves the authors include, and for what reasons they include themselves. The author's voice emerges to demonstrate that they are writing. Though it is more frequently considered as a subgenre of creative nonfiction, the terms literary journalism and creative nonfiction are occasionally used interchangeably. Currently, in the United States, John McPhee, Jane Kramer, Mark Singer, and Richard Rhodes are recognised literary journalists. During the last century, renowned literary journalists include Tom Wolfe, Jack London, George Orwell, and Stephen Crane. It has developed from objective, factually graphic reporting found in newspapers and magazines. Additionally, in Literary Journalism, newspaper feature clichés are avoided. Instead, it presents details in the mode of realistic fiction that reflects ordinary life. The book combines journalism with literature to give readers the most comprehensive and complex view of modern society. This substitutes narrative storytelling and literary approaches for traditional reporting's objectivity, plain language, and inverted pyramid form. Intimate journalism, literary nonfiction, new journalism, and creative nonfiction are all terms used to describe this trend.

Writing in the style of reports, these journalists creatively craft their data making the non-familiar things familiar to us so that it sounds more like a work of fiction than fact. It becomes a form of nonfiction that combines traditional journalism with fictional storytelling techniques. This further turns to an amalgamation of two genres combining fiction and nonfiction. Literature tends to distort the truth, whereas journalism focuses on reporting the facts. Many people dismiss journalism as little more than a factual account because they assume it lacks the nuance and complexity of literary works. Martha Gellhorn's writing, however, demonstrates the same while portraying the facts as any novel. This book will further show how Gellhorn's writing goes beyond the conventions of journalism and touches the realm of literature through an analysis of some of her works.

Journalism by Gellhorn is distinguished by her dedication to accuracy and her role as an impartial witness to historical events. She reported on the atrocities of war from the front lines in Spain, China, and across Europe during World War II. Her writing is known for its forthright, unflinching tone. On the other hand, Gellhorn's work reflects her compassion for the victims of these catastrophes and her attention to the minute nuances of human experience that make these stories come to life. Gellhorn's language is a major factor in elevating her journalism to the level of literature. Her writing seems ordinarily extraordinary because of her talent for picking the perfect words to express the mood of a scene. For instance, in her report from the front lines of the Spanish Civil War, she writes in eerily beautiful prose on the bombing of a tiny town.

Another literary quality of Gellhorn's work is the care she takes in developing her characters. Gellhorn infuses in her prose a sense of depth and complexity beyond a simple retelling of what she sees. For instance, in her account of the London Blitz during WWII, she introduces us to a diverse cast of individuals, from regular people attempting to go about their lives despite the carnage to powerful politicians whose decisions will determine the war's outcome. By painting vivid pictures of these people, Gellhorn shows us the humanity at the centre of the struggle.

Gellhorn's journalism is literary because of the depth with which she delves into broader topics and concepts in her writing. For instance, she does not limit herself to reporting on the violence and carnage that characterise the European theatre of battle in her writing. Instead, she analyses the essence of war and its effects on those who are caught up in it through the lens of her own experiences. This strong declaration, which confronts the romanticisation of war so prevalent in literature, is only one manner in which Gellhorn utilises her journalism to explore the bigger questions of her day.

Martha Gellhorn's writing shows that journalism has the potential to be just as literary as any other genre. Gellhorn's journalism, which focuses on the events of her day, rises to the level of literature due to her use of clear and evocative language, attention to character development, and examination of bigger ideas.

American writer Martha Ellis Gellhorn is widely regarded as one of this genre's finest war journalist writers. She spent her 60-year career reporting from combat zones around the world. She was one of the first female war correspondents and one of the finest American reporters of the 20th century, covering a wide range of conflicts across the globe during her 60-year career. Her status as the former wife of celebrated American author Ernest Hemingway brought her widespread recognition. Reporting from Czechoslovakia, England, Burma, Finland, and Hong Kong, Gellhorn covered the rise of Adolf Hitler in 1938. No formal press credentials or approval from her husband Ernest Hemingway could stop Gellhorn from reporting on the Allies' D-Day landing at Normandy in World War II's closing days. The truth is that he undermined her attempts to obtain credentials, but she was undeterred. She hid in the ship's restroom until they were well out to sea, and then pretended to be a stretcher carrier when the medical ship landed. Unexpectedly, on D-Day, June 6, 1994, she was the sole female journalist stationed at Normandy. Following the Allied liberation of the Dachau concentration camp, Gellhorn was one of the first journalists to report on the situation there. In Caroline Morehead's edited book, *Selected Letters of Martha Gellhorn*, she wrote: "Where I want to be, boy, is where it is all blowing up," she wrote to a friend. "She hated not to be a part of history." (112)

In addition to her extensive body of work in journalism, Gellhorn also wrote several novels, novellas, and short tales based on her own experiences, as well as memoirs of the conflicts and journeys she covered. Her first novels included *What Mad Pursuit* (1934) and *The Trouble I've Seen* (1936), are both based on personal experience. *Vietnam: A New Kind of War* (1966) is representative of her brand of hard-hitting journalism in long form; and *Travels with Myself and Another* (1978) is a lively memoir of her journeys.

She put a human face on the suffering caused by war and exposed the lies told by those in power that led to conflicts she reported on during her 60-year career, which spanned from the Spanish Civil War to Vietnam and beyond. After covering the Central American wars in Panama, El Salvador, and Nicaragua in her 80s, she decided she was too old for the kind of work. After a wonderful life that was lived and ended on her terms, Gellhorn, who was practically blind and tormented with ovarian cancer, took a cyanide capsule to take her own life at the age of eighty-nine.

As one of the finest journalists of the 20th century, Martha Gellhorn was honoured with the annual Gellhorn Prize. The Martha Gellhorn Prize for Journalism was established in her memory to distinguish itself from the many other journalism awards given out each year by recognising journalists whose works excel beyond the norm. When Martha Gellhorn showed up in Madrid in 1937, she had a backpack, fifty euros, and an assignment to cover the Spanish Civil War for the magazine *Collier*. In 1940, she married Ernest Hemingway, who was also serving as a correspondent in Spain. They were married for five years, the longest of any of Hemingway's marriages, and Gellhorn was the only wife to leave.

During the D-Day landings in Normandy, Gellhorn stowed away on a medical ship and snuck ashore as a stretcher bearer. Later, she tagged along with British bombers on night bombing flights over Germany and assisted Allied soldiers in the liberation of Dachau. Yet she seemed to have an endless supply of vitality; in 1989, at the ripe old age of 81, she was covering the front lines of the US invasion of Panama. Due to the war, she was unable to accept a position in Bosnia because she was too old and clumsy to fight. One of the most written-about events in history is the start of World War II. There has been a lot written about the turbulent 30s, so it's hard to think of anything that might be said about the era that hasn't already been said. A new perspective emerges, however, when one revisits an early narrative of Hitler's Germany's rise to power. Experiencing the battle through Martha Gellhorn's reportage from 1938 Czechoslovakia is like looking up at the sky from the ashes of Depression-era Europe.

In 1938, Gellhorn was a fearless 30-year-old American war correspondent with a talent for finding conflict zones. After travelling across the Atlantic to report on the Spanish Civil War, Gellhorn found herself in Czechoslovakia just before the Sudetenland's takeover by the Nazis. Gellhorn's writing style is complex and full of atmosphere and emotion. She writes with the kind of realism that could only come from an eyewitness, capturing the day-to-day existence and intricacy of occurrences while putting the impending military assault that the Nazi regime was about to impose on Europe in the foreground.

Gellhorn's approach was to narrate events literally, with the deeper meaning and interpretation concealed beneath the surface. With the heart-breaking opening of *The Face of War*, she describes a pro-democracy parade led by Czechoslovak social democrats in her article on Czechoslovakia for Collier's magazine published on August 6, 1938: Slovak peasants with embroidered blouses, scarlet skirts, and high boots dance past while the Baker's Union marches with enormous breakfast rolls on their heads. They shout, "We want democracy!" (Gellhorn, *The Face of War* 75) and salute the president as they march through the streets, with banners and signs bearing the slogan democracy over and over again. They fear they will have to stage a battle for democracy in the Czech Republic. So, its citizens talk a lot about it. Setting the stage, Gellhorn has caught the spirit of the 1930s and the impending great clash without being blatantly monolithic.

Reading her work, it is clear that the outbreak of World War II and the epoch-defining clash between democracy and totalitarianism, epitomised in the most brutal form by the Nazi regime, was not a sudden event that caught the sleeping masses by surprise; rather, alarm bells were ringing across the continent, and commentators like Gellhorn, who had just witnessed the rise of fascism in Spain, were well aware of the dangers ahead.

Here, the prose gracefully weaves in and out of peaceful-sounding descriptions of the land to be broken by icy allusions to impending conflict: "The area is flat along the border between Silesia and Czechoslovakia, and small hills reminiscent of the Ozarks curl around the farms behind the village of Troppan. Both men and women are bending over in the beet fields and forking the grain" (Gellhorn, *The Face of War* 131).

In addition to the haystacks, there are other objects that, from a distance, appear to be haystacks, but upon closer inspection, are camouflaged pillboxes containing machine guns and anti-tank guns and manned by troops who stand as still as scarecrows among the hard at work peasants. You can see a new fort being constructed as you drive through the pine forests behind Troppan near Haj. It will be broad and flat on the top of the hill, and along the road, you will see dozens of still spikes buried into concrete blocks.

Later, the path leaves the woods behind, crosses a river, and emerges into a level plain. That plain separates Czechoslovakia from Germany, and across the nearest field is a triple row of barbed wire, on huge spools, and beside the river is a black cement and steel gun fortress where, alongside machine guns, and anti-tank guns, there are also the highly perfected anti-aircraft guns that all of Czechoslovakia believes in. The girls are drying their hair after a swim in the river as three soldiers chat with them (Gellhorn, *The Face of War* 91)

Gellhorn's report on the global depression demonstrates her in-depth research into the military build-up and the political and social unrest of the time, and she provides concrete examples of the latter. She addresses the Social Democratic Party, whose membership has declined precipitously since the Great Depression. She records conversations she had with the German minority among the Slavic population of Czechoslovakia who, she writes, had only minimal support for the Nazi party before falling prey to the fascists who used nationalism to scapegoat solves and Jews for the onset of the economic depression. Around two million of the 3.5 million Germans living in Czechoslovakia are Nazis, and they are the reason for all this unrest.

Eighty per cent of Germans up until 1935 were social democrats who believed in democracy and got along fine in Czechoslovakia. Then 500 factories collapsed, putting thousands of people out of work. These were the factories that made glassware, beads, porcelain, jute, sugar, and textiles, all of which were sent over the world (Gellhorn,

The Face of War 77). The Nazis believed they were being intentionally malnourished and held the Czechs responsible for the global downturn. She meets the local Nazi party's leader.

He's a decent guy who reads the newspaper to stay up to date on current events. He claims that the people there are not seeking conflict but rather employment. That no one wants to visit Gottesgabe anymore, she says, is the fault of the Czechs, who have kept relations with Germany so tense as to discourage visitors. Gellhorn shows compassion for all of her interviewees, including the Nazi party man, despite her knowledge of his nefarious political ties. She describes the miserable conditions in which party supporters lived, including children going hungry in huts where they were given only hot bread and water to eat. She comforts two terrified people: the wife of a wine merchant and a Jewish lawyer. They were content, helpful members of the neighbourhood community before the Great Depression. They'd been in the area for many years. However, in only a few short months, their formerly cordial customer base had dried up completely.

Gellhorn records the talk in an unfiltered manner. She claims that since May 1st, not a single customer has made a purchase, and nobody has bothered to engage them in conversation on the street. They may have lost contact with their pals, but they were content in this place even before the war, she explains. We are terrified of the crowd. Many Czechs, Gellhorn reports, had high hopes that they could withstand the German invasion.

However, Gellhorn considered these preparations as woefully inadequate after witnessing the horror of modern battles in Spain.

Gellhorn describes seeing a young lad ride along the street with his horn honking like an air-raid siren. The Central Chunk of Barcelona was destroyed in 95 seconds, and several hundred people were buried alive as a result. As a result of her keen strategic and geopolitical analysis, she has pessimistic expectations for peace in Czechoslovakia. The country is located in a slant over central Europe, beyond which lie the oil fields of Romania, the wheat of the Ukraine, and the Black Sea. If a major power ruled Czechoslovakia, it would have a favourable base from which to launch an attack on Western Europe and the Mediterranean. The tragedy of Czechoslovakia is that it is an obstacle.

While Gellhorn was present on D-Day to see the start of the war, that was just the beginning of her remarkable achievements, she was not allowed to cover the D-Day landings due to the prevailing patriarchal attitudes of the 20th century, despite Gellhorn's track record as a competent and courageous journalist. Not even sneaking onto a medical boat headed for Normandy, locking herself in a toilet, and wading onto the coast with the crew from the water ambulances could deter her from making her way to safety. Her description of the landings was published in *Collier's*, making her the first female correspondent to do so and ironically beating out her then-husband Ernest Hemingway who had been commissioned to report for *Collier's*.

Later, Gellhorn was one of the first journalists to enter the Dachau concentration camp after its liberation. Despite the terrible circumstances, she was determined to cover the conflict for the newspaper. She kept writing about the Arab-Israeli conflict, the Vietnam War, the American invasion of Panama, and other major world events. When she was elderly and ill, she committed suicide in her London apartment.

Shortly after her return to the United States, she met the writer Ernest Hemingway and the two of them embarked on a journey to Europe to cover the Spanish Civil War.

They tied the knot in 1940, but their marriage was doomed from the start when Hemingway began to resent Gellhorn's frequent business trips and when Gellhorn realised that her husband's literary fame overshadowed her independent work as a war correspondent, she began to resent being labelled simply as Hemingway's wife.

In 1945, after their divorce, Gellhorn moved to London. She worked as a journalist far into the 1990s before retiring due to declining eyesight. For a woman to make her mark in the male-dominated field of war reporting as Martha Gellhorn did was ground-breaking. She matured alongside the twentieth-century coverings, practically every major international crisis throughout her 60-year career and forever altering the field of journalism. She always knew from birth that she wanted to be a writer and she wanted to go everywhere, and see everything. She left Brynmawr College in 1930, just after turning 21 years old, to work as a cub reporter for the Albany, New York-based Times Union.

Martha wrote about the police beat, women's clubs, and even the morgue. She was the only female reporter on staff and often had to rely on the sexual approaches of her editor to keep herself comfortable in the raucous, alcoholic atmosphere of the office.

Until the same lecherous editor demanded that she

abandon a story she was passionate about. The story's protagonist, a waitress and smoker who plays bridge in her spare time, loses custody of her kids after getting in trouble with a local judge for the things she does for fun. Martha saw a victim who needed her support from another mother. But that internal monologue and her moral compass were useless to her. That's not how it works in Albany.

Martha wanted to be taken seriously as a writer, but the only articles that sold well during the following four years were about fashion or the woman angle for American magazines she had little respect for. Her conscience, intelligence, and skill finally found a fitting target when she took a job with the Federal Relief Administration collecting the experiences of the collapsing villages and dispossessed families devastated by the Depression. She used what she'd witnessed while writing the critically acclaimed book *The Trouble I've Seen*, which catapulted her to fame as a writer in 1936.

Later, in a Key West Bar, she happened to meet her literary idol, Ernest Hemingway. She was determined to join him in Madrid to cover the Spanish Civil War after learning of his impending trip there. A few months later, in the spring of 1937, she crossed the border from France into Spain on her own, carrying just a knapsack, $50 in cash, and a fake letter of credentials she'd gotten from a friend who worked in publishing in New York.

The siege of Madrid had reached its fifth month. There, as the stench of explosives filled the air, she began to record what she had witnessed: boys in shambles in makeshift hospitals, women waiting in bread lines, children making their way to school through bloody trails, and citizens carrying on with their lives bravely as their city crumbled around them. She was firm in her belief that if you loved something deeply enough, you could convince people of its importance simply by writing plainly and from the heart.

Collier's magazine's publication of Martha's work during her time in Spain not only established her as a writer but also revolutionised coverage of war. As the world descended into World War II, Martha turned her attention away from the typical topics of war tactics, generals, arsenals, and weaponry and towards the people.

She was Hemingway's third wife, and she eventually became his enemy due to his frustration with her drive. After Martha consistently put her career ahead of her husband's, Hemingway retaliated in 1944 by offering his by-line to *Collier's* as senior correspondent for D-Day, thus replacing Martha on the masthead.

Several people worked against Martha's resolve, not simply Hemingway. Only 178 out of the thousands of reporters covering the battle from around the world were female, and they were all denied entry to the front lines because the military did not recognise their credentials. Martha used her wits and grit to sneak aboard the first hospital barge to reach Omaha Beach. She helped bring injured people back to the ship by serving as a stretcher carrier onshore. Since her husband didn't show up to Normandy, she ended up getting first dibs and being the only female present.

After being jailed and having her documents revoked, Martha discarded her passport and joined a mobile regiment, travelling in jeeps and sleeping in fields. She lied, cajoled, and chatted quickly when she got into difficulty, making up boyfriends she had to visit for the final time. When American troops freed Dachau in May of 1945, she was there, among the first reporters. What she saw there, she would later argue, shattered a fundamental part of her, robbing her of optimism and faith in humanity. The world may have been a difficult one to observe, but Martha never closed her eyes. Explaining all the sufferings women face in war field reporting, Elizalde wrote in the article "Enough with All That Objectivity Shit":

… here go again why do women always have to look for orphanages? She wanted to do a book on Vietnam that would mirror the structure of The Trouble I've seen, but she could not get a visa back into the country, possibly because she was 'too emotional', angry and contentious. This is how women's lib was born. (Elizalde)

Martha always preferred that people remember her for the work she did and not as a symbol for feminists. Today's leading women share these sentiments, including Christiane Amanpour, Marie Colvin, Jacky Rowland, and Maggie O'Kane. Amanpour and her colleagues were very adamant in a 2012 Vanity Fair profile that they would be recognised as only reporters, not women reporters. These journalists have demonstrated vast stores of Martha's courage and grace under fire, and they all have war stories to back it up, from Pakistan to Afghanistan to Kosovo to Sarajevo. It's a good thing, too, because they still have a long way to go before females can expect equality in what is still predominantly a male-dominated field, 70 years after she broke new ground. While it's difficult to generalise about how women and men perceive war, it's certainly not a coincidence that Amanpour and her colleagues worship Martha's undeniable contribution to journalism and essentially do what she did first by looking past the bombs and shell, litter, to see the people. It's also not a coincidence that the handful of women who cover war today use strategies Martha helped develop.

For example, former reporter of *the Guardian* Maggie O'Kane freely admits to being armed with conveniently deployed lies and fake, embarrassingly sexual letters to pass through airport security. Martha persisted in her writing until her eyes gave up and she had to stop transporting herself to regions of war and violence. For the *Daily Telegraph's* thriller review in 1990, she sneaked herself into Panama under the guise of her partner.

In late 1989, when news of an American invasion of Belize broke, she was snorkelling alone there. She later recruited a friend who was an editor to write a fake letter on her behalf, claiming that she was in the country as a special correspondent. It was an identical form letter to the one she had pleaded with a friend to write her 50 years earlier to cross into Spain. Even though Martha was 81 years old at the time, she heard the tale.

A group of several dozen people gathered on a windy afternoon earlier this month in London, outside of 72 Cadogan Square, a large red-brick townhouse not far from Sloane Square. War correspondent and author Martha Gellhorn spent the final twenty-eight years of her life in a penthouse and attic apartment that could be viewed by stooping over or walking into the street. Most of the young chaps in attendance were publishers and authors whom Gellhorn had met and been friends with in London throughout the 1980s.

They went to see a blue plaque dedicated to Gellhorn unveiled.

Blue plaques honouring the lives of London's famous

dead have been installed at their former residences since 1866. Number 948 belonged to Gellhorn. Somebody has fastened a little velvet curtain to the wall. She spent fifty years covering conflicts and died at her apartment in 1998. As a makeshift stage was being prepared for the ceremony, the loudspeakers erupted with an unexpectedly dramatic bang. The audience crouched instinctively as shots rang out. At over eighty years old, Roosevelt and Gellhorn got close after staying up talking and smoking until 2 in the morning at a dinner party in Kentish Town. Claiming that the agony and the sacrifice of the war had brought men and women closer together, Margaret contends:

...the situation changed forever as a result of the First World War. In August 1914 Emmeline Pankhurst sensibly announced that the campaign for the vote was suspended. Christabel - whose sojourn in France seemed to have atrophied her ability to think clearly - remarked melodramatically that 'a man-made civilization, hideous and cruel in time of peace, is to be destroyed? The war, she continued, was 'God's vengeance upon the people who held women in subjection'...remarked in The Suffragette Movement that men and woman had been drawn closer together by the suffering and sacrifice of the war. Awed and humbled by the great catastrophe, and by the huge economic problems it had thrown into naked prominence, the women of the suffrage movement had learnt that social regeneration is a long and mighty work. In 1918, women over the age of 30 were given the vote; and in March 1928, under a Conservative government, they finally won it on equal terms with men. (qtd. in Knight)

The year of Gellhorn's birth is 1908, and St. Louis, Missouri, is the place of her birth. At the age of twenty-one, she came to Paris in pursuit of a career as a novelist, but it was during the Great Depression that she discovered her voice as a journalist, reporting on the plight of the textile workers for the Federal Emergency Relief Association. When she befriended Eleanor Roosevelt, she was invited to stay in the White House for a period.

After he received criticism on a BBC show for his honest reporting on the Vietnam War, Gellhorn sent him a postcard. The message read, "Do not ever let the bastards get you down. Let's get together and enjoy a beverage" (qtd. in Knight) as Pilger's response indicated. "My promise to never again bring up Ernest Hemingway was broken during many unforgettable hours spent here with good friends and a bottle of the famed Grouse whiskey. True, we did that rather frequently" (qtd. in Knight).

After her death in 1999, the Martha Gellhorn Prize for Journalism was established to honour journalists whose work exposed official pushes as Gellhorn termed them.

According to Pilger, never again would a journalist be as widely respected as Martha Gellhorn. Despite Gellhorn's professional toughness, many of the speakers recalled her kindness toward others, her neat attic, and her eclectic group of acquaintances. Pilger remembered an incident where he and Gellhorn were kicked out of Selfridges because Gellhorn was smoking and how she would loudly criticise movie trailers.

John Hatt, a travel writer and publisher, recalled visiting Cuba in the sixties with Martha Gellhorn, where he heard a senior community official wax poetic over the country's magnificent Billboards. Hatt remarked that

Martha gave him a blocking about Cuban cuisine when he stopped, making her appear furious. Hatt inquired of Gellhorn after their time in Turkey as to whether or not she had made an effort to study the local tongue.

During the 1990s, as Gellhorn's eyesight was deteriorating, John Simpson, the BBC's world affairs editor, became friends with her after reporting on the first Gulf War. He learned of Gellhorn's experience at the inauguration ball for President John F. Kennedy. By herself and feeling out of place, Gellhorn suddenly became aware of the president and his entourage approaching.

There was Kennedy himself coming towards her with all the hangers-on and the freaks and the creeps, Simpson said. And, as he walks up to her, and she said, oh, fuck. He's going to make me secretary of state. It was not that Kennedy had heard that Gellhorn used to live in the White House and might know of a way to sneak out from time to time. Gellhorn told the President about a small gate at the back of the property. "There's only one guy in charge of it, (qtd. in Knight) she said. "Roosevelt used to just give him money all the time. She was very mysterious, I think, socially", Glendinning said. "There were hinterlands" beyond her hinterlands (qtd. in Knight):

Like H.G. Wells, Leonard Bernstein, and the twenties London social beauty Lady Diana Cooper, Gellhorn liked to see friends alone, wrote letters often, cooked rarely, and did not care about clothes. One of our favourite phrases was, 'I hate the kitchen of life,' Glendinning said. "We did not usually eat in the flat, I have to say. But, when we did, her signature dish was opening two tins, one of tuna and one sweet corn, and mixing them both together. And it was peculiarly disgusting." Over whiskey and cigarettes,

Gellhorn's young chaps found themselves telling her things that they had not told anybody else. (qtd. in Knight)

Gellhorn took a cyanide tablet at the age of 89. As well as losing her eyesight, she also had cancer of the liver and ovaries. Gellhorn was discovered by Glendinning and her husband on Valentine's Eve. She recalled that they had gotten up, walked around to where they were standing, and then stood in the square, staring up at the skyscraper in the darkness. She did it precisely and thoughtfully, with all the windows open and the lights on high. A few years ago, during a book festival in Toronto, Glendinning decided to reflect on the Gellhorn of back then. She was delicate and nervous.

She and Glendinning had to get down on the floor and scramble around for her missing earring. However, Gellhorn seemed completely different while performing. She confidently discussed the massive scale of the international armaments trade without using any notes. So, she was a real trooper and pro, Glendinning concluded. "Martha was not a perfect person by any stretch of the imagination. Though she was the moral compass for many of us" (Knight). After everyone had finished speaking, Simpson did a Lord on the velvet curtain to reveal Gellhorn's plaque and the young men posed for pictures. There were no hiccups. During her lifetime (1908-1998), war correspondent and author Martha Gellhorn called this building home.

The novel *A Stricken Field* by Martha Gellhorn, published in 1940, was doomed to be ignored. It's already down because of the following reasons:

1) It's an unpopular tale that reveals uncomfortable truths about our nation's history.

2) The work fell prey to the trend away from sentimentality in literature (nearly always associated with books written by women).

3) Its creator has been unfairly overshadowed by Ernest Hemingway's stature.

Many of the women authors were also treated less favourably than their male counterparts when compared to the literary canon. Nevertheless, we thought that this novel deserved and needed to be remembered the most of all the novels we read. This story is an emotional knockout because it so vividly depicts the failure of Western countries to protect the most helpless members of our society, namely stateless and destitute refugees.

When *A Stricken Field* came out in 1940, which is set during the Czechoslovak refugee crisis of 1938 after the Munich Pact handed the country over to Nazi Germany, served as a powerful warning about the magnitude of the war's humanitarian crisis, which countries like Britain, France, and the United States had proven they were unwilling to facilitate.

At the Evian Conference in July 1938, before the Munich Pact in September 1938, 31 of the 32 countries declined to increase their inadequate refugee quotas, helping to prepare the stage for the Holocaust. Gellhorn's story remains relevant now as a result of the refugee crisis in Europe and along the southern border of the United States. Gellhorn wrote the novel in her new home with Ernest Hemingway in Cuba in 1939; while she wrote, he was typing away in another part of the house on *For Whom the Bell Tolls*, even though the number of refugees worldwide is at its highest point since World War II. The United States has reduced its refugee ceiling to 18,000, down from 85,000 in 2016.

Gellhorn had been profoundly affected by her experiences in Spain during the civil war, but she had felt too raw to write about them at the time of their meeting of course not wanting to compete directly with Hemingway may also have had something to do with it. Though dedicated to Hemingway and featuring prose that, at times, echoes his famously spare style, *A Stricken Field* owes all credit for its profound impact to Gellhorn herself, not Hemingway. When we read the book now, we could experience the same helplessness that Mary had when she first read it. All she can do is take the stories of the refugees she helps out of Prague and tell them. Journalistic history is the subject of this book.

Gellhorn's experience in the Czech Republic parallels that of Mary Douglas. In 1938, she made two trips there to report on the situation, writing a total of two articles for coal miners' magazines. However, she believed that they had not adequately depicted the human situation that she had seen. Gellhorn understood very well that when refugees are reduced to abstract numbers, or worse, stereotypical undesirables, it is much easier for people to close their doors and hearts.

About 10,000 political and Jewish refugees were brought back to Nazi Germany and Austria to face their inevitable deaths, and only fiction had the power to make their plights real. Mary didn't care that an unpronounceable Czech manufacturing town had become German, as Gellhorn puts it; instead, she was concerned about the workers who had lost their jobs and were now wandering the roads with their oversized bags, looking for work that no longer existed behind an unreasonable line of barbed wire.

Gellhorn brings us face-to-face with those on the move, including men who have had to leave their wives, lovers who must part, and children who have been taken from their mothers. She portrays the hopelessness and panic that often lead to suicide in these people's eyes. Until the narrative takes a surprising and powerful turn, we see these people through Mary's eyes as she gets to know a particular immigrant. Mary tags along as Rita takes her on a nightmare tour of the factories housing the refugees visits her hotel, and spends time there while we remain at the base. Several new magazines directed at women appeared in the 1920s, though their titles - Woman and Home, Good Housekeeping signal the limited expectations of their audience. But there were also dissenting voices, with a more radical take on women's position, in Time and Tide, which was launched in 1920, its distinguished contributors including Virginia Woolf, Rebecca West, and Rose Macaulay. This magazine argued that women should act, independently, to put pressure on all the political parties to tackle women's concerns, and it raised a whole range of women's issues, including the position of unmarried mothers and of widows, and the guardianship of children. Martha asked the readers to put themselves in Mary or Rita's position to realise how crazily they crave peace and stability. This switch makes *A Stricken Field* an experimental novel, evocative of the alternating viewpoints in Mrs. Dalloway by Virginia Woolf. Mary is our entry into this world, but the real story is what it's like to be one of those people known to the rest of the world only as a number, and Gellhorn thought it would be inadequate to tell the story only from an outsider's perspective as Hemmingway does in *For Whom the Bell Tolls*. This dual viewpoint helps the reader to feel both the anguish of the pursued and the helplessness of the American reporter, who knows she can do little to alter Rita's or anyone else's destinies. Mary asks, "What good did it do?" (Gellhorn, *A Stricken Field* 77) as Rita urges her to report on the atrocities, she has witnessed in order to help change public opinion. Gellhorn's heart-string-pulling is never gratuitous; she writes, "It was extremely easy to make people detest, but it was almost impossible to make them help" (Gellhorn *A Stricken Field* 77). All we have to do is put ourselves in Mary or Rita's shoes to understand that their desire for quiet and stability is also our own most fundamental need.

Mary witnesses a group of immigrants kneeling and squatting on the mattresses, bowed together over a map. When Mary pays a visit to Rita and Peter's makeshift home, we observe a small flat with slanted furnishings but filled with their love for each other, even though it looks like they could be planning a vacation, but in reality, they are looking for a country, any country that might take them in. Mary is encouraged by the brief vision of their future selves before they are taken away from them, declaring, "We will prevail in the end" because "no one has yet discovered how to corrupt decent souls or convert love into meaningless slogans" (Gellhorn, *A Stricken Field* 136). Although she has doubts, she finally believes that love will triumph over hatred. You can label that attitude as romantic if you choose, but Mary also demonstrates an urge to connect with others beyond the basis of survival, an attitude that undoubtedly helped bring down the fascism of that time.

Manuscripts, letters, notebooks, professional files, financial records, photographs, audio recordings, and videos are all part of the Martha Gellhorn archive. Manuscripts in the collection include book-length works, short stories, articles, and other works. Novels and other fiction include *Peace on Earth* (unpublished, 1937); *The Wine of Astonishment* (Scribner, 1948), and *Point of No Return* (New American Library, 1989), an unfinished novel set in Mexico (1952-1966); *Two by Two* (Simon and Schuster, 1958); *On Balance*, an unfinished novel set in Africa (1963-1964); *Pretty Tales for Tired People* (Simon and Schuster, 1965); an unfinished novel about Diana Jamieson (1973- 1975); *The Weather in Africa* (Penguin, 1978; Dodd, 1980); *Ways and Means*, an unfinished novel set in the Caribbean; *Package Tons*, a novella; and various short stories and fragments. Non-fiction includes *The Face of War* (Simon and Schuster, 1959; revised edition, Atlantic Monthly Press, 1986); *Travels with Myself and Another* (Penguin, 1978; Dodd, 1979); *The View from the Ground* (Atlantic Monthly Press, 1986); and numerous articles for various periodicals, some unpublished.

Correspondence in the collection includes both personal and professional letters dating from 1914 to 1997. Included here are letters to and from Ernest Hemingway (dated 1932-1947); some are copies. Also present are numerous letters received from various unemployed people, received while working on *The Trouble I've Seen*; four notes exchanged with Lauren Bacall at a meeting of the U.N. Security Council (May 1965); several letters from readers; and many letters to and from her parents. Notable correspondents include H.G. Wells, Eleanor Roosevelt, Nelson Algren, Leonard Bernstein, Adlai Stevenson, Patrick Hemingway, Anthony Eden, Bernard Berenson, Irwin Shaw, Jane Bowles, J. W. Fulbright, Ernest Gruening, George Kennan, Robert Graves, Moshe Dayan, Ward Just, Eugene J. McCarthy, Jules Dassin, George S. McGovern, Stuart Symington, and Jacqueline Kennedy Onassis. Journals and diaries in the collection are extensive.

Included are Gellhorn's diary notes from Mexico (June 1931); notes on England (ca. 1933); notes on the Spanish Civil War (1937-1938); her diary of a trip from France to Spain (1937); notes on World War II (1937-1945); notes on Berlin, used as the basis for an article for Collier's (1945); notes on Poland, used as the basis for an article for the Atlantic Monthly (1960-1961); notes on Palestinian refugees (1961); diary notes on Spain (1961); notes on Germany, used as the basis for an article for the Atlantic Monthly (1962); notebooks on Africa (1962); notes on Uganda, used as the basis for an article for the Saturday Evening Post (1964); notebooks on Paris (1969); a journal (1969-1970); notes and notebooks on Israel (1971), the Arab-Israeli War, and the Six Day War; a diary for Paul Theroux regarding a trip by Gellhorn to Cuba; notes on sleep disturbances in torture survivors; notes on a lawsuit by Gellhorn against Hamilton (1993-1994); and other notes on various subjects (1929-1954).

Printed material in the collection includes material regarding the Spanish Civil War, including many articles and clippings; published wartime articles by Gellhorn from various periodicals (1936-1942) Vietnam: A New Kind of War (1966) and Aspects of the Arab-Israeli War, pamphlets with text by Gellhorn, reprinted from her original articles for the Manchester Guardian, with clippings of the articles; a program for a dinner to celebrate the bicentenary of the prohibition of slavery in Great Britain (1972); and various published articles by Gellhorn for *The Guardian, The New York Times, Collier's, Atlantic Monthly,*

The Saturday Evening Post, The New Republic, Harper's Weekly, The Observer, and the St. Louis Post Dispatch.

Professional material in the collection includes various passports, press passes, and visas; address books and engagement books (1960-1961); desk diaries (1965-1967); copy of a press release for a press conference in England (1967); appointment books (1970- 1972); date books (1973-1986, 1988-1992); and an inaugural committee press kit (1977).

Financial material in the collection includes stock certificates for Associated Magazine Contributors (1946); a notebook regarding Gellhorn's finances (1963-1964); check books with stubs and financial statements (1963-1964); bills, receipts, and cancelled checks (1963-1964); various records and tax data (1962-1967); tax records, banking records, and receipts (1968-1994); and royalty records. Photographs in the collection include various images of Gellhorn (colour and black and white), as well as her friends and family; these date from 1940 to 1991.

Other photos include several black and white prints and negatives regarding Vietnam, as well as an autographed photo of Harry S. Truman, two photos of refugees from the Spanish Civil War, photographs of Ernest Hemingway, and photos of China, Germany, Italy, and other locations.

Audio recordings in the collection include a reel-to-reel recording of Gellhorn at the Mugar Memorial Library dedication dinner (1966); cassette tapes of letters to Daniel Ellsberg from Israel (1970s); and cassette tapes of an oral history interview with Gellhorn, transcript included (1980).

The collected Video recordings include VHS cassettes of interviews with Gellhorn conducted by the BBC in 1991 and ca. 1995. Other items in the collection include Gellhorn's exam books from Bryn Mawr; a certificate of appreciation from the U.S. War Department (1947); a notebook kept by VellzIlling (a German), with photos; papers regarding safaris and the building of Gellhorn's home in Kenya; essays by African children from the Longonot Village School in Kenya, written for an essay contest sponsored by Gellhorn (1972); a scrapbook with various items on Gellhorn's career; and research material on Vietnam, Spain, Cuba, and Latin America.

In the opening chapter titled "Introduction", I have introduced the risk-taking war reporter, Martha Gellhorn who was a well-known and dependable American journalist, war correspondent, novelist and travel writer. Throughout her writing career, she used her pen to highlight nearly every combat zone of different wars that occurred in her era. Not giving much importance to the chronology of the war, the chapter explains how she was able to get herself closer to the locations affected by the conflict and lift the blinds so that everyone might see the terrifying and severely damaging tactics used in battle. She became the most genuine, lovable and widely read war journalist worldwide as a result of her brave and candid journalism.

The second chapter titled "Reporting as a Journalist: Gender and War" explains how, in former times, women journalists were prohibited from covering wars on the front lines because of their gender. In those days, reporting from the front lines of battle was only permitted for males. It also explains why she was trusted and well-liked by the public: although she was among the most reputable national journalists, she never undervalued the problems that the average person faced and the failings of the ruling classes, which were thriving throughout her era. In addition, she declined to use her pen's ink to curry favour with important figures and prominent politicians. She never compromised her morals and conducted herself as a trustworthy journalist when writing her articles so that the oppressed and underprivileged may be heard by the powerful. She was well aware of the responsibilities of journalists and believed that their job served as a clear mirror in which society and the government could observe all of their attitudes and working methods. She believed that journalism should be free of any blemishes.

The third chapter of this book is titled "Frontline Female Reporters: A Study of Gellhorn's Non-Fictional Writings" which discusses Martha Gellhorn's firsthand account of War field reporting in her non-fictional works such as *The View from the Ground*, *The Face of War* and *Travels with Myself and Another*. It explains how female war reporters face risks on the frontlines that their male counterparts do not. It also highlights the manners in which they resist being reduced to stereotypes. This chapter focuses on the frontline female reporters along with Gellhorn's personal experiences of covering armed conflicts and the challenges they encounter on the job.

The fourth chapter titled "Women and War Work: A Study through Gellhorn's Short Stories and Novellas" examines Gellhorn's short tales and novels such as *What Mad Pursuit, A Stricken Field, The Heart of Another, Liana,* and *The Wine of Astonishment* as well as women and their war works. The idea of the female war correspondent as a woman working in a man's world and having an adventurous life is arguably founded in the Gellhorn legend, and it is today promoted by the media and Hollywood. Journalism was not much simpler for the first female war correspondents who frequently had to resort to extraordinary tactics to get access to the frontlines. Along with Martha, there were a few more female journalists who led the way in live conflict reporting on the battlefield.

In the last chapter it is concluded that in her long 60-year career in journalism, Gellhorn's unique brand of nerve was as uncommon as radium. She didn't seem to be suppressed by fear; instead, it seemed to make her more courageous in the face of injustice. Her voice was a blade, sharpened by wrath and used to serve others. Women war journalists have gone a long way from Bourke-White and Irwin breaking down obstacles that males put in their way to Christiane Amanpour, the highest-paid foreign correspondent on television news. However, this does not suggest that women reporters have become indifferent to war with progress and advancement. There will always be battles to be won in the newsroom, on the military range, and in the media itself. Chauvinistic tendencies and strong, independent women's need to report on the world as they see it remain constant over time. Women war correspondents of the future will have to push just as many doors open as the women of the past. But by nature, they have it in them. There is a drive, a certainty in conviction, that women war correspondents have amongst them and they won't stop until they prove it to the world.

CHAPTER II

Reporting as a Journalist: Gender and War

When Martha was younger, she looked to journalism as a beacon of hope and believed in the inherent goodness of man and the march of progress. People would immediately demand rescue efforts, punishment for wrongdoers, and protection for the innocent if they were convinced that truth, dishonour and justice would be upheld. Thus, in *The Face of War*, the writer contends: "When I was young, I believed in the perfectibility of man, and in progress and thought of journalism as a guiding light. If people were told the truth, if dishonour and justice were clearly shown, to them, they would at once demand the saving action, punishment of wrong-doers, and care for the innocent (Gellhorn 79)."

Martha also writes on the conflicting emotions created by demonstrations of these weapons' destruction in her 1959 anthology *The Face of War*: "They were apprehensive... But their looks and voices were pained as they spoke of rescuing our lads and bringing them home and it was good the war was finished" (Gellhorn 189). She further adds, that she lost some of her idealism after WWII, but that she still believes telling the stories of the tragedies of war might prevent further atrocities. She spent the better part of her life reporting on conflicts like the Vietnam War, the Arab-Israeli War, the Civil Wars in Central America, and the US Invasion of Panama. The way war is portrayed in media has implications for everyone. The position of the war recorder has a substantial impact on the portrayal; however, this is rarely considered in the vast field of literature on war representation.

As a woman, Gellhorn's gender puts a limit on some of her options for how to position herself about the fighting, but it was not the only one. It was intriguing to follow her as she stowed away on dynamite Latin seeping over imaginary oceans, flew in vintage planes and deadly fighter jets, mucked in and stood out, and generally avoided direct battle. Her writing moves in a similar range, from detached observation to intense immersion to detached distancing, as if seen through a camera. Martha has always had a burning urge to see the globe, live every moment fully, and document her adventures through writing. She wanted to be seen seriously as a writer. Her fears, intelligence, and skill became obvious or the target when she took a job with the government relief administration, documenting reports of disintegrating villages and getting rid of simply the family that was most impacted by the depression. She used what she witnessed to become a literary sensation in 1936 with her book *The Trouble I Have Seen*. She travelled from France to Spain on her own with a small backpack, a falsified document verifying her qualifications, a desire to beg from an editor friend in Newark, and a rolled and hidden 50 dollars in her boot.

Martha Gellhorn never really believed in the neutral eye. As she famously remarked during the Spanish Civil War when she and Hemingway wrote only about the atrocities committed by the Nationalists, and never about those carried out by the Republicans: "Only fools resorted to all that objectivity shit" (Moorehead, *Gellhorn: A Twentieth Century Life* 64).

Gellhorn never found writing easy. To a remarkable extent, given their taut, polished, confidant final form, she laboured and agonized over her articles, writing and rewriting them dozens of times, complaining to friends of blocks and setbacks. As she grew older, she was worried that her writing was pedestrian and unadventurous and that younger writers, such as John Updike and Saul Bellow, were bringing forth tigers out of their cocoons. In the dozens of her notebooks held in the Howard Gotlieb Archival Research Centre at Boston University, there are endless entries about her hopes and uncertainties, about characters and plots, and herself as a writer. She never thinks about herself. Even when helpless to change the world, she observes, people have no right to the comfort of ignorance: it was the duty of writers, at whatever personal cost, to break through that ignorance. (Moorehead, *Gellhorn: A Twentieth Century Life* 62)

For Gellhorn, to fail as a writer was to fail at life, to be adrift in an uncertain and hostile world with nothing to hold on to. When she had what she called lockjaw of the brain, when she sat at her typewriter for weeks and was unable to write, or when she thought that what she had written was worthless, she despaired: not just of herself as a writer, but Mauro and probably writer, but as a friend, a human being. She lost her eye, ear, and nerve, and probably was no longer a writer, she told a friend in the early 1980s in one form or another, again and again. She talked of the writing muscle, which had to be kept strong and well exercised, and the need for total solitude and compulsion and discipline. Style, she told a friend, was important because the function of writing is to snare and to lure, never to bore, and to give out information in the form of pleasure and excitement. More than many writers, she believed not in the determining power of thought, but in action: people were what they did, not what they thought (Moorehead, *Gellhorn: A Twentieth Century Life* 62).

Right up until the end of her life, despite ill health and increasingly bad eyesight, Gellhorn kept travelling and writing. Being seventy or even eighty never seemed to her a reason to give up war reporting, and when in 1982 she was cast down, she could find no paper prepared to send her to report the Israeli invasion of Lebanon. Early in 1994, soon after her eighty-fifth birthday, she decided that she wanted to write about street children in Brazil. She was by now slightly deaf, almost blind in one eye and suffered from back problems. For weeks she travelled around, interviewing people, visiting courts and prisons, and asking questions. Though she could barely see the typewriter keys and had trouble reading her notes, she persevered. The article took her many weeks and many drafts and was turned down by *Granta*, but then published in the London Review of Books: "'This,' she told a friend, 'is a historical document ... It is my last and worst article!'" (Shute)

Gellhorn wrote several novels and a great many short stories and novellas.

Often, they were re-tellings, in barely concealed form, of her own experiences or those of her friends: what stands out in her diaries and notebooks is how little she imagined, how much she observed, and then used as fiction. Her characters do not lack subtlety, but it was what they did and not what they thought that interested her. In the sense that she lacked the transforming magic of a true novelist, she was not a great writer of fiction. But as the collections of her journalism prove, she was a superb reporter, and at her best occupied that delicate line where fact ends and fiction begins. As the writer Gerald Rosen once remarked, "She had a cold eye and a warm heart" (CGA Winter 2016 Magazine)

She started documenting the scenes she witnessed, including boys with broken bodies being treated in makeshift hospitals, women waiting for food, children making their way to school amid blood trails, and inhabitants bravely keeping on with their lives while their city fell apart. She was confident from the outset that anyone who cared enough about an issue could persuade others of the necessity of addressing it, and so she wrote clearly and passionately. Journalist Martha's voice and style were defined by *Collier's* magazine's coverage of her time in Spain which also had a profound impact on how conflict was covered in the publication. Martha married Hemingway and became his third wife but gradually this marriage turned tumultuous when Hemingway raised questions about Martha working as a frontline journalist, "why should I be a footnote to somebody else's life?"(Atlas, "Martha Gellhorn: War Correspondent, and Memoirist") Instead of focusing on the usual issues of war, practice, generals, arsenals, and artillery, Martha focused on the people, and she should have continued to do so for the next several years, while nations teetered on the brink of World War II. In 1944, Hemingway's marriage to Martha ended when he offered his by-line to *Collier's* as a senior correspondent for D-Day, thus replacing Martha on the masthead.

Martha was not merely inspired by Hemingway when it came to her tenacity. The military refused to authorise women, therefore only 178 of the thousands of reporters covering the fight abroad were able to enter the front lines. Martha used her wits and grit to escape on the first medical barge to reach Omaha Beach. She volunteered to help bring the deceased back to the ship by carrying stretchers ashore. She was the only lady in sight and ended up saving her husband, who had perished before reaching the beaches of Normandy. Martha was arrested and deported, but she managed to join a mobile unit by using her charisma to get rides in jeeps and bunk in fields with the other members. One of the first journalists on the scene as American soldiers freed Dachau in May 1945, she subsequently said that the experience shattered something fundamental in her, taking with it her idealism and hope for humanity. Even though Martha found it more challenging to keep her eyes open, she continued to do so.

Gellhorn's first article, on the courage of ordinary civilians caught up in the conflict, marked her first step into war journalism. *Collier* loved it and put her name on their masthead; other articles followed and she began to write for *The New Yorker* as well. Soon, it was clear that she was writing a good deal better than many of the seasoned war reporters in Spain, and in many ways better than Hemingway, whose prose often felt contrived and self-centred: "I like writing, she noted in her diary. In the end, it is the only thing which does not bore or dismay me, or fill me with doubt. It is the only thing I know absolutely and irrevocably to be good in itself, no matter what the result" (Moorehead, *Selected Letters of Martha Gellhorn* 317).

Martha's only goal was to do her job; she had no interest in becoming a symbol of feminism. Today's leading female journalists share this view, including Christiane Amanpour, Marie Colvin, Jacky Roland, and Maggie O'Kane. Amanpour and her colleagues have fought to be recognised as reporters, not women reporters and they have stories of hardship to prove it. These journalists have shown what it means to keep up Martha amounts courage and grace in places like Pakistan, Afghanistan, Kosovo, and Sarajevo. It's a good thing, too, because they confront many of the same hurdles she had - 70 years after she blazed the way – in a world that is still dominated by men. Although it may be a stretch to say that women have a different perspective on war than men, it's not a coincidence that Amanpour and her fellow journalists hold Martha in such high esteem and continue to do what she pioneered by seeing past the bombs and shell litter to locate people. It's therefore not shocking that the few women who cover conflict today use tactics that Martha first developed. As a war correspondent, Martha Gellhorn often broke rules set by the government, the armed forces, and even common sense in her pursuit of a good story. Martha was all set on covering D-Day and wasn't about to let something as trivial as the presence of American troops stand in her way. After being denied press credentials, she hid in the bathroom of a hospital ship that had anchored off Omaha Beach on June 7, 1944. Martha awoke with the sun to see a seascape crowded with ships, the biggest maritime traffic bottleneck in history. The scale and grandeur of it made it seem more like a natural phenomenon than a man-built structure. Soon after, she waded ashore to help the ship's crew bring in injured soldiers (Hartley, "Martha Gellhorn: Eyewitness to War").

In a century that was defined by conflict, Martha Gellhorn found her calling. In the broad confusion of war, she wrote, she finally discovered her private disorderly place in the universe. From the Spanish Civil War through the invasion of Panama in 1981, she was a journalist covering wars. World War II, however, would prove to be her defining fight, and Martha was among the war's outstanding chroniclers. From the political manoeuvring in Czechoslovakia in 1939 through the Nuremberg trials, she wrote about it all.

Without complaining, Gellhorn enjoyed the anarchy of war and the deprivations it imposed. In March of 1944, when Gellhorn had already sent numerous articles from the front to various periodicals, the first of these appeared. Among all female correspondents, she is known not only for her writing but also for her attractive looks. "Blonde, tall, and dashing, she comes dangerously close to embodying Hollywood's vision of a major-league female reporter should be," (qtd. in Moorehead, *Gellhorn: A Twentieth Century Life*) the editors wrote.

After breaking up with Bertrand de Jouvenel, she moved to the United States and began working for the Federal Emergency Relief Administration, reporting on the conditions in North Carolina and New England. She interviewed mill workers, sharecroppers, teachers, and doctors while trudging through muddy roads in her Parisian shoes, and she saw malnourished children and entire families rendered powerless by diseases like syphilis. There is some relevance to the term 'American stock' if the phrase has any sense at all. They have strong judgement and a decent sense of humour, and they are generous and dependable.

John Pilger, a journalist, said of Gellhorn, "She would have nothing to do with the kind of bogus objectivity that media schools love" (Shute). Gellhorn was angered by the tragedies she witnessed and the government's failure to alleviate the suffering. This anger drove her war journalism for decades and helped her develop a keen, almost frigid eye. Her reports are sharply drawn and moving portraits of people who were buckling, swinging free of all hope and yet too proud to go on relief. She admired their grit and wept for them, and shook with rage. All of this comes through in the writing, which was being sent by Hopkins, without Gellhorn's knowledge, to Eleanor Roosevelt as well as FDR. She was invited to dinner at the White House to share stories of what she had seen. "Franklin, talk to that girl," Eleanor urged, starting a conversation that became an open invitation to visit anytime and tell them both more. This meeting marked the beginning of a long and fruitful friendship between the two ladies, who communicated with each other for decades. (Mclain, "The Extraordinary Life of Martha Gellhorn, the Woman Ernest Hemingway Tried to Erase")

Nearly a year into her post Gellhorn was fired for inciting a riot among unemployed workers in rural Idaho, and Eleanor wrote to say that she was welcome to live at the White House until she could find her feet again. For two months Gellhorn stayed in what would later be named the Lincoln Bedroom, helping Eleanor answer sheaves of mail from people in dire straits.

Gellhorn claimed Eleanor as a private hero and became galvanized during her time at the White House to use her voice and considerable energy to expose the suffering she had seen and give it a broad, loud platform. She would write fiction, using real-life models. The resulting book, thrown off in a few short, burning months, became *The Trouble I've Seen*, a collection of four novellas that was praised far and wide. (Mclain, "The Extraordinary Life of Martha Gellhorn, the Woman Ernest Hemingway Tried to Erase")

It was the spring of 1937, and Gellhorn was getting ready to embark on a trip to Europe. Like a lot of young Americans, she was captivated by the unfolding civil war in Spain. The 27-year-old woman wrote an article for *Vogue* titled "Beauty Problems of the Middle-Aged Woman" to help raise the money she required. Hemingway insisted that Gellhorn focused her writing on civilian casualties rather than military strategy, an area in which she felt she was woefully uninformed. While walking through a square, she saw an elderly woman with a small child in her arms. As a reader, you can guess what's going through her mind. She wants to get the kid back home, where she feels safer among the familiar sights, sounds, and smells. She'll be standing in the middle of the square when the next assassin arrives. A tiny shard of twisted steel, hot and exceedingly sharp, shoots out of the shell and pierces the little kid in the throat. While the men rush out to transfer the child, the elderly mother stands there, holding the dead child's hand and staring at him incomprehensibly. An enormous, illuminated sign reading "Get out of Madrid" stands to their left on the square's side. (Gellhorn, "Reporting America at War")

The New Yorker and Collier's both begged for an increase. At the age of 28, Gellhorn had already established herself as a prominent war correspondent. Gellhorn reflected on her experiences in Madrid, saying, "There are practically no words to describe Madrid, it was heaven, far and away the nicest thing I have ever seen or lived through" (Valis, "Martha Gellhorn: High Explosive for Everyone"). She was reluctant to go even as the war's end drew near, but she had been tasked with reporting on the potential for renewed hostilities in France, England, and the Czech Republic for her magazine. She warned Eleanor Roosevelt that the next World War would be "the most stupid, deceptive, and violent sell-out of our time," contrasting it with the "kind of war" seen in the Spanish-American War. (Valis, "Martha Gellhorn: High Explosive for Everyone")

Following the Japanese attack on Pearl Harbour on December 7, 1941, *Collier's* reached out to Gellhorn and asked if she would be interested in covering the United States' involvement in the war. Women reporters were not given credentials to cover military events in the United States. Gellhorn told the *Collier's* Editor, Charles Colepaugh, "As you say, it is late to do anything about my sex. That's a disadvantage I've had to deal with since I was five, but I'm going to keep going anyhow, army or no army.... This is going to be a great long war," she said, "And sooner or later they are going to want to make it popular, and then folks like us can work" (Gellhorn, "Night life in the Sky").

Having spent time with Hemingway in Cuba and helping Liana win the Nobel Prize in Literature in New York, she can attest to both of these claims. After her book was released in November 1943, she went back to England. After returning home, Gellhorn wasted no time in visiting Lincolnshire to open an account of the British unit with the worst survival odds in September 1943, Bomber Command's young and inexperienced pilots. She travelled from Algiers to Naples after joining the Allied invasion of Italy. She teamed up with the French transportation officer and made the trip to the front near Cassino by car, braving the elements and driving over dead animals and wrecked lorries in the north. There was a cable from Hemingway asking, "Are you a war correspondent or wife in my bed?" (McLain, "The Extraordinary Life of Martha Gellhorn, the woman Earnest Hemingway tried to erase") suggesting that she return to Cuba.

There was no alcohol on board. So Gellhorn couldn't drink away her sorrows, and she limited herself to smoking outside. She read *Lady Chatterley's Lover* and thought about her failed marriage. In *Selected Letters of Martha Gellhorn*, she wrote to her mother, "Stayed in bed till afternoon" on May 10, 1944, and went on to describe her "severe despair last night" and how she "can't sleep for sadness" and how she "regrets it" just as much (Moorehead 137).

Injured service members were taken to the sheep in landing craft and water ambulances. Despite her aversion to the German inmates, Gellhorn helped with translation by shouting 'Ruhig!' (Silence!) whenever they chatted or laughed. "We are helpless against our own decency, truly," (Shute), she subsequently wrote. As mentioned in the article "Martha Gellhorn: A Women at War", Gellhorn and the medical teams waded ashore, as night fell, to start collecting the wounded. "An abandoned junkyard, with boxy black outlines of tanks, trucks, and weapons depots," (Shute), she saw. "A sweet smell of summer grasses; a smell of cattle and serenity and the sun that had warmed the ground some other time, when summer was real" (Shute).

The sound of exploding cells was used as a defensive mechanism. The next morning, the hospital ship weighed anchor so it could begin the journey back to England with the injured. Gellhorn was arrested upon her arrival in London for entering France without military permission. Her travel documents and ration coupons were confiscated and sent to a nurses' training camp with instructions to return to Normandy only when the nurses were ready to depart. In *The Face of War*, the author says:

> I date from an older America and I remember with longing the day when a President said to the American people, 'We have nothing to fear but fear itself.' That wasn't any form of propaganda, it was truth, and is just as valid now if only we knew it. I wish I could ask George Orwell's opinion, but it seems to me that propaganda is a sign of fear. We ought to give the Communists a world-wide monopoly of propaganda and let them founder in it; not us. (Gellhorn 246)

Gellhorn's pace was unaffected by these orders. She left the nurse's base and flew to Naples in the cockpit of an RAF plane. Before leaving London, she wrote a letter of protest to Colonel Lawrence, expressing her displeasure with the Army's continued refusal to permit the return to France of the nineteen women correspondents who had been accredited by the SHAEF. She argued that this weird patronising behaviour was as ridiculous as it was undignified, and she prevented veteran reporters from doing their jobs and helping millions of people in the United States who are in dire need of seeing but cannot see for themselves.

She travelled throughout Europe, visiting Paris again soon after its liberation, then moving on to Brussels and Arnhem where she was found by the 82nd Airborne, with a notebook in hand but without identification or uniform.

She was handed up to their leader, James Gavin. As she put it, her documents had been revoked because she had tried to sneak away from the invasion.

Gellhorn spent the final year of the war travelling alone, flying a P-61 over Germany at night to speak with Germans who claimed to have never been Nazis, and looping down to the Spanish border to speak with the refuseniks. In the May 1945 episode of Dachau, which had only been liberated a few days before, she combed through everything, including the skeleton remains of the survivors. In the article "Martha Gellhorn: A Great War Reporter", Szanton wrote about Martha and other war correspondents, "We have seen too many wars and too much violent dying; we have seen hospitals, bloody and messy as butcher shops. We have seen the dead like bundles lying on all the roads of half the earth. But now here, was there anything like this? Nothing about the war was ever as insanely weird as these starved and outraged, naked, nameless dead" (Szanton).

After World War II, Gellhorn's fortunes declined. She was bouncing around between Italy, Mexico, and Kenya because she was restless and had nothing to focus on. Although she deeply cared for the Italian war orphan she adopted, she hated being a mother and frequently left him for months at a time. She tied the knot with T.S. Matthews, a former Time editor, only to realise that marriage wasn't enough to keep her a second time.

In *The Face of War* Gellhorn wrote, "Luckily Vietnamese do not believe propaganda; they believe what they know from their own experience, and that is terrible enough. But Vietcong-fear-syndrome propaganda is an insult to the incredible courage and endurance of the Vietnamese people. And it deforms our understanding of all their varied anguish. Misunderstanding alienates; it does not "win the hearts and minds of the people" (243).

Martha's impact on war reportage is immense. Though she had to fight for recognition in a male-dominated sector, she ultimately revised the guidelines for covering war. Gellhorn kept covering hostilities in Vietnam, the Six-Day War, and the Central American region. The Martha Gellhorn Journalism Prize is named after her, and the biopic Hemingway and Gellhorn (2012) is about her life with the famous American writer. In *Selected Letters of Martha Gellhorn,* Martha wrote: "The only way I can pay back for what fate and society have handed me is to try, in minor totally useless ways, to make an angry sound against injustice" (Moorehead 121).

As discovered from the *Selected Letters of Martha Gellhorn,* she had started writing in 1937 while she was in Spain. In the beginning, she says, "I was a part of a Federation of Cassandras, using my typewriter to warn democracies of imminent Fascist danger," but "in the end, we became single stretcher bearers," saving as many lives as possible from the blaze. (Moorehead 129)

Shell-shocked Barcelona, Helsinki, Canton and Bastogne—the prelude and shattering Symphony of World War II come back—with almost unbearable vividness, thanks to Gellhorn's art which has an unwavering, dazzling, even cruel honesty: "At the time, I was a pacifist, and the use of my eyes would have been a violation of my values," (Gellhorn, *The Face of War* 213). By 1936, she had worked it out and become a most vocal opponent of fascism. Her heart was never far from the ordinary soldier, the injured, or the children. But she was never mushy or sentimental, and her works almost universally remain fresh and relevant even after half a century. Gellhorn further explains: "Gradually I came to realize that people will more readily swallow lie than truth, as if the taste of lies was honey, appetizing, a habit" (*The Face of War* 214).

When Gellhorn penned *Travels with Myself and Another*, she was in her seventies. Because no one is interested in trips that go smoothly, she states in the prologue that this book is about horror excursions. Her trip to Africa is one example. She sells a short tale to a television network in the early 1960s and uses the money to go on a vacation. She uses her signature brand of sarcasm, as in Travel for pleasure, the most audacious notion yet.

She doesn't say that she abandoned her adopted son or that she was in her fifties at the time. Sadly, most of her African horror stories are set in West Africa, specifically Cameroon and Chad. When she finally arrives in Nairobi, Kenya, she opts out of going on a guided safari and instead decides to get a Land Rover and see the country at her own pace. The British safari guide insisted that Martha travel with a companion to hire a car, so he selected Joshua, a young man, to accompany her.

Gellhorn is at the height of her comedic abilities when she gradually discovers how Joshua, her self-proclaimed protector, is actually of very little assistance. He does not demonstrate any initiative. He is petrified of the wild creatures that she yearns to interact with. He is concerned about the possibility of soiling his fake Italian silk pants and sharp black shoes. Martha is the one who winds up wading into rivers up to her knees to determine whether or not they are passable by vehicle. Martha is the one who clears the way by removing trunks from the roadway when there are lions and rhinos nearby. As time goes on, she also concludes that Joseph has been lying about his ability to drive in order to get the job.

Joseph's assistance to Martha consists, in the end, of little more than putting her suitcase into and out of the car and interpreting a few words of Swahili here and there. However, it would appear that he is the one watching out for her. However, Gellhorn rarely opens up about the challenges she faced while working as a war correspondent. She mocks the American media executives and military authorities who tried to keep her off the battlefield in passing remarks. However, she sneaked into Holland to watch the superb 82nd Airborne Division of the United States of America in action.

Gellhorn is one of the few women who has never struggled to relate to men in battle, and this honesty is what sets her work apart. After covering the Six-Day War in Israel as she is an ardent supporter of Israel, she announced a separate private peace to create fiction. She believes that journalism has no borders and ceases only with death. However, reporting on the Vietnam War, which was the only war she covered from the opposing side, cut her flesh and reawakened her immoral radicalism. Vietnam was the one war she covered from the wrong side. The latter few chapters of this book are full of vitriolic criticism intended against the United States government's attitude toward Central America. Gellhorn in the "Preface" of *Travels with Myself and Another* says that: "Nothing is better for self-esteem than survival".

The way Gellhorn crafts her sentences is captivating. This is because she belonged to the generation of Edward R. Murrow and James Cameron, who used declamatory, even propagandistic writing as a personal weapon while shunning bravado and macho.

Similarly, when we talk of The Spanish Civil War which affected English-language writing, focusing on the experiences of three female writers, Sylvia Townsend Warner, and Nancy Cunard including Martha Gellhorn, who went to Spain as war correspondents or volunteers. The Spanish Civil War broke out in 1936 and sparked a worldwide cultural reaction unlike any other. Artists of all stripes were moved to create works in response to the war, which they saw as a battle between democracy and fascism in many countries.

Cunard, Gellhorn and Warner argued in favour of the democratically elected Republican administration and warned of the global consequences of a win for fascists in Spain. In *The Face of War* Martha says:

Before going to Vietnam, I had many unanswered questions, but was obliged to make my picture of this war, like everybody else, from a composite of news reports and the pronouncements of American leaders: Vietcong assassinations and atrocities. Grenades thrown continuously on the helpless populace. The countryside and the roads strewn with mines. Vietcong raids on the towns at any moment. All the young American soldiers open to massacre in the jungles, or to incessant surprise attacks wherever they were quartered. Snipers following every move.

Terror by day and night. Saigon a city of awful hazards. If this picture of the war was my private invention, I would now think myself certifiable; but it is not. It is average American, perhaps average British, too; the result of fear-syndrome propaganda. (Gellhorn 213)

After the Death of Don Juan by Sylvia Townsend Warner, Martha Gellhorn's articles for Collier's Weekly, and the poetry of Nancy Cunard are just a few of the works that this book analyses, all of which have been virtually ignored by critical research. This book places the poetry and publishing of Cunard into the context of socialist internationalism, the ideology at the centre of the transnational solidarity that drove so many writers to Spain. Next, Warner's depiction of the war's fuelling factors, class inequalities and competing conceptions of tradition and development are examined in the context of her historical fiction. Martha Gellhorn's work as a journalist and the development of the subgenre of reporters covering the Spanish Civil War are also discussed. Their writings about the Spanish-American War complement those of well-known authors like Orwell, Hemingway, Auden, and Spender, and they shed light on the several ways that the battle was portrayed in literature during the 1930s.

From Czechoslovakia, England, Burma, Finland and Hong Kong, Gellhorn reported on Adolf Hitler's rise to power in 1938. Despite not having official press credentials or the approval of her then-husband, Ernest Hemingway, Gellhorn was eager to report on the Allies' D-Day landing in Normandy during the later stages of WWII. Though he had harmed her credential-gathering abilities, she was still invincible.

In *The Face of War*, middle-class Vietnamese cling to their status by wearing neat, fresh, though cheap clothes. The new poor, whom she saw were paper thin. She explains:

... In Vietnam, everyone suspects everyone else. Even so, I defend the government, we must have it for stability. But, you see, the government has no confidence in the people who have no confidence in the government. Our rulers like to be flattered; they surround themselves with yes-men. Twenty per cent of their minds want to help the country; eighty per cent want to make money ... I am pro-American; they have good intentions. Many of their theories don't work in practice but they are re-modernizing the country. The people are too ignorant to appreciate that.

Scandinavian socialism is the ideal way of life. The North Vietnamese have not understood how to exploit the economic suffering of the people (he gestured towards his stomach) but they sail learn ... Here everyone still calls Ho 'Monsieur' They call our topical of South Vietnam's black humor.) He is respected because Sin Laders ces marques. He is respected because of defeating the French. And all the same, it is amazing the way he stops the Americans. Nationalism enters into it, a sort of pride. But Communists have no sense of the dignity of man. For that, I detest them; as a Catholic. Though this government has no feeling for the individual either ... My greatest fear is a world war. We would all be annihilated. No, the human race is not mad. The rulers are mad ..." (Gellhorn 229)

She hid in the ship's bathroom until the medical transport was far from land, and then she posed as a stretcher bearer to be closer to the action when the ship docked. She found herself to be the only female journalist covering the Normandy invasion in June of 1944.

Also, after the Dachau concentration camp was freed, Martha was one of the first journalists there to report on it. She put a human face to the suffering that war brings. Her goals as a journalist were twofold: to act as an eyewitness and portray the stories of regular people caught up in violent conflicts, and to expose the lies perpetrated by those in authority that contributed to the onset of wars. Also, she often said that she hoped to "Let the bad guys have it" (Lyman).

To make a small, ultimately futile noise against injustice is the only way she can make amends for the hand that fate and society have dealt her. Having an opinion and being willing to defend it is part of being a citizen, and that's why it has become a tough occupation. There is never enough time in life, although the days are very long.

A conflict, according to Martha Gellhorn, renders the actions of the vast majority of people meaningless. She finally concludes that the chaotic nature of history is due to the short lifespans of its protagonists. The only way to get better is to try things out and see what works, but there just isn't enough time in the day to implement even the most sensible and reliable of these experiments. From her experience, she could tell us that the hardest obstacle is learning to be alone. It's easy to tame the scary and brave parts, the ones about love and dying, after the fact. Martha's hope in accepting her loneliness will lead to a sense of calm and safety. Like poverty and failure and the incurable diseases that are likewise deforming, a broken heart is such a shabby thing. As a tough but slightly terrified operational organ, she despises and is embarrassed by the fact that she needs to fix this heart and return it to working order. So, she says: "The worst bed partner on five continents? That would be me, I dare guess. If I engage in sexual activity, out of moral conviction, that is one thing; but to enjoy it ... seemed a failure" (Jasmine, "Martha Gellhorn: Quotes by A Courageous Woman").

As Gellhorn was always in support of humanity,

she, with a heavy heart, explained the affected people's condition in the war field:

>...the father is killed to the war; the woman has four children. pen children, she is too poor. The mothers cry, when they give as their children. They cry very much?"

"Soeur Jeanne's crèche, beyond the cost of the babies, small children crawled on the floor, or sat with outstretched legs, or stood alone; all thin, all silent, all with dark, sad eyes. Sour Jeanne said: The misery, the misery. Everything is here. War orphans. War wounded. (Gellhorn, *A Stricken Field* 310)

Officially, eighty thousand orphans are registered now in different institutions, and an institution is the last desperate resort. The Vietnamese exist as all-inclusive families, and they love children. No one could guess how many orphans are sheltered by relatives. The Ministry of Social Welfare predicts an average of two thousand more orphans every month. It is not strange that we count and proclaim only military casualties as she said.

According to Martha, those homeless children should be listed as wounded; and wounded forever.

The school-age children were down the road at a school where the nuns teach. Older girls and women sat or lay on the hardwood beds in their building; they had nothing else to do, month after month. Most of the adults are too sick or frail or old or handicapped to work. They were relatively able to do maintenance jobs around the aisle and were rewarded with an extra food ration. The Vietnam Government contributes twelve piastres a day per person which would not prevent general starvation.

In contrast to the ancient ruins and churches that

can be seen in Greece and Italy, the people and culture of Israel are what truly set this country apart from others. All individuals are impacted by war. The only other thing that comes to her mind is that she feels as though she has been repeating herself for an unimaginably long time. The majority of individuals, unless they are directly touched by a dispute, behave as if it is inevitable and beyond their control, or as if it has nothing to do with them even when they are directly affected. The human mind is not yet wired in such a way that it can fully comprehend the horrors of war. They worry about it, but just in the general, hazy sense that children worry about their dreams, without any distinct mental images of what might take place as a result of their concerns.

This wouldn't bother her so much if she were a top-notch author. The thing that really gets her down is that writing is so incredibly difficult, obsessive, and lonely that all you want in return is a modicum of satisfaction for yourself. That will never happen because she does not deserve it. She said that she would never be a competent writer. It's tough to feel lonely again after you've managed to avoid it for a time. That was okay with her; she was accustomed to being alone and could handle the harshness. She was waiting for a voice, a face, a body that would not be there, is not hers, and does not feel homesick in the same way that she does. To put it simply, she didn't want to lose her mind over it, so she educated herself to be strong and apathetic. As a journalist, Martha Gellhorn saw no necessity for objectivity. She believed that reporting the truth, disproving the liars' claims, and delivering the goods to the bad guys were the primary purpose of going anywhere to cover anything. In the novel *A Stricken Field* she once remarked: "You go into a hospital, and it's full of wounded kids. Therefore, you record reality as you perceive it. You don't state that there are 37 injured kids here, but there might be 38 more on the opposite side.

What you see is what you write about" (Gellhorn 85).

Although Martha Gellhorn's reputation rests on her ground-breaking journalism, she was also a talented fiction writer who penned five novels, fourteen novellas, and two collections of short stories, many of which were inspired by people she met and situations she witnessed during her extensive travels. Published in 1959 as *The Face of War*, Martha Gellhorn's war diary shows how she focused on the lives of ordinary troops and civilians while ignoring the actions of the generals. Her reporting during times of relative calm was published in *The View from the Ground* in 1988. Her works include *A Stricken Field* (1940), set among refugees in Prague just before the Nazi invasion of Czechoslovakia, and *Liana* (1944), which follows a mulatto woman as she marries a wealthy white man in the French Caribbean. It has been noted that Ms Gellhorn's novellas, such as *The Weather in Africa* (1988), a collection of three stories set in Africa, and *The Novellas of Martha Gellhorn*, are even better than her nonfiction works (1993). Ms Gellhorn felt that the press's involvement in ending the Vietnam War had not been adequately reflected in subsequent coverage, despite her belief that military leaders had learned their lesson.

In the article "Martha Gellhorn: A Daring Writer", Layman talked of Gellhorn: "It seems to me that they feed war reporters at these ludicrous briefings in the ballroom of hotels miles from everywhere, and she stressed that the public needs to realise that it is not getting the full picture" (Layman).

Martha Gellhorn once said, reflecting on a life that would have been interesting fodder for any fiction or reportage: "I am overprivileged. My life has been fantastic.

Though I didn't earn it, here I am. I really don't ever want to hear his name uttered again; she told her mom in a letter. To compensate for being such a horrible person, a man would have to be extraordinarily brilliant" (Moorehead, *Selected Letters of Martha Gellhorn* 412).

When Martha was reporting in May 1945 from Dachau, she said: "Behind the barbed wire and the electric fence, the skeletons sat in the sun and inspected themselves for lice" (Mundsh). In another message from a freshly invaded Germany, she criticized the self-pity and denial of average Germans, saying: "I concealed a Jew for six weeks. For eight weeks, I sheltered a Jewish man. In other words, I hid a Jew, He sheltered a Jew, all God's children concealed Jews" (Mundsh).

Journalism students are frequently taken aback by the extreme rage portrayed in her stories; Gellhorn would later describe the tales to the Germans as 'paeans of hatred', and it's difficult to imagine a piece of this calibre being published or even produced today.

Nonetheless, nothing in her delivery would have surprised American readers at the time or those in England, France, Holland, Greece, Hungary, Czechoslovakia, Yugoslavia, or Russia, to name a few. It's quite hard to picture Dachau providing a balanced account.

It is fascinating to revisit Gellhorn's approach to journalism in light of the recent deaths of journalists Anthony Shadid and Marie Colvin in Syria and photojournalists Tim Hetherington and Chris Hondros in Libya not to mention the hundreds of journalists and media workers killed in Iraq since 2004 and dozens in Mexico in recent years. Reading her work and talking to modern war correspondents makes it clear that Gellhorn's approach to reporting on battle was up-to-date, even prescient, but is now absolutely out-of-date.

For the sole purpose of aiding *The Republic*, Gellhorn arrived in Spain in 1937. But she had no idea what she was doing and certainly not how to be a war correspondent. A fellow journalist friend of hers recommended her to produce an article on Madrid. So, upon further reflection many years later, in the article "Madrid to Morata" she asked, "What made a story, to begin with? Didn't a major turning point need to occur before an article could be written? Nobody should care about that. My curiosity got the better of me, so I inquired. It had become routine. What was new and prophetic about the war in Spain was the lives of the civilians, who stayed at home and had conflict delivered to them" (Gellhorn).

The data support Gellhorn's viewpoint. Marxist historians such as Eric Hobsbawm estimated that while soldiers accounted for 95% of casualties in World War I, 80-90% of victims in today's conflicts (the majority of which are intranational) are unarmed civilians. These estimates are based on the fact that soldiers accounted for 95% of casualties in World War I. The militias in the Democratic Republic of the Congo that routinely engage in mass rape and female genital mutilation, the Lord's Resistance Army in Uganda that uses children as slaves, the Taliban's bombing of markets and schools, Al Qaeda's attacks on mosques in Iraq, and Al Shabaab's attack on medical students and teachers. Political theorist John Keane has referred to these conflicts as total wars.

These new wars, according to Mary Kaldor of the London School of Economics, replace ideas politics with identity politics, making it impossible to understand them in traditional political terms because there isn't a unifying ideology or goal. This makes recent wars one of the most perplexing developments in recent history. Traditional modern wars, such as guerrilla wars and liberation movements sought to win over indigenous populations and establish new states, whereas new warriors sought to perpetuate failed or imploding states, expel or murder civilian populations, and sow fear and hatred among their own countrymen. Kaldor argues that new warriors seek to sow fear and hatred among their countrymen. The manner in which battles are fought has progressed, and so has the way in which the media reports on them. When it comes to combat, the aspect that fascinates the most is not how individuals perish but rather how they emerge victorious:

... We were suddenly, enormously involved in a war, without any explanation that made sense to me. Instead of reason and fact, we got exhortation and propaganda. All the war reports I could find sounded inhuman, like describing a deadly football game between a team of heroes and a team of devils and chalking up the score by body counts and kill ratio. The American dead were mourned, but not enough; they should have been mourned with bitter unceasing questions about the value of sacrificing these young lives. The Vietnamese people were apparently forgotten except as clichés in speeches. American bombing missions were announced as if bombs were a selective weapon, or as if only the proclaimed enemy lived on the ground. Vietnamese civilians lived all over the ground, under that rain of bombs.

They were being freed from aggression' mercilessly. I did not want to learn about new techniques of warfare, nor ever again see young men killing each other on the orders of old men. Finally, I went to South Vietnam because I had to learn for myself, since I could not learn from anyone else, what was happening to the voiceless Vietnamese people…" (Gellhorn, *Travels with Myself and Another* 213).

But there is another reason for the contemporary focus on civilians. Gellhorn referred to Spain as Causa. Reporting commitment was the source of her deepest insights and her greatest failures: she did not report on the atrocities and executions perpetrated by the Loyalists. In fact, Gellhorn took a clearly partisan stance in virtually every war she covered; as her biographer wrote: Gellhorn was "more committed than almost any journalist of her generation to promoting the cause of oppressed people everywhere" (Moorehead, *Martha Gellhorn: A Life* 327). Martha was fervently pro-Israeli (in 1948, in 1967, and after) and equally fervent in her opposition to U.S. policies and actions in Vietnam, Nicaragua, El Salvador, and Panama. This is what Martha Gellhorn teaches us about the morality of contemporary war reportage as mentioned in the article "The Hubris and Despair of War Journalism:"

I can't predict what she would say about any particular contemporary war— speaking for the dead is always dangerous—but I'm pretty sure she agreed with her friend Robert Capa when he told her, "In a war, you must hate somebody or love somebody, you must have a position or you cannot stand what goes on" (Linfield).

However, many contemporary journalists lack Gellhorn's understanding of the political subjects that motivated her writing, particularly fascism and antifascism. In no way does this imply that there is some kind of apathetic middle ground. The Bosnian War was not only the final conflict of the old era but also one of the earliest manifestations of the post-Cold War world order. Millions of people are affected by wars that are more like auto-exterminations than traditional wars and which can last for decades.

They were divided into two camps, the Government and the Rebels. The woman who confronted the narcissistic Nobel laureate on both an academic and emotional level has finally been recognised for her efforts. Martha Gellhorn, a journalist known for her platinum blonde hair, was a ferociously ambitious woman who was never short on grand notions about debate, politics, and social issues. Her oeuvre includes five novels, fourteen novellas and two collections of short tales. She also broke ground as a war reporter for women.

She went to nearly 50 different countries and was known for brazenly risking her life to get articles, including hiding on boats and penetrating enemy territory. Their explosive five-year marriage made headlines because of the tension and rivalry between them. She believed, incorrectly, that a man's need for sex was as essential to his survival as food, and that denying him sex was a selfish act on par with starving him. She has always been interested in what's going on in the wider world. They introduced me to the more energetic and outgoing side of life that she had discovered among lads. Although sex did not seem to be their pleasure, she did experience the joy of being desired and the type of care that a satisfied male offers. Despite their love for one another, Gellhorn left Hemingway suddenly and radically during World War II due to their acrimonious relationship. In *Selected Letters of Martha Gellhorn* edited by Caroline Moorehead, Martha says: "A bet is on: I daresay I was the worst bed partner on five continents" (214).

Ten years later, having read *Across the River and Into the Trees* by Hemingway, Gellhorn wrote an enraged letter to a friend about the time she had wasted trying to appease her childish, tantrum-throwing husband. She says: I'm so sick that I can't even put it into words. Cold and sickly. I watch as he meticulously decorates his likeness... I'm sad about the eight years I wasted serving him and worshipping his statue, and about anything else I may have lost because of it. Though her hostility and wrath lessened over time, her famous cookie personality stayed the same, creating issues in her subsequent relationships and political writing. (Moorehead, *Selected Letters of Martha Gellhorn* 329)

After a protracted struggle with cancer, the journalist took her own life in 1998, although she was completely committed to her profession to the end. She lasted to the ripe old age of 89. In 1937, General Franco's Nationalists and Republicans on the right controlled a severely fractured Spain. Martha, whose earlier work had centred on politics, wrote about the effects of the war on the villagers while in Spain with Hemingway. Her work as a war correspondent began when her reports were published in the American magazine *Collier's*. Martha had an affair with Hemingway and met the famed war photographer Robert Capa in Spain. Following their time in Spain, Hemingway and Martha spent the spring of 1939 in Cuba, where Martha wrote messages from the Czech Republic and the United Kingdom as war loomed. Their wedding in November 1940 took place in the Union Pacific Dining Room in Wyoming, not long after the September 1940 publication of *For Whom the Bell Tolls*, which featured a tribute to Martha.

Even though the military at the time did not allow women to do so, Martha was eager to report on the war from the front lines. Despite being denied press credentials, she continued to chronicle the war in Europe, having previously reported on submarine warfare from the Caribbean. While things were rocky in Hemingway and Martha's marriage, he was *Collier's* main workplace correspondent. Martha was denied permission to participate in the Omaha Beach invasion, so she slipped away on a medical transport ship.

She landed in Normandy and later contributed twice to Collier's, with one story focused on the German captives she interviewed.

Hemingway was permitted to visit Omaha Beach, but he never showed up. They parted in 1945, and Martha went on to report from the Nuremberg trials and the liberation of concentration camps across Europe. After moving to Mexico from the United States in 1948, Martha adopted her son Sandy from an Italian orphanage the following year. Martha married Tom Matthews in 1954 and stayed home with their three children until their divorce in the late 1960s. Sandy Gellhorn's connection with Martha deteriorated as he entered adolescence. Martha's dedication to a healthy lifestyle was in stark contrast to Sandy's struggle with his weight. After Sandy's adult arrest for drug possession, he and his mom had no further contact. They reconciled somewhat later in her life.

In the novel *A Stricken Field*, while sharing her woeful war field experience, Martha explains:

You see it is very difficult. You and I are just people,

and it is easy for us to say, we want peace, we want nothing else, the whole world wants peace: Why didn't those men in the Luxembourg set a good example? It is true that peace never seemed farther away than in the splendid halls of the Luxembourg. It would be wonderful if it were only the delegates' fault, because then we could fire them, we could say we want better, more competent men. It was not their fault. They were human beings, like you and me, just as anxious and twice as prejudiced. They know that their people are exhausted, hurt and poisoned by war. They themselves were not living in some delicious Shangri-La during those cruel years. The Norwegian chief delegate spent the war in Sachsenhausen, one of the great death concentration camps of Germany. The second-ranking Dutchman was in a Jap prison camp in Java. Bevin was as vulnerable to the bombs that fell on London as any cab driver. The Italian prime minister, who served his apprenticeship in a Fascist prison, took his chances in Rome like anyone else who opposed the Fascist and Nazi regimes. The Yugoslav, who is very young, went to prison as an anti-Fascist before the war, and fought as a partisan during the war. The Pole was imprisoned by the Germans in both wars. Bidault was probably more wanted by the Gestapo than any man in France. And so, the list goes on... (206)

It was in 1966 when Martha went to Vietnam to cover the conflict as a journalist.

She did what she had done previously during the Spanish Civil War and travelled to various locations such as hospitals and rubbish dumps to document the effects of the violence on the local populace. Her distressing reporting contributed to a rising discontent with the Vietnam War. Martha never returned to Vietnam after her anti-war poem was published there, instead spent her time raising money for Vietnamese orphans. After the Vietnam War was over, Martha continued to report on world events. In 1994, she submitted a dispatch from Brazil to the London Review of Books describing the abuse of homeless children by police.

Martha settled in the United Kingdom's London and Wales area. She was widely regarded as one of the best war journalists of her era with the 1978 publication of her books *The Weather in Africa* and *Travels with Myself and Another*. Later in life, Martha grew close to a group of writers and journalists known as the Guys which included names like John Pilger, Rosie Boycott, Victoria Glendinning, John Simpson, and Jon Snow.

Martha passed away on 15 February 1998, at the age of 89, and her ashes were dispersed in the Thames. During the Great Depression, the line between fact and fiction was blurry in Martha Gellhorn's 1936 anthology *The Trouble I've Seen*. According to Martha:

… because no one got killed anymore and foolishly, in those early days we thought we had learned enough not to start killing again. During the war, the rule was never to discuss casualties; people mourned in silence. Grief was always there and always heavier but contained, from necessity. Now the survivors had time, suddenly too much time, to count their losses. In old-fashioned wars, men went off to fight and parents, widows, fatherless children wept for them. Since modern total war was first practiced in Spain, men could return safe from the battles to find their families and homes wiped out. Bombs, artillery, mines, deportation, hunger killed non- combatants and combatants alike. In its entire history, Europe had not known such appalling loss. By unspoken agreement, people kept their sorrow to themselves.

The past could not be changed and though it was no longer legally a crime in England to spread despondency and alarm, it was wrong to spread darkness of spirit. Everyone had his own share of memory to live with. And many had to live with the worst memory in all experience, the Nazi concentration camps; nothing else in war was as evil, as bestially subhuman. We did not talk of the dead and the destruction; we were determinedly cheerful about the present. Still, peace did not feel quite natural or comfortable; one couldn't think what to do with oneself, having fixed one's mind for so many years on the single aim of finishing Nazism. Soon after VE Day, a friend and I wandered around London musing on the question: What next? What next indeed? As a beginning, one might try to settle somewhere. I bought a little house in London that afternoon and imagined I had taken a sensible step in the right direction. An expert surveyed my property and said that a land mine had dropped across the street, blowing a large gap in the row of houses. had also shaken my dwelling to its foundations and dry rot had set in everywhere and it wasn't the best bargain of the century... (Gellhorn, *The Face of War* 177)

In November of 1938, Gellhorn was quoted by Lyman as saying that the weather in Barcelona was ideal for bombing, referring to the advance of Franco's bombers on Republican territory. Every single cafe along the Ramblas was overflowing with customers. Orangeade, a poison that is sweet and fizzy, and a terrible counterfeit for sherry were the only drink that was accessible. Naturally, there was not a single morsel of food to be found anywhere. The brisk afternoon light encouraged people to venture outside in large numbers. She felt deprived in 1939 when fascist Spain triumphed over the rest of the world in the war it was fighting. According to Weingarten, in a letter to her friend Hortense Flexner, she stated that she had declared nothing in her life had so impacted her thinking as the closing of the war. To quote the late great Leonard Cohen: "It's quite commonplace, like the death of all cherished things. She reportedly wrote to Flexner, Earnest and I genuinely are scared of one other, each knowing that the other is the most aggressive person each one of us knows as described by Weingarten" (Moorehead, *Selected Letters of Martha Gellhorn* 224).

Her defenders believe that Gellhorn demonstrated courage by first accepting advocacy journalism and then criticising traditional war media for having an excessive amount of faith in generals and governments. According to an article written by Susie Linfield and published in *The Nation*, Martha Gellhorn and other journalists, such as the British journalist George Orwell, believed that journalism was synonymous with the truth and that the truth would encourage people, especially those living in ostensibly civilised democracies to protest and take action. According to a phrase attributed to Gellhorn, the function of a reporter is to confine one's thinking about a topic to what one sees or hears about it. According to a remark made by one of Martha's biographers, Caroline Moorehead, who was cited by Jonathan Yardley of the Washington Post, Martha never faced the fundamental dilemma of omitting to write what you believed to be true in order to uphold a higher cause throughout her life. Rosen reported that Moorehead's statement was true (Rosen, "Cold eye, warm heart" 124).

She had previously reported on the invasion of Panama by the United States in 1989, but by the time the war broke out in Bosnia in 1993, she had concluded that she was too elderly to go there. She had previously reported on the invasion of Panama by the United States in 1989. She was sent to Brazil in the middle of the 1990s as part of an international reporting assignment, and while there, she reported on the violence that was committed against the homeless people of that country. Due to her impaired eyesight and the consequent inability to look back over her work, she had a very difficult time including a letter in the article about Brazil that was published in the literary magazine *Granta*. She worked immensely to do so.

Not only did the publishing of Martha's writings from her time spent in Spain in *Collier's* Magazine define her voice and style, but it also had a huge impact on the way the conflict was reported. Martha's attention was drawn to the people rather than the typical aspects of war, such as strategies, generals, arsenals, and armament, as the globe was teetering on the brink of World War II. After being turned away from the country using the more conventional entrance procedures, she gained access to Panama illegally in 1990 by pretending to be a thriller reviewer for the *Daily Telegraph*. She by herself did scuba diving in Belize at the time of the U.S. invasion in late 1989, and so she asked a friend who was an editor to forge a letter for her that would make it seem like she was there on official business as a special correspondent. This made it appear as though she was covering the invasion for a news organisation. She had urged a friend 50 years ago to help her get to Spain by writing her a letter just like this one. The letter was a request for assistance in travelling to Spain. You may put your faith in Martha's advice even though she was 81 years old at the time she gave it since she was aware of what she was talking about.

The primary criticisms that were levelled against Gellhorn, Cowles, and Herbst about *The Face of War, Looking for Trouble* and *The Starched Blue Sky of Spain and Other Memoirs* were that they did not tell the entire story, that they omitted significant names and dates, and that they did not provide sufficient information regarding the politics and propaganda of Spain. Despite this, the women who travelled to Spain and subsequently republished their reports from the Spanish Civil War did not have these objectives in mind when they set out on their journey.

While a reporter is responsible for gathering facts to write about for a magazine, a foreign correspondent is responsible for filing dispatches or longer stories on unfolding events on a worldwide scale. As long as the news from overseas does not alter the situation at home, a foreign journalist is also afforded a greater degree of flexibility. Describing the woeful sufferings in the field of war, she says in her book *The Face of War:*

These articles are in no way adequate descriptions of the indescribable misery of war. War was always worse than I knew how to say always. And probably from an instinct of self-preservation, one tried to write most often of what was brave and decent. Perhaps now my articles on Germany and on the behaviour of the Gestapo, the SS and other sections of the German Army will seem untimely paeans of hate. I reported what I saw, and hate was the only reaction such sights could produce. (Gellhorn 84).

Through their coverage of stories about the lives of Americans living on a low income, young female reporters in the 1930s made a significant contribution to the creation of the language of social observation. This was the phrase used by government agencies such as FERA, RA/FSA, and WPA, which sent unemployed men and women as well as journalists and photographers to document the lives of those living in the areas that were severely hit by the Great Depression. Women reporters made significant contributions to the greater discourse for social change as a result of the work they did. These contributions influenced how people viewed the world and how stories were told about it. In 1934, when Martha Gellhorn was working as a field researcher for FERA, she witnessed first-hand the ineffectiveness of many government programmes that were intended to address social concerns. Her first-hand accounts of the Great Depression among factory strikers in Albany and New York at the turn of the century enrich her accounts of poverty, disease, and starvation in the Carolinas, New Jersey, and Massachusetts during that period.

She felt compelled to express her displeasure at the sight of American workers and their families becoming victims of resource mismanagement at the hands of uniformed aid workers who were biased towards the affected population.

The Spanish Civil War was everything but peaceful, even though it began with conventional Nationalists staging an unlawful coup against an elected Republican government in July 1936. The conflict lasted until 1939. There was a significant gap in economic and social resources, ownership of property, and the ability to vote that existed in Spain. As a result of this gap, the country was divided into many camps. Even though people from all over the world were actively supporting one side or the other in the Spanish Civil War, Germany and Italy used the conflict as a testing ground for a new form of warfare, which involved the bombing of civilian and civilian-occupied areas from the air.

This was done even though Germany and Italy were the two fastest-growing European powers at the time. Because the objectives of the new warfare strategy, the destruction of non-military targets and the infliction of large fatalities were inverted in the Spanish Civil War, this conflict has been labelled as a modern total war. This is the first time in history that these objectives have been inverted. In March of 1937, a large number of writers, activists, and journalists travelled to Spain. Since the coup in July 1936 that ignited the civil war, Madrid had been the 'Holy Grail' for the Nationalists who made repeated attacks against the seat of the Republican government which had been evacuated to Valencia in November 1936. This conflict lasted from July 1936 to May 1939. Herbert Matthews described Madrid as the one location above all others where a man was concerned about the state of the globe he would wish to be. Herbert Matthews described Madrid as the one location above all others where a man was concerned about the state of the globe he would wish to be. The three veteran women namely Alice Schalek, Louise Mack and Mary Boyle O'Reilly arrived in Spain in the spring of 1937 as press tourists with letters of introduction or letters indicating interest in articles from news organisations or weekly journals; this was not their first conflict to cover, as they had all spent the first part of the 1930s travelling throughout the United States and abroad, reporting on social and political issues. arrived in Spain in the spring of 1937 as press tourists with letters of introduction or letters indicating interest in articles from news organisations or weekly journals; this was not their first conflict to cover, as they had all spent the first part of the 1930s travelling throughout the United States and abroad, reporting on social and political issues. Gendered assumptions impacted editors' expectations of what female reporters should write, and women were tasked with reflecting women's perspectives and voices in their work. There was a lot of censorship of correspondents who were meant to send out daily dispatches in Spain, and anything that made it into newspapers in Europe and the United States was viewed as propaganda.

However, as Gellhorn, Cowles, and Herbst found out in Spain, freelancing for weekly periodicals, weekly columns, or illustrated publications have a variety of benefits. After a friendly dispatcher at the Telefonica Building in Madrid suggested that Martha Gellhorn focuses her radio show on human interest rather than conflict, Gellhorn stormed off in a huff. However, as Cowles points out, the Spanish writer only had leeway in covering human-interest stories and was restricted from providing extensive coverage of the bombings. Gellhorn and Cowles were able to gain access to the front lines and build an audience despite their lack of combat experience because of their extensive education, familiarity with international events and legislation surrounding the Spanish Civil War, and middle-class upbringing. High-ranking military leaders singled out Gellhorn and Cowles when they summoned them, but this came at the expense of criticism from other correspondents, both women and men. What got people's attention and made people try to rein in their influence was their foray into the public sphere. Tabea Alexa Linhard argues that women's story production during times of revolution and conflict vacillates between resistance and accommodation, reflecting the testing and reinforcement of the public-private gender divide. For the first three months of the Spanish Civil War, Republican forces allowed women to fight alongside their male counterparts. Although general mobilisation was initiated early on and the ranks of the people's army were gender-integrated, six months into the conflict, women were sent away from the front and behind fighting lines.

Women war correspondents knew well that the New Woman's image had not yet been translated into various visual languages, even though many images produced by authors, photographers, and magazine editors between 1870 and 1960 emphasised her presence and authority. In a hotel in Prague, American journalist Mary Douglas is met by a group of foreign correspondents who inform her that the Czechoslovakia story is already dead. Mary strives to learn as much as she can from the correspondents who have witnessed concentration camps and signs of torture but are unable to file their pieces without censor approval. Martha Gellhorn's commitment to documenting people's struggles began in Spain at the start of the decade, and her work as a war correspondent has been widely praised, but the fact that both she and her collaborator, Taro, are attractive women hampered their efforts to have their focus on the citizen exile experience recognised as uniquely their own. Due to a lack of permanent assignments or short-term visas, Gellhorn and Taro were forced to travel frequently rather than remain in Spain, and while in Spain, they were constantly on the move. Nonetheless, their experience and observation went beyond the limitations of their mobility. They were able to break down barriers of race, gender, and class because of their good looks, self-assurance, and forthrightness, which were all products of their privileged upbringing. Gellhorn was born in the United States to German-Jewish parents who were active in the movement for women's suffrage and social reform which provided her with early exposure to these issues.

As self-educated committed witnesses, Martha Gellhorn and Gerda Taro's writing, photography, and filmmaking all explore the complexities of the citizen/exile experience in Spain. However, as attractive foreign women and non-party members, Gellhorn and Taro's relationships with Hemingway and Cuba provided a measure of security and access to basic as well as professional resources.

Even in the "Preface" to the first 1959 edition of *The Face of War*, Martha Gellhorn describes herself as "an undamaged tourist of wars". Gellhorn was acutely aware of her status as an outsider, a woman, and a spectator when she arrived in Madrid on March 27, 1937. She was neither an accredited journalist nor a member of the military. As a result of the efforts of her biographers to disprove the version of events presented by Hemingway's historians, in which he is represented as the benevolent sponsor who arranged for Gellhorn's admission into Spain on March 23, 1937, the story has taken on mythical proportions. This is because her biographers have tried to disprove the version of events presented by Hemingway's historians. Gellhorn discusses these issues while travelling on a train from Paris to Puigcerda, the final station before entering Spain. Puigcerda is the last station before entering Spain. There, she did not understand what the young Spanish man was saying, but she continued to follow him with the backpack full of canned goods she was carrying. She paid them fifteen cents for the bag of non-perishable goods and they let her board the train to Barcelona despite their initial confusion about her being an American woman The man accompanied her to the border patrol, where they took the money and let her board the train.

She then spent the next day, March 25, travelling to Valencia with a journalist and a Polish woman. Before that, she had spent the previous two days in Barcelona touring schools, meeting with refugee children, and going to the Women's Union. The following day, she visited students as well as Italian fascist inmates. Later the same day, she attended a party held in honour of M. Alvarez del Vayo to commemorate his appointment to the position of minister of foreign affairs. It was on March 27 when she picked up three press passes from Ted, which marked the beginning of her trip to Madrid with Sidney Franklin.

In their unpublished autobiographies, both Arturo Barea, the censor who reviewed dispatches filed by correspondents in Madrid, and Ted Allan, a twenty-year-old Canadian who wrote for Federated Press and worked with Dr. Norman Bethune's mobile blood transfusion unit, described their initial encounters with Gellhorn upon her arrival in Madrid. Barea was responsible for reviewing the dispatches filed by correspondents in Madrid, and Allan was a writer for Federated Press (1946).

The entry in Gellhorn's diary that she made while she was in Spain provides evidence that she did meet Allan and that, following their initial encounter in Valencia, he did provide her with press credentials. However, Allan asserts that on the same day, he travelled with Gellhorn to Madrid at the request of Constancia De la Mora, the censor in Valencia, to provide Gellhorn with advice regarding the state of the war. *The Trouble I've Seen*, a collection of short stories written by Gellhorn and published in 1936, was promoted in the media with images that the author had taken while travelling to and from Spain. During the war in Spain, just a handful of images were taken of Gellhorn, and none of them portray her in the way that Barea and Josephine Herbst describe. Not only does the fact that Gellhorn made four visits to Spain during the conflict illustrates her loyalty to the Republican cause, but it also demonstrates the challenges she faced there as a result of the lack of a definite position. Gellhorn's first voyage to Spain was taken between March 27 and May 1937 and lasted for a total of five months.

In addition to Martha Gellhorn, other female correspondents were accorded the status of celebrities in Spain, garnering equal degrees of love and ridicule. It is possible that Ms Gellhorn was referring to the fact that the reporter would never have been allowed to cover a war if she hadn't taken such risks when she stated that she accepted the invitation knowing very well what the Commandant's intentions were.

Before being taken back to the civilian zone, the correspondent is finally given the opportunity to observe the dead bodies of the four soldiers who served under the Commandant on the front line. This will improve the credibility of the account as a fresh story from the front, even if the real story is about the hazardous condition of women in combat, which the reporter will not write about. This will increase the credibility of the account as a fresh story from the front. As there were significantly more men than women working as correspondents, Gellhorn and Taro were able to capitalise on their attractiveness and their femininity. The morale of the troops was much improved as a result of their excursions to the front, which were modelled after those of female celebrities.

Hemingway has done more than anybody else to establish Gellhorn as the archetypal attractive but dim-witted girl. Gellhorn is one of his most famous characters. Dorothy Bridges is a Vassar-educated, lazy Cosmopolitan correspondent who, when she is not sleeping, fantasises about a home life with Philip Rawlins, a glorified version of Hemingway, or takes advantage of the war-torn economy to buy a silver fox cape for a song. This is how Hemingway portrayed Martha Gellhorn in his novel *The Sun Also Rises*. The report "Fresh Air on an Inside Story from Spain" demonstrates that Gellhorn did not do much better in Hemingway's non-fiction. In the "Afterword" of *A Stricken Field* Martha contends:

I was well along in a new book of short stories when I wrote from Cuba on May 22, 1940: I know something very wrong happened to me about this last book but as yet I don't know how or why. If you work for a long time on a book, you should get something out of it for yourself, some sense of triumph. But I had nothing. I had the feeling I had dropped my work, the hard months of my life, into a well, and there they were, muffled and lost. I do not know why this came about but it did and I am surely suffering from it now, both in a sense of personal futility and a lack of confidence in my work ... As I don't know what it is, I cannot write it ... with a little time I will find it and correct it. I buried A Stricken Field, never again mentioned it; and got on with the job (Gellhorn 314).

CHAPTER III

Frontline Female Reporters: A Study of Gellhorn's Non-Fictional Writings

Throughout her nearly six-decade career, Martha Gellhorn has written about a wide range of topics including the Great Depression in the United States, the anxious aftermath of Franco's death in Spain, the Christmas celebrated with the have-nots in London, the weekend in Israel, the magnificent protests at the White House, the memoir of domestic life in Africa, the return to Cuba after forty-one years etc. Inspired by the horrors of fascism in Spain and Germany and the highly modern terror in Central America and by the courage of those defenders of decency who stand up to the thugs both in and out of government, *The View from the Ground*, like its companion volume *The Face of War*, is a singular act of testimony that is unique in our time. In this updated and expanded edition of her 1959 classic, Gellhorn reflects on political, civil, and social issues and crises spanning six decades, from a lynching in the American South to a recent visit to Cuba to see what is new and what is still the same in a country that is still off limits to most Americans. In the "Afterword" of the novel, *A Stricken Field*, Martha wrote: "I think that England is a kid glove fascism, worse because of its hypocrisy and the fact that all of the people are fooled all of the time" (309).

At the age of 21, Gellhorn, an accomplished writer and journalist, packed a bag and $75 and flew to Paris, expecting to start work as a foreign correspondent within a few weeks. The articles penned by Martha span sixty years of the modern period. In the ensuing 58 years, she has seen many historical events first-hand, including a lynching in Mississippi, the collapse of Czechoslovakia in the 1930s, the suffering of Italian war orphans in the 1940s, the rise of Israel and the Palestinian problem in the 1950s and 1960s, post-Franco Spain in the 1970s, and the new Cuba in the 1980s. Throughout her career, Gellhorn has reported on a wide variety of topics, from the McCarthy hearings and the Eichmann trial to the peace negotiations in Vietnam and, more recently, the anti-nuclear rallies by women in Greenham Common, England, and the torture in El Salvador. To her, writing has always been the price to be paid for the privilege of observing and learning, making her an expert on the topic of personal journalism and a fierce advocate for human rights. *Travels with Myself and Another*, a companion to Gellhorn's *The Face of War* is a memorial to the interruptions in everyday life during times of peace brought out by the ugly, polarising politics of this century. Gellhorn's anonymity is absolutely unwarranted; she is a smart woman and a gifted writer.

The short story collection *The Trouble I've Seen* (1936) was penned by the author during the Great Depression. The Great Depression as experienced by Martha Gellhorn is condensed into these interrelated tales. These fictional works, created with documentary realism, powerfully depict the progressive spiritual breakdown of the basic, homely adequacy of American life in the face of abrupt unemployment, acute poverty, and pessimism. At the age of twenty-one, Martha was the youngest of the sixteen reporters chosen to make covert reports to the Roosevelt administration. They reflect the sentiment of a generation lost to apathy, of young men who have lost faith in humanity and God and who shun the idea of private enterprise. Martha Gellhorn returned to the United States in 1934 after three years abroad during which she had a bohemian love affair and lived among the city's intellectuals. At the age of 25, Gellhorn was the youngest of the 16 reporters Roosevelt secretly tasked with covering the human effects of the Great Depression. Gellhorn was dispatched to the Carolina mill towns, where she combed the slums and Hoovervilles for clues as to the origin of the newfound, unwarranted panic. She saw people lose faith, pride, and morals with time. Gellhorn started writing articles that would become *The Trouble I've Seen* while she was a visitor at the White House. Gellhorn started writing the articles that would become *The Trouble I've Seen* while she was a visitor at the White House. Gellhorn started writing the interwoven short stories that were finally transformed into *The Trouble I've Seen* while staying as a guest at the White House. In them she captures the desperation of men emasculated by lack of work, women worn away by the effort of eking out the relief and children who had to learn to let go of their "got to have, got to have, can't have" desires and become adults before their time. (Ransley, "The Trouble I Have Seen: Review")

But destitution never quite extinguishes the human spark: a mother makes a feast of canned salmon for her downtrodden daughter; a young girl digs eagerly through slops and filth in search of a go-cart wheel; a young man becomes a thief to make his wedding day a final, exuberant shot at how life should have been. Gellhorn wrote that her reports gave only "a bird's eye view: a bird flying hard and fast" (Ransley).

With the same documentary clarity, *The Trouble I've Seen* by Gellhorn occasionally achieves an imaginative insight that goes beyond the project from which it grew and anticipates Gellhorn's eventual career as one of the most brilliant war correspondents of the 20th century. Martha Gellhorn's *The Heart of Another* is a collection of short stories that are the outgrowth of her own experiences and those of her associates in wartime Europe. These include the Spanish Civil War, the French occupation, the front in Finland, the Mannerheim Line, the air base, Corsica, the Tyrol, and many other places. Compared to her earlier works, these stories are emotionally and humanly barren because she is more aware of the agonies of unexpressed feelings that this war seems to produce. Both Luigi's House about a Corsican vineyard hand who gives up everything to safeguard what he believes is his, and *A Portrait of a Lady*, about a female writer who resorts to sex to get her story, are among the best of them.

Explaining the democracy of the country in the time of Hitler back then, she wrote in her renowned novel *A Stricken Field:* "This is a very remarkable and exciting country. Without Hitler, it might have been the model democracy of Europe. With Hitler, it is a fortress. And Hitler knows it. I seriously believe that on May 21, when the Czechs mobilized and called Hitler's bluff—the first nation to do so—the war was indefinitely postponed. Indefinitely means a year or two but anything may happen in that time: good or bad. I feel hopeful now, though it is inconceivable that this armed piece—with the armaments' burden and the exhausting tension—can endure for long. There are four Russian divisions and 1000 planes on the Romanian frontier and every key road in this country is barricaded and barbed-wired and all bridges mined. The air itself is unbreathable but at least the Czechs are not afraid and conf dent" (Gellhorn 304).

When it came to war reporting in the early 20th century, many English-speaking countries only considered combat reporting to be worthy of coverage and did not think women were capable of writing about such a manly subject. Most English-speaking Allied nations during WWII believed that female reporters were less reliable than their male colleagues. As a result, women's wartime journalism during World War II was unjustly devalued in the classroom. The twenty-first century has seen a rise in studies of women's and minorities' pasts, but most of this research has been conducted at the national level.

This book, with a focus on English-speaking Allied war correspondent Martha Gellhorn, argues that women's coverage of the Second World War in journalism is crucial to our understanding of the struggle as a whole. This book draws from two distinct types of secondary literature. The first set of biographies falls under the jurisdiction of specific nations. Here, these works examine the difficulties women faced in gaining access to battle zones and other military locations, as well as the limits placed on them by governments and military authorities throughout WWII and the treatment of female authors in the media. Institutionalised sexism is examined in this piece as a factor that hampered the credibility of female war correspondents and prevented them from having equal access to the conflict as their male colleagues. Rather than focusing solely on female reporters, it would be more beneficial to take into account female experience. Some determined women were able to break through to the front lines of their chosen fields. Yet they frequently displayed a style distinct from that of their male counterparts. There were a lot of first-person journalistic accounts during WWII because writers felt it was the best way to convey what it was like to be there. Female journalists adopted this strategy, but male reporters were more successful at making themselves look like a vital part of the team or the struggle by using this strategy. Though women reporters, even when writing in the first person, often wrote as bystanders of soldiers at work rather than being a part of the action, their pieces were true in-the-moment observations of the violence, terror, chaos, and misery of war.

Martha Gellhorn, by her own account, travelled to the front lines whenever possible and wrote extensively about the battle. Her works not only described the consequences of battle strategies, but also the sights, sounds, and even smells of the battlefield. Gellhorn was one of the only female reporters to ever fly above a battle zone. As a passenger in a P-61 Black Widow night fighter over Germany in January of 1945, she kept a diary detailing her experience. Gellhorn plays the role of the innocent outsider in this narrative, getting dressed in flying gear and sitting on a box in the plane while the troops give her a parachute and explain how to use it in case the plane gets shot down. However, Gellhorn's reporting reveals that she would have been an effective journalist even if she hadn't been integrated with the military. She went into great depth describing how night fighter pilots used radar to locate their targets but still had to get close enough to see their quarry before opening fire. Gellhorn praised the pilots for their dedication to duty and professionalism in her article. In the tale, Gellhorn emphasises the men and boys' selflessness by saying: "They performed their duty, and that was all there was to it" (Gellhorn, *A Stricken Field* 221) echoing the sentiments of many combat reporters who write about the bravery of troops under fire. There are soldiers, of course, but there are also daytime pilots and night-time pilots, tank crews and skydivers, and so on. They don't think things through; they act on impulse. Gellhorn witnessed the battle for the Gothic Line, a massive German defensive line encompassing Italy's boot, as the Eighth Army moved up the Italian peninsula.

Gellhorn, unlike an embedded battle writer, focused on the immense hodgepodge of humanity that was the Eighth Army which necessitated the creation of road signs in the form of pictures and code numbers. Tank traps, barbed wire, mines, subterranean pill bunkers, and tank turrets hidden in trenches were just some of the German defences she detailed. From a neighbouring hill, she communicated with the Canadian brigadier in charge of the operation, telling him that the sight looked unbelievable, small, crystal clear before them. after the fighting had ended. Men might be found hiding in tanks, beneath explosives, and under trees where shells landed.

She, along with the other survivors, walked the battlefield after the fighting had stopped. She went into greater detail about particular elements, such as the chunks of flesh and blood caked inside a Sherman tank turret, the young Italian girl laughing wildly on the porch of her bombed-out shack, and the Canadian soldier's coat spread tenderly across his body. It dealt with the horrors of war, yet was written in such a way that the reader cared about the characters. Although they were restricted in their access to the battlefield, women still managed to offer in-depth reporting that provided a multifaceted look at the war. While the wartime reporting of women is now recognised as crucial to comprehending the war, their contributions were frequently disregarded at the time. The role of journalists has changed significantly since 1945, but the stereotype of the strong female reporter remains popular in the United States. The emergence of women war correspondents, especially in broadcast news, demonstrates a continuing impulse to spice up the drama of combat reporting in a market-driven profession, despite the backlash that has resulted from portrayals of women in peril. They imperil their lives because they know that what the major networks want is a front-line narrative from a preferably lovely lady in a flak jacket, says one female war correspondent. Beyond the commercial viability of the lady reporter cliché, women have made significant contributions to journalism and military correspondence. Stories like those penned by Bly and Gellhorn about refugees, injured soldiers, and their exploits are more in line with the sensibilities of modern readers than the subjective reporting of their male colleagues who set the requirements for the twentieth-century norm. War correspondent Marie Colvin has said that forgetting the horrors and injustices of the past terrifies her more than any conflict. She spent the better part of four decades covering virtually every major conflict of the contemporary era, from the Iran-Iraq War to the Kosovo War and the engagement in Libya, Sierra Leone, Afghanistan, and Gaza. The complete list is both horrifying and impressive. Colvin drove into the heart of the battle, putting her life in danger so that the stories of ordinary people who were caught in the crossfire might be told. Even though Marie had lost an eye in the grenade explosion that occurred in Sri Lanka,

Colvin's friends thought with a sarcastic tone that she still had an eye for it.

In the backdrop of this chaotic century, reporting requires either bearing witness or immersing oneself in the action and then writing about it with honesty and compassion in the hopes of motivating readers to take action themselves. The genre of reportage differs from the verb to report, which designates the action of relating, recounting, describing, and telling a story. Speaking of Mary Douglas, who in Martha's work is a representation of herself, she wrote:

> She tried, leaning back and closing her eyes, to put in order what she had seen, heard, and what she had known before. She wanted to place her knowledge in paragraphs (a good opening sentence? she thought), so that it would be easy to handle when she came to write it. But it did not fit in paragraphs and she could not see it, plain and informative, colourful but unimpassioned, on a page. There was no beginning, no middle, no end. (Gellhorn *A Stricken Field* 118)

Reading for pleasure and to uncover hidden relationships between works by other writers or between authors' utilisation of similar or entirely different methodologies is what we currently refer to as intertextuality, a term derived from literary theory. You should try to obtain a sense of the author's history and thought processes rather than merely hunting for quotes to utilise in an essay or to impress your literary professor. The popularity of the memoir *In Extremis* written by Lindsey Hilsum and the film *The Private Combat* has contributed significantly to the widespread acclaim that has been bestowed upon Colvin's war communication as one of the finest examples of its kind. Her remarkable reporting is in line with a broader tradition of journalism that has, via a variety of writing styles and research methods, investigated the ethical repercussions of being a witness to war.

Before you start reading nonfiction, the reason you want to do so should be the first and most significant item you think about. When one is faced with a broad choice of reading and creative alternatives, one often finds oneself drawn to the ones that keep one firmly rooted in reality rather than those that lull him/her into the arms of fantasy. These questions assist us in defining our general expectations for the reading of nonfiction and in determining whether or not those expectations reflect our actual experiences.

Martha Gellhorn, an American journalist and reporter for *Collier's* magazine, was one of the first non-fiction writers, with her great eye for detail and polished prose. Her writing in the early 1940s had a significant effect on the growth of wartime communication and was a major contribution to this development. In the majority of her journalism, Gellhorn possesses a remarkable ability to write effortlessly and vividly about situations that take place in combat zones. After a brief period that was devoted to the presenting of factual information, she turns her focus to a more personal depiction of what it was like to be at the epicentres of conflict and, more crucially, to listen to people's tales. Narrating about how Martha Gellhorn saw the Normandy invasion, she recounts:

As the engines warmed up, they produced a buzzing sound and felt very heavy. The massive jets, most of which are black in colour, are about to take their spots on the runway one at a time as they roll out. After the first plane had disappeared into the distance and did not appear to be moving very quickly, we noticed that its tail light had begun to rise. Soon after, all thirteen planes that were taking off from this location gave the impression that they were floating against the sky as though it were water. They finally evolved into distant stars that moved at their own leisure. The conversation had reached its conclusion at that point. The activity came to a halt, and the guys went their separate ways. It appeared as though they would be absent for the entirety of the night. The strategy called for them to fly over France and drop bombs on marshalling yards in the hopes of severing one of the two rail lines that connected France and Italy for the shortest amount of time possible. In the event that they were successful, the soldiers in southern Italy would have an easier time of things for a period of time. (Gellhorn "There is a point where you feel so small and helpless in an enormous, insane nightmare of a world that you cease to give a hoot and start laughing")

The author paints the scenario with wide strokes, interweaving very short words with elaborate, novelistic descriptions to create a work of writing that has a rhythmic quality and a lyrical tone as well. Such cinematic approaches are utilised to completely submerge the reader in the action and give them the impression that they, too are present at the scene. Methods such as realism even if the dialogue was eavesdropped on, scene-by-scene reconstruction, backstory for characters, and flipping between first-person and third-person narratives were utilised in the 1960s as the forerunner of the so-called New Journalism. Even if the author strongly condemns any forms of violence, the use of vivid prose raises concerns about the possible fetishisation of war and conflict, particularly if it is accompanied by a depiction of cruel yet heroic fighting: "Be careful, Mary Douglas told herself, you're only a working journalist. It is better not to see too much if no one will listen to you" (Gellhorn, *A Stricken Field* 83).

This brief selection does not do justice to Gellhorn's stylistic range, but it is easy to see that her writing does not pretend to be objective. Gellhorn's entire oeuvre is infused with introspection on the role of the author's subjectivity within the reportage genre.

Gellhorn noted for her biting wit, hated the rules of writing dispassionately, calling them as objectivity garbage. *The Trouble I've Seen* (1936), a collection of short stories set in America during the Great Depression, *A Stricken Field* (1940), a novel set in war-torn Czechoslovakia, and *The Face of War* (1959), a comprehensive collection of war journalism, are some of her most well-known works. *Travels with Myself and Another* (1978) is the sole overtly autobiographical work of hers, and the other in the title is a reference to Gellhorn's late spouse, Ernest Hemingway.

Marie titled Gellhorn's acceptance speech for one of her many journalism awards "Courage Knows No Gender" because of her firm belief in the fact that war reporting of female correspondents is hardly different than that of men:

Does gender play a role in how wars are reported? Once upon a time, that question would make my skin crawl. Taking the same risks and covering the same story as my male colleagues, the idea that I would be judged as a woman war correspondent rather than a writer upset me. Those sentiments of mine were not novel. "Feminists nark me," wrote one of the century's greatest war correspondents, Martha Gellhorn. To label us as women's writers is an insult to women, and I believe that is what they have done. In the past, there was no such thing as a male writer. The reality of gender roles in warfare is stark and ancient. With few exceptions, armies are primarily male, even though as some of those exceptions amply demonstrate women are just as capable of fighting. (Colvin, "Courage Knows No Gender")

According to some critics, Gellhorn was the only female journalist to reach the Normandy landing beaches. When no publisher would send her to the front lines on D-Day during World War II, Martha Gellhorn sneaked aboard a hospital ship and became the only woman in the field and the only journalist to set foot on shore, as noted in the Oxford Companion to American Literature.

At first glance, Colvin's proposal of writing without reference to either sex may seem simple and straightforward. Among second and third-wave feminists and cultural theorists, the argument on this subject has a rich and storied history or more precisely, HER story, but it is undeniably idealistic. Literature and gender studies could benefit from beginning with the Poetry Foundation's suggested reading list. Writing about these two female war correspondents is not only fascinating in its own right but also offers a rare chance to rethink how we debate literary influences. "Anxieties of Influence", written by Harold Bloom, is the most frequently read book on the topic of literary dialogues. In this influential and somewhat stressful essay, Bloom portrays literature as a battlefield where modern writers contend with their predecessors. But is this really the only result that might occur? What if the authors stopped seeing themselves as the ones who need to mark, alter, and challenge the text and instead saw themselves as the ones who need to battle authority and tradition? What if, instead of competition, creative exchanges take the form of inspired teamwork? Describing her struggles of war reporting in the novel *A Stricken Field*, Gellhorn says:

No propaganda, they would say. We want the inside story. Make it clear, make it colourful, make it lively, If I knew how, I would write a lament. I would tell how J I heard the children sing once in Spain, in Barcelona, that cold and blowing March when the bombers came over faster than wind, so that it would all happen in here unending minutes, but if you saw them, they were hanging in the sky not moving, slow and easy, taking their time, you'd think, not worried about anything. But usually, the planes were higher than you could see or hear, and suddenly the streets beneath them fountained up, in a deep round echoing underground all-over-the-sky roaring that seemed never to finish, and the windows bent inward and the furniture shook on the floor and in the stillness afterwards you would hear one voice, wild and thin and alone, crying out sharply, and then silence. I heard the children at school, between air raids, sitting obediently on small red-painted chairs around a low piano; between air raids. The teacher struck chords on the piano and the children stood and lifted their faces to the dangerous sky and sang as softly and sweetly as you will ever hear an old song about being a good child, and sleep now, sleep well. I heard them again today. It is all the same. So, who wants to know that, and I better get to work. (82-83)

Gellhorn began working as a full-time journalist in the early 1930s. From the Spanish Civil War through the wars in Vietnam to wars in Central America, she covered it all as a journalist. In the end, the fact, that she had been married to Ernest Hemingway, her unwilling companion, affected how people viewed her later works. Mournfully describing the bloodshed and loss of lives in the field she wrote:

"It is like being buried alive, Mary Douglas thought, people deserted everywhere, scattered about in empty houses going crazy, and alone, and no one knowing who they are and no one hearing them, and no one helping. And no way to help, she thought. But it cannot be. It cannot be. What is worst is not to know what will happen," Rita said, who remembered too well. "Not to know whether it is concentration camp, or death, or torture. And then not to know where are their families, or what happens to the women, or if the men are still alive" (Gellhorn *A Stricken Field* 71).

Martha Ellis Gellhorn is the daughter of renowned gynaecologist George Gellhorn and his wife, Edna Fischell Gellhorn, and was born in St. Louis, Missouri. Her parents were both politically active. For a year, Gellhorn studied at Bryn Mawr College in Pennsylvania after finishing at John Burroughs School. She dropped out of college because she wanted to pursue a career in journalism instead. In 1929, she worked for the New Republic and the Hearst Times Union, but she had no training in journalism.

Gellhorn began her career as a foreign correspondent in Europe in the early 1930s. She was able to save money by negotiating free passage on the Holland America ship line in exchange for an article in the company's trade magazine. In Paris, she contributed to publications like *Vogue*, the Associated Press, and the St. Louis Post-Dispatch. Since she believed there could be no peace in Europe without the Franco-German rapprochement, she also affiliated herself with a group of young French pacifists. Bertrand, a French political scientist, journalist, and marquis, was her first husband during this time. Colette was his stepmother.

One possible reason for Gellhorn's 1934 return to the United States was to undergo an abortion. *What Mad Pursuit* (1934), a novel she wrote while living in Europe, marked her literary debut. The *New York Times* described it as a very personal piece about the lives of three American students after college which is vulgar, new, and engaging. In retrospect, Gellhorn says that she now regrets writing the bizarre account. She was employed by Federal Emergency Relief Administration (FERA) director Harry Hopkins to provide reports on the agency's Relief program's work in urban and industrial settings. Her report, written in the style of four stories, was published in 1936 under the title *The Trouble I've Seen*. H.G. Wells, with whom she was allegedly having an affair, penned the book's foreword.

Gellhorn met the President and Eleanor Roosevelt, who became lifelong friends, because of her job. In 1934 and 1935, Wells and Gellhorn were invited as guests of the first family to the White House, where Wells had an open invitation to visit. Wells started writing to Gellhorn after meeting her on his trip to the nation's capital. Gellhorn used the nickname 'Stooge' when writing to Wells. Wells and Gellhorn moved to Connecticut after spending time in Hollywood at Charlie Chaplin's house. Gellhorn began writing a new novel when she was in Germany. After the Nazis took control three years prior, Gellhorn felt it too tense to create fiction. Gellhorn visited Key West, Florida, near the year's conclusion in 1936 and met Ernest Hemingway there at the bar Sloppy Joe's. Gellhorn, at twenty-eight years old, was a successful author and aspiring journalist whose natural blonde hair and long legs caught Hemingway's eye. She ran upon Hemingway again in Madrid in 1937 and 1938 while reporting on the Spanish Civil War for Collier's Weekly.

Gellhorn visited Czechoslovakia and Finland in the late 1930s. When the Winter War broke out between Finland and the Soviet Union in 1939, she was there to see it unfold. She was visiting Helsinki when the city was bombarded as a declaration of war by the Soviet air forces. We concluded with admiration that the Finns were a hardy and unyielding race after hearing an Italian reporter say in Helsinki that anyone who could survive the Finnish climate could survive anything and after witnessing them treat this war as if three million people fighting against a nation of 180 million was nothing particularly remarkable. Small apples from Svinhufvud's orchard were presented to the visitors.

Gellhorn was surprised by the age of the Finnish fighter pilots she interviewed at the Karelian front and said that they ought to be going to college dances. Finnish public opinion was significantly swayed by Gellhorn's reporting which highlighted that Helsinki was not the aggressor. Describing the affected people's conditions in the war, she observes in A *Stricken Field:*

She imagined that on the faces of the women, there would be some sign of what had happened, even despair would be better than this, despair would have shaped, and brought the faces to life. But these people looked grey and empty and she thought, so that's the way it goes; they learn to keep quiet fast. ... She was walking quickly now, as if to leave behind whatever had silenced these others. She swerved to avoid a woman with a black felt hat, pulled down like a pot, and cracking shoes and a loose black coat, who carried a bundle wrapped in newspaper. A cleaning woman, Mary decided, going home from some office building to get supper, and tired anyhow as she is every day, but now more than tired. Two young girls, with their hair chopped into stiff short bobs, very blonde, unpainted, walked along not noticing the men or the shop windows. They must be salesgirls, Mary said to herself. (13)

Hemingway accompanied Gellhorn on her 30,000-mile trek to China in 1941.

When the war between China and Japan broke out, *Collier's* dispatched reporter Martha Gellhorn to China to cover the conflict. They went to Burma after seeing General Chiang Kai-shek and stayed there for a while. Gellhorn went to Singapore and Java, while Hemingway went back to Hong Kong. Hemingway told the magazine's readers that Gellhorn gets to the location, gets the tale, writes it, and comes home. Gellhorn later recounted her travels with her 'Unwilling Companion', in *Travels with Myself and Another* (1978). Besides Ernest the monster, Ernest the myth and E, she also referred to him as Hemingway by a few other nicknames. According to Hemmingway, Gellhorn was the most ambitious lady who ever lived. Both Hemingway and Gellhorn covered the outbreak of World War II in England in the early 1940s; Hemingway was searching for German submarines in the Caribbean, while Gellhorn was reporting from the United Kingdom. She came on his boat, the Pilar, a 38-foot diesel-powered vessel, with him in 1942. She hoped that by telling him that the place was crying out for you in Europe, she could entice Hemingway to go there. From 1943 to 1945, Gellhorn reported on the European theatre of war from various countries, including England, Italy, France, and Germany. Even though Hemingway was in England on assignment before the Normandy Invasion in 1944, he did not help Martha book a flight. Even better, he had surpassed Gellhorn as *Collier's* most senior reporter.

It took her two weeks, but she finally made it to London aboard a Norwegian cargo laden with explosives and amphibious personnel carriers. Gellhorn's interest in the continent began and continued during those thirteen years.

Now including a foreword by Bill Buford and photographs of Gellhorn with Hemingway, Dorothy Parker, Madame Chiang Kai-shek, Gary Cooper, and others, the new edition titled *Travels with Myself and Another* rediscovers the voice of an extraordinary woman and brings back into print an irresistibly entertaining classic: "Martha Gellhorn was so fearless in a male way, and yet utterly capable of making men melt," writes *New Yorker* literary editor Bill Buford. As a journalist, Gellhorn covered every military conflict from the Spanish Civil War to Vietnam and Nicaragua. She also bewitched Eleanor Roosevelt's secret love and enraptured Ernest Hemingway with her courage as they dodged shell fire together" (Gellhorn, *Travels with Myself and Another: A Memoir*).

Gellhorn released six novels between the years of 1934 and 1967. For the *Guardian* of London, she covered the Vietnam War in the 1960s and the Arab-Israeli War in 1967. Later, she would write that the American force in Vietnam was an army of occupation- victims and victimizers alike. As a result of political aggressiveness thousands of miles from home, they became victims and were forced to work as cashiers, clerks, or cooks. They oppressed Vietnamese people due to their racist views. It was during the 1962–1963 school year that Gellhorn made her way around to various universities in Germany. Now that she was away from the dutiful children singing the authorised opinions, she vowed she would never go back to Germany. She met Mrs. Mandelstam, the widow of poet and essayist Osip

Mandelstam (1891-1838), on a trip to the Soviet Union in 1972 concluded that the Russians seemed to have a special historical genius for oppressing and being oppressed. In the mid-1980s, she covered the conflicts in Central America for a news outlet. She went to Panama during the U.S. invasion without booking a hotel, according to a letter she penned at age 81.

Being more and more cautious when it comes to optimism and learnt that sentiments are more dangerous for the travellers Martha realises:

It is high time that I learn to be more careful about hope, a reckless emotion for travellers. The sensible approach would be to the expect the worst, the very worst, that way you avoid grievous disappointment and who knows with a tiny bit of luck, you might even have a moderately pleasant surprise, like the difference between hell and purgatory. (Gellhorn *Travels with Myself and Another: A Memoir* 306).

Her second collection of nonfiction, *The View from the Ground*, was published in 1988. Reporter Martha Gellhorn passed away in London on February 15th, 1998. Like any excellent journalist, Gellhorn could spot the crucial information in a crowd and convey it in a way that was easy to understand, witty, and precise. Even many years after the fact, she had a perfect memory for details like people's outfits and the topics of conversation on special occasions. On the other hand, she was often complaining about how poor her memory was. She lamented that there is no use of living so long, travelling so extensively, listening and looking so intently if, in the end, one might know what you know. In her essay "Memories", she added: "But I have no grip of time and no control over my memory" (05). It is published in December 1996's *London*

Review of Books. In 2012, Philip Kaufman's film on the love affair between Gellhorn and Hemingway, starring Nicole Kidman and Clive Owen, made its debut. One of the first female war correspondents in the world, Martha Gellhorn, had her collected letters, *Selected Letters of Martha Gellhorn*, published that summer. For over thirty years, Gellhorn wrote for The *Atlantic Monthly*.

She arrived in Madrid in 1937 with a rucksack, fifty euros, and an assignment to cover the Spanish Civil War for *Collier's* Weekly, and that was the beginning of Gellhorn's career as a writer. During this time, she met Ernest Hemingway, who was also working as a journalist in Spain. They eventually married in 1940, making Hemingway her second husband and she as his third wife. Gellhorn was a fearless journalist who would go to any length to get the story she needed, including stowing away on a hospital ship and sneaking ashore as a stretcher bearer during the D-Day landings in Normandy, riding along with British pilots on night bombing raids over Germany, and accompanying Allied troops during the liberation of Dachau. And her supplies of vitality seemed bottomless: at the incredible age of eighty-one, she was still reporting from the front lines in 1989, covering the U.S. invasion of Panama. The arrival of conflict in Bosnia was the only time she was unable to accept an assignment, justifying her decision by saying she was too old and not nimble enough for combat anymore.

She left for the Middle East in 1961 to spend time among the Arabs who had been uprooted by the establishment of Israel. In The Arabs of Palestine, she extensively described her research. The Palestinian refugees have the unenviable fate of being used as a tool in an endless conflict. There are growing red flags suggesting that Palestinian refugees could become more than just a pretext for a cold conflict with Israel. The Palestinian refugees in the Middle East, about whom we are told over, are just the beginning, not the end. Their job is to stick around and serve as an ever-present prod.

Humanitarian goals like returning refugees to their home countries are not the end game.

Although Gellhorn's coverage for *Atlantic* of the Adolf Eichmann trial is not technically speaking war reporting, it reveals the extent to which her experiences during World War II shaped her reporting style. Gellhorn wrestled with the themes of good and evil that the trial inevitably raised in Eichmann and the Private Conscience.

A letter that is quoted in *Gellhorn: A Twentieth Century Life* speaks about people's inhuman behaviour towards the war:

War happens to people, one by one. That is really all I have to say and it seems to me I have been saying it forever. Unless they are immediate victims, the majority of mankind behaves as if war was an act of God which could not be prevented; or they behave as if war elsewhere was none of their business. It would be a bitter cosmic joke if we destroy ourselves due to atrophy of the imagination. (Moorehead 280)

Adults in Germany, who were aware of Nazism and who cheered and admired Hitler in the millions until he started losing, have committed a national act of forgetfulness, pretending that they had nothing to do with the atrocities committed by the Hitlerian government. The youth know this is implausible, but one by one they defend their fathers' innocence, insisting that someone else's dad must have done the dirty work. Santayana observed that if one does not remember the past, one is doomed to repeat it. Germans are not a new people, and they are not trustworthy partners since they are taught in obedience and dedicated to moral whitewashing. While Gellhorn's reputation rests on her journalism, she was also a skilled novelist. Several of her works appeared in the *Atlantic* throughout her lifetime, and she went on to publish a total of five novels, fourteen novellas, and two collections of short stories. The August 1956 story titled "The Smell of Lilies" won the inaugural O. Henry Award for Best Short Story in 1958. The narrative follows the interactions between a cheating husband and his dying, oblivious wife. In typical Gellhorn fashion, it is brutally honest.

Today, female journalists are frequently present in active conflict zones, but this was not the case eight decades ago. World War II saw a small but significant number of female war correspondents about hundreds go to the front lines to report on the fighting. Just a small number of them, like Martha Gellhorn, have been honoured over the years. During her 50-year career as a correspondent, she covered numerous critical moments during World War II and subsequent conflicts, but is most remembered for being the third wife of the journalist and the literary genius Ernest Hemingway.

While writing a letter, talking about being lonely and being indifferent to others Martha says: "It is much harder to be lonely, when you have for a while stopped being lonely. I was used to having only myself, cold and hard as that is; I could live with it. And now I wait, for a voice, a face, a body, that is not going to be here, is not mine, does not in any case wait as I do, nor share this homesickness

.... How to explain that I taught myself to be tough and indifferent, because it mattered too much and learned not even to weep in my mind not to notice" (Gellhorn, *Selected Letters of Martha Gellhorn* 236).

Once back in the United States in the early 1930s, Martha struck up a friendship with none other than Eleanor Roosevelt. She stayed with the Roosevelts for two months, helping Mrs Roosevelt with her mail and her column for Woman's Home Companion in the evenings. That connection helped Martha get a job as a federal field investigator for the Federal Emergency Relief Administration. She later worked with Dorothea Lange to capture the effects of the Great Depression on ordinary Americans, including the plight of the homeless and the hungry. Martha was given a rare chance as a woman in the 1930s to research controversial themes before landing a coveted position as a foreign reporter.

She reported from the front lines, the hospitals where injured soldiers were treated, and the explosions in Barcelona. Martha was sent to cover the invasions of Czechoslovakia and Finland as Nazi Germany rearmed and became a greater danger to European security in the late 1930s. *A Stricken Field* details the harsh torture she endured at the hands of the Gestapo in Prague and her thoughts on reporting the events of that time.

In 1943, she accepted a job that would take her to Cassino, Italy, where she would report on orphans and the French Army's fight against the Nazis. Hemingway cabled her plaintively: "Are you a war correspondent or wife in my bed?" (Fergusson, "Are you a war correspondent or wife in my bed"). He got his answer on D-Day, June 6, 1944, when she stowed away on a hospital ship and landed on Omaha Beach soon after the invasion.

Hemingway was furious that she scooped him. The couple's marital problems reached a peak in 1944 when Hemingway used Martha's press credentials to cover the upcoming Allied assault of Normandy in England. After Hemingway stymied her efforts to obtain a press pass to catch a trip to Europe to cover the opening of a Second Front, she crossed the Atlantic in a ship full of explosives. In England, she learned that her spouse was cheating on her. Martha's divorce allowed her to devote more time to her career as a journalist. She discussed how youngsters were coping with the war and told the stories of pilots rescued from fiery accidents in the days leading up to D-Day. Since Hemingway now worked for the *Collier's*, Martha had to struggle to get a position in the press to cover the June 6, 1944 invasion of France. The southern British coast was, when she first spotted the hospital ship, prompting her to make haste. She deceived the military police into letting her on board by saying she had been assigned to conduct interviews with the ship's nurses. Once on board, she hid out in a lavatory for the duration of the crossing of the English Channel. Martha made her way aboard a landing boat functioning as a water ambulance once the ship had anchored off Omaha Beach. As a result of her efforts, on June 6, 1944, she was one of just a handful of women and journalists to set foot on the ground. She waded ashore to assist the medical staff in transporting the injured servicemen back to the hospital ship. After returning to the hospital ship, she recorded the talks of wounded men waiting to be removed from the beach on D-Day, demonstrating once again the resilience of the human spirit in the face of war and destruction.

British military police arrested Martha after D-Day and revoked her credentials. But she was not deterred by that failure. She was unhappy with the timeline. She wanted to return to the action as soon as possible and the military eventually granted her permission to cover the fight again. She travelled to every front of the battle she could find. She was dispatched to Europe to fulfil her duty, which did not include reporting on the privates or the lady's perspective. She went on to cover the Battle of the Bulge and other critical events in the European theatre of the war, but the liberation of Dachau was her crowning achievement. Dachau seemed to her the most ideal site in Europe to hear the news of victory as she wrote in *The Face of War*. The war was fought, without a doubt, to put an end to Dachau and all concentration camps like it. *TIME* magazine recognised Martha as one of *Collier's* rising stars during the war. Part of the reason for her success was her determination to share the experiences of regular people who lived during the war. She is an inspiration for her resilience and determination. She demonstrated, through her writing, the far-reaching effects of war on civilian life. After World War II, Martha reported on countless wars and military conflicts, such as the Arab-Israeli War, the Vietnam War, and the Invasion of Panama. While approaching retirement in 1988, she reflected on her career reporting the worst of humanity and stated: "There has to be a better way to govern the world and we had better see that we get it" (Gellhorn *The Face of War* 189).

Of all the things Martha Gellhorn did correspondence of wars stands out as her most significant achievement. Neither did she have a white robe nor did she act like a saint. The seductive power of war stories was something she was well aware of. Given that she was married to Ernest

Hemingway, one of the great spinners of self-aggrandizing narratives, for five years, it's not surprising that Gellhorn coined the word 'Apocrypha' to describe the habitual inventors of such fictions as detailed in Caroline Morehead's marvellous 2003 biography of Gellhorn. In the 'Preface' to her remarkable collection of reports, *The Face of War*, she described herself as a special type of war profiteer showing that she was not immune to the self-contempt inherent in the business of converting bloodshed and suffering into stories and money. The start of World War II is probably one of the most documented events in human history. With so much already written about the turbulent 1930s, it's hard to think of anything fresh that could be added to the canon.

Explaining about final battles in our species' war history in the "Introduction" of her book, Martha contends: "No wars, in the war-logged record of our species, have been terminal.

Until now, when we know that nuclear war would be the death of our planet. It is beyond belief that any governments–those brief political figures–arrogate to themselves the right to stop history, at their discretion" (Gellhorn, *The Face of War*).

Discussing the thoughtless, listless, lethargic, violent and destructive attitudes of the young people in her selected letters, Martha says:

According to temperament and surroundings, they are becoming careless, listless, inert or unruly, violent and destructive. What haunted Bruère was this spectacle of a lost generation for whom economic recovery would simply come too late. Talking of the young, Gellhorn wrote: They don't believe in man or God, let alone private industry; the only thing that keeps them from suicide is this amazing loss of vitality; they exist. (Moorehead *Selected Letters of Martha Gellhorn* 14)

A new perspective emerges, however, when one revisits an early narrative of Hitler's Germany's rise to power. Reading Martha Gellhorn's 1938 reporting from Czechoslovakia is like witnessing the rebirth of war in Europe from the ashes of the Great Depression. In 1938, Gellhorn was a fearless 30-year-old American war correspondent who had a penchant for finding the most dangerous conflict zones. After crossing the Atlantic to report on the Spanish Civil War, Gellhorn found herself in what was then Czechoslovakia, reporting on the German invasion of what was then called the Sudetenland. Gellhorn's writing style is ominous and full of atmosphere and emotion.

Foregrounding the military aggression that the Nazi regime was about to impose upon Europe, she portrays the day-to-day existence and the intricacy of events with a reality that only an eyewitness could have built.

As demonstrated in *The Trouble I Have Seen*, Martha Gellhorn was angry and despondent about the misery and poverty she had witnessed. She got herself fired for inciting a group of men on work relief, who were being exploited by a crooked contractor, to rise and break the windows of the FERA office in protest. Described as a dangerous communist, she was summoned back to Washington.

Gellhorn's approach was to merely narrate occurrences, with the deeper meaning and interpretation concealed. The Czechoslovak Social Democrats led a pro-democracy procession, and she describes it movingly at the beginning of her *Collier's* magazine report on the country from August 6, 1938. Slovak peasants in embroidered blouses, scarlet skirts, and high boots dance beside the

Bakers' Union as they march with enormous breakfast rolls on their heads. They perform for the president and the crowd with songs and cheers.

Democracy appears on every banner and sign. As a result of fears that they may have to fight for it, Czechs and Slovaks talk a lot about democracy. Without being overtly moralistic, Gellhorn successfully paints a picture of the 1930s and the impending big struggle. It is clear from reading Gellhorn's work that the Second World War and the epoch-defining clash between democracy and totalitarianism, epitomised in the most brutal form by the Nazi regime, was not a sudden event that caught the sleeping masses by surprise; rather, alarm bells were ringing across the continent, and commentators like Gellhorn, who had just witnessed the rise of fascism in Spain, were well aware of the dangers ahead. Her prose gracefully weaves in and out of peaceful country imagery, broken up by icy allusions to potential conflict. Describing the hardships behind her war reporting Martha says:

If I were a first-rate writer, I wouldn't mind a bit. What does depress me is this: it is so desperately hard and so obsessive and so lonely to write that, in return for all this work, one would like a little self-satisfaction. And that is never going to come, for the simple reason that I do not deserve it. I cannot be a good enough writer. You, see? I call it grim. But the future looks awfully clear to me. (Gellhorn, *Travels with Myself and Another* 217)

Behind the village of Troppau, which is on the border between Silesia and Czechoslovakia, are a few small hills that resemble the Ozarks and curl around the fields. While men use forks to harvest grain, women bend over in the beet fields. There are pillboxes hidden amid the haystacks, armed with machine guns and anti-tank guns, and soldiers standing as still as scarecrows among the toiling peasants. If you take a drive through the pine forests behind Troppau, not far from Haj, you'll spot a brand-new fort being constructed up on the hilltop and dozens of steel spikes set into concrete blocks along the road, where the barbed wire will be strung once it's finished. After passing over the river, the road emerges into a plain, having descended from the forest. That plain separates Czechoslovakia from Germany; across the nearest field is a triple row of barbed wire on enormous spools; and beside the river is a black cement-and-steel gun fortress containing machine guns, antitank guns, and the highly perfected antiaircraft guns in which all of Czechoslovakia has faith. The girls are drying their hair after a swim in the river as three soldiers chat with them. Gellhorn did her homework on the political and social unrest in addition to the military build-up, as evidenced by her story. In her speech, she addresses the dwindling membership of the Social Democratic Party, which has been hit hard by the Great Depression. She keeps a journal of her interactions with the Heinlein Nazis, a German minority among the Slavic population of Czechoslovakia who, she writes, had expressed limited support for the Nazi party until the fascists, who used nationalism to scapegoat Slavs and Jews for the onset of economic depression, pushed them into their hands. All of this unrest can be attributed to the small but vocal German minority in the area. Two million of the 3.5 million Germans living in what is now called Czechoslovakia were identified as Henlein Nazis. Social Democrats made up 80% of Germans up until 1935; these individuals were firmly committed to democracy and lived comfortably in Czechoslovakia. Afterwards, 500 factories collapsed, including those that made glass, beads, porcelain, jute, sugar, and textiles, all of which employed these people and sent their products all over the world. During the Great Depression, the Henleinists believed they were being deliberately starved by the Czechs, whom they held responsible. She wrote about the local Nazi party's leader she met: "He is a good guy who reads the paper to learn about politics. He claims they do not seek conflict but rather employment. No one cares to visit Gottesgabe because the Czechs have such poor relations with Germany" (Malloryk).

Gellhorn is compassionate toward every person she writes about. While she does not deny the Nazi party man's sinister political ties, she does detail the miserable conditions in which party supporters lived, including huts where children went hungry on heated bread and water and nightmare poorhouses full of the elderly. A Jewish lawyer and the wife of a wine merchant both listen to her, and both reveal their apprehensions. In the years before the Great Depression, they had been contributing members of the community. Since the beginning of recorded history, they have called that place home. Customers had dried up, however. Previously cordial ties become antagonistic in months. There is no sugar-coating in Gellhorn's transcription of the conversation. She claims that since the beginning of May, nobody has bought from them or even acknowledged them in passing. However, even though they now appear to be lonely, everyone here used to find happiness.

Many Czechs, Gellhorn notes, had hope that they might withstand the German invasion. However, Gellhorn considered these preparations as woefully inadequate after experiencing the horror of contemporary battle in Spain, as seen by her commentary.

Gellhorn describes feeling uneasy as he watches a young boy ride up a street on his bicycle while honking his horn like an air-raid siren. He reflects on how 95 seconds were all it took to destroy a significant portion of Barcelona and bury alive hundreds of people. The child can make the journey up the village street on his bicycle within 95 seconds.

When she considers the oil riches of Romania, the wheat of the Ukraine, and the Black Sea beyond, her assessment of the possibilities for peace in Czechoslovakia becomes even more pessimistic. If a major power ruled Czechoslovakia, it would be well-positioned to launch attacks across Western Europe and into the Mediterranean. The tragedy of Czechoslovakia is that it stands in the way.

Present for the start of hostilities, Gellhorn's exploits continued even after the conflict began. Despite Gellhorn's track record of success as a journalist and her undeniable bravery, she was not given access to cover the D-Day landings due to the prevailing sexism of the 20th century. Despite this, she continued her war reporting. She secretly boarded a ship carrying medical personnel to Normandy, hid in a restroom, and then waded ashore with the water ambulances' staff. As the first female correspondent to cover the landings, her narrative appeared in *Collier's* magazine before that of Ernest Hemingway, who had been commissioned to write for the magazine. Later, Gellhorn was one of the first journalists to enter the Dachau concentration camp after its liberation. Despite the atrocities of World War II, she was nevertheless eager to cover the conflict as a journalist. She continued to write about the Arab-Israeli conflict, the US invasion of Panama, the Vietnam War, and the assault on Cambodia. She was elderly and ill at the time of her 1998 death in London, which all signs point to being a suicide. In 2018, a blue plaque maintained by English Heritage at her 28-year-old London home on Cadogan Square was unveiled in her honour.

Reporting the misery of the sufferers on the battlefield she writes:

The newspapers said it was the hottest summer on record, and every day, braggingly, listed deaths by sunstroke, heat prostration. The people on the block suffered like animals, going leadenly through the days, their eyes aching and glazed from heat, thirsty, unable to sleep at night in the closed, airless rooms. The pavement burned through shoe soles, and the slight, unhealthy grass withered into a brown crust. Mrs Mayer endured this summer, as she had others before it. (Gellhorn, *The Trouble I Have Seen* 227)

She said nothing, since it was useless to complain, and looked forward to nothing, realizing that the winter would merely be a change to enduring cold.

The riveting, untold history of a group of heroic women reporters who revolutionized the narrative of World War II from Martha Gellhorn, who out-scooped her husband, Ernest Hemingway, to Lee Miller, a *Vogue* cover model turned war correspondent. On the front lines of the Second World War, a contingent of female journalists were bravely waging their own battle. Barred from combat zones and faced with entrenched prejudice and bureaucratic restrictions, these women were forced to fight for the right to work on equal terms with men.

The Correspondents: Six Women Writers on the Front Lines of World War II by Judith Mackrell follows six remarkable women as their lives and careers intertwined: Martha Gellhorn who got the scoop on Ernest Hemingway on D-Day by travelling to Normandy as a stowaway on a Red Cross ship; Lee Miller, who went from being a *Vogue* cover model to the magazine's official war correspondent; Sigrid Schultz, who hid her Jewish identity and risked her life by reporting on the Nazi regime; Virginia Cowles, a society girl columnist turned combat reporter; Clare Hollingworth, the first English journalist to break the news of World War II; and Helen Kirkpatrick, the first woman to report from an Allied war zone with equal privileges to men.

CHAPTER IV

Women and War Work: A Study through Gellhorn's Short Stories and Novellas

Even though Martha Gellhorn is more renowned for her outstanding journalism, the collection of her short stories and novellas highlights her exceptional abilities as a social observer of customs and cultural differences in locations that include the United States, England, Italy and Africa. The four novellas from *The Trouble I've Seen* (1936), her work from the Great Depression, to the three novellas from *The Weather in Africa* (1978), are all included in *The Novellas of Martha Gellhorn*. The novel is a result of Gellhorn's obsession with travel and desire to learn about different cultures. The novels she wrote for President Franklin D. Roosevelt's Federal Emergency Relief Administration are first-person stories of the people she met while doing her war work. The thoughts and attire of these people are described in fine detail and with empathy, but astonishingly little of the sentimentality that frequently taints proletariat fiction from the 1930s. The tales seem to be recent.

Gellhorn's later fiction often focuses on the subject of marriage; indeed, her second book of novellas, *Two by Two* (1958), takes the titles of its four stories from the marriage service: "For Better for Worse," "For Richer or Poorer," "In Sickness and in Health," and "Till Death Us Do Part." Here she shows a wonderful ear for dialogue, revealing the joys and tensions of courtship and marriage through the exchanges of lovers who often misunderstand the import of each other's words. She continues this interest in the vagaries of marriage in the three novellas included in *Pretty Tales for Tired People* (1956).

Gellhorn lived many different lives in her well-travelled career, but it is a tribute to her imagination that she was able to create whole worlds and independent personalities that transcend their roots in her biography. Although Gellhorn does not adopt an explicitly feminist stance, her delicate depictions of men and women invariably bring up concerns regarding women. Her male and female characters repeatedly circle around the problem of commitment to each other. There are happily married couples in her fiction, but they are a rarity, serving only as fixed points in an unstable marital universe in which the most urbane couples take lovers and treat marriage as a form of convenience, as a necessary (even comfortable) institution, but rarely as a permanently romantic or inviolable union.

Women in Gellhorn's fiction frequently find themselves alone, having been rejected and occasionally tricked by their male loves and husbands. However, males are not necessarily villains, and women can be fools. Gellhorn's depiction of the sexes is devoid of sentimentality. Women are alone because marriage, in her opinion, is a tough institution to maintain. Her ladies can be lost both inside and outside of marriage since it can disclose or worsen their flaws, but it is not a cause of human failing.

Gellhorn has never written a programmatic piece. Her values stem from her meticulous observations of people and situations. She may be just as harsh on her female characters as she is on her male counterparts. She has spent little time lamenting the injustice of male privilege, preferring to strive for her place in traditionally masculine domains. Gellhorn's interest is social justice as her stories demonstrate. She argues that if humans are treated correctly, topics such as gender equality and women's rights will receive adequate attention.

Gellhorn abandoned the security of her wealthy family in St. Louis, Missouri, at an early age in pursuit of a life of adventure, most notably as a fearless war correspondent. To top it all off, he manages to debunk the Hemingway myth by depicting herself as a multifaceted, courageous and maverick. Despite her privileged upbringing in St. Louis and her marriage to Ernest Hemingway, one of the literary giants of the twentieth century, Martha Gellhorn rose to prominence as a war correspondent for the international press, as well as a novelist and short story writer of considerable skill and vision.

Edna Fischer Gellhorn, the author's mother, was a prominent suffragist and close friend of Eleanor Roosevelt's due to their shared belief in the importance of women's emancipation and social standing. Gellhorn worked as a journalist and social activist for the Roosevelt administration throughout Franklin D. Roosevelt's twelve years in office. She attended Bryn Mawr University for two years, from 1926 to 1929, where she published poems in the student literary magazine. Gellhorn was transferred from Bryn Mawr to the Albany Times Union as a cub reporter in her senior year. Bertrand de Jouvenel, a French pacifist and internationalist, became her first spouse while she was reporting on female delegates to the League of Nations for the St. Louis Post Dispatch in 1930. The wedding took place in the summer of 1933. For her first book, Gellhorn used her own experiences as a young journalist to write *What Mad Pursuit*. Some reviewers criticised the autobiography's phoney attempts at literary pretensions. Reviews for Gellhorn's second book, an anthology of short stories based on her time as a FEMA investigator exposing corruption and abuse, were more positive. Critics praised the story for being so obviously based on the author's actual life experiences. The journalistic urgency that permeated Gellhorn's subsequent novels began with her debut. Hemingway and Gellhorn happened upon each other in Key West in 1936. Gellhorn and Hemingway had an affair after her divorce from Jouvenel, even though Hemingway was still legally married to his second wife, Pauline Pfeiffer. They both happened to be in Spain in May 1937, while *Collier's* Weekly reporter Martha Gellhorn was there covering the Spanish Civil War for the magazine. When the bombing of Madrid by the Loyalists began, she and Hemingway stayed at the Hotel Florida. Gellhorn, who had grown fond of the Republican cause, tried to convince Roosevelt to take a stand against the fascist invaders. She supported the Spanish Republican movement by visiting the United States in 1938 and making radio broadcasts from Spain. Gellhorn, a strong-willed and independent woman, altered the landscape of journalism by proving that women might succeed where males were once supposed to have a monopoly. Eight years before World War II, Gellhorn covered major events for *Collier's*, beginning in Spain and continuing through Czechoslovakia, Finland, China, the United Kingdom, France, Italy, Germany, and Java. Being a journalist has helped her become a more astute observer and reporter, but it has also taken a toll on her personal life. She and Hemingway married in 1940, but they divorced in November 1945.

Her novel, *A Stricken Field*, recounts her time spent in Czechoslovakia during the terrible Munich Agreement. She wrote the novel *Liana* in response to Hemingway's claims that she had been unfaithful to him while they were in Cuba. In 1966, Gellhorn went to *The Guardian* of London as a war reporter to cover the Vietnam War and the Israeli-Palestinian conflict, both of which she had witnessed firsthand during her four years spent in Mexico which formed the subject of her memoir *The Lowest Trees Have Tops*. She was against the United States getting involved in Vietnam but cheered on Israel's success in their conflict with the Arab world. Even when her marriage to *Time* magazine's former editor Tom S. Matthews ended in 1963, Gellhorn continued her trips across the world.

After a journey to Africa in 1978, the author published *Travels with Myself and Another*, a collection of three stories with a common thread. Two books, *The Face of War* and *The View from the Ground* collected her war reporting from the front lines. She kept up her career as a writer and social critic even as she became older. Gellhorn passed away at the age of 89 in 1998. Pearl K. Bell evaluates the novellas of Martha Gellhorn, with extensive coverage of Gellhorn's life and career, giving special emphasis on her novellas. The American economic collapse of the 1930s was devastating on many levels.

Unemployment, hopelessness and horrific poverty were captured by a lady who would go on to become one of the finest war correspondents of the twentieth century. Gellhorn's writing in this style is as direct, vivid, and empathetic as her later reporting, especially when it comes to the plight of regular individuals thrust into extraordinary situations. In 1936, *The Trouble I've Seen* was praised by critics. *The Trouble I've Seen: Four Stories from the Great Depression* was the subject of an initial October 1936 review by John Selby for the Wilkes-Barre Record. Looking at the halftone on Gellhorn's book cover, the readers may think that she is a debuting socialite.

All the tales are equally interesting. It's hard to find the right adjective, but the word superb comes to mind. After three years and a bohemian love affair in Paris, Martha Gellhorn came home to take a job that would take her far from the city's intellectuals on the Left Bank. Gellhorn, then 25 years old, was one of 16 reporters selected to cover the black hour of our national existence in briefings to Roosevelt's White House. Gellhorn went to the Carolina mill towns to investigate the cause of the nameless, unreasoning terror that had risen in the place of the American ideal where she saw the slow but steady erosion of faith, pride, and morals.

With the same level of documentary accuracy, *The Trouble I Have Seen* occasionally reaches a level of imaginative understanding that goes beyond the project from which it was born and provides insight into Gellhorn's subsequent career as one of the most outstanding war correspondents of the 20th century. These four related essays capture Martha Gellhorn's first-hand experience of the Great Depression as she saw it. In the face of sudden unemployment, horrible poverty and pessimism, the stories illustrate the slow breakdown of the simple, homely sufficiency of American life in a startling way.

These photos show a generation of men who have lost faith in both society and the private sector.

Sixteen reporters were selected and paid to furnish Roosevelt with confidential reports on the human stories underlying the Great Depression's statistics. Martha was the most recent addition. The financial toll of unexpected ruin is laid bare here. One may hear the early cadence of the woman widely regarded as the best war correspondent this century. (Mackrell, *The Correspondents: Six Women Writers on the Front Lines of World War II* 128) In the mid-1930s, Gellhorn was among a group of authors tasked with painting a realistic picture of the plight of the poor for the leaders of the new welfare programmes, in addition to her work covering travel and war. Four novellas she authored as a result of her experience are included here.

Each story depicts desperation and poverty with no sugar-coating, and tackles racial attitudes and injustices head-on, without offering any pat solutions or false hope like Harry Crews' autobiography *Childhood*, but written from a cold, dispassionate third-person perspective. When compared to Crews' story, Gellhorn's characters are realistic about their failure and the impending collapse of a civilization that, in their eyes, has already failed. (Mackrell, *The Correspondents: Six Women Writers on the Front Lines of World War II* 128)

Martha Gellhorn has published 15 novellas and 2 story collections (1908-1998). Despite her best efforts, most people will remember her for her brief marriage to Ernest Hemingway during World War II rather than her novels.

She covered conflicts as diverse as the Spanish Civil War and the American invasion of Panama in 1989 for major news outlets over nearly four decades. *The Trouble I Have Seen* is Gellhorn's first work of fiction, and it was published in 1936.

Gellhorn was motivated by the Great Depression to write four short stories about the challenges of the common man and his family. She writes of the agony endured by those families during the war:

Farming is a family affair for Mrs. Madison, her son, and her daughter-in-law. Mrs. Maddison concluded that everyone had a better time at some point in their lives.

Once upon a time, we were actual people; we had homes, families, and plans for the following year and the next, the author writes. Joe, Peter Joe, and everyone else named Joe all work for a labour union. Pete, being a union member, has gone on strike. They both end up in a sticky situation. (Gellhorn, *The Trouble I Have Seen* 87)

The character Jim's efforts in *The Trouble I Have Seen* to keep his employment are unsuccessful, and as a result, his family suffers a devastating blow. Ten-year-old entrepreneur Ruby comes up with an idea to make money. It is quite evident that Gellhorn has a soft spot in her heart for victims of wrongdoing. Moreover, that is a great deal of information that was both useful and fascinating about that era. It's important to note that the NRA is actually an acronym for the National Rifle Association, not the National Relief Association. Surprisingly, the vast majority of people didn't welcome the opportunity to receive aid. An underlying resentment of the questions and the powerlessness that came with being on medication was obvious. (Gellhorn, *The Trouble I Have Seen* 97)

Other writers began to admire Gellhorn after reading Paula McLain's *Love and Ruin*. All acquired great insight into her writing process which was a result of her determination to complete this and other works. A journalist's perspective on poverty's pessimism is what reflected in *The Trouble I Have Seen* published in 1936 which takes a sobering look at the real people who suffered during the Great Depression. FERA administrator Harry Hopkins chose a group of sixteen people, including Gellhorn to travel to areas with the worst unemployment and poverty rates, conduct thorough interviews with as many locals as possible, and document their results.

Gellhorn wrote the four tales in this *The Trouble I Have Seen* collection based on the classified reports she gave to Hopkins. There are stories here about kids who had to drop out of school to make ends meet, young adults who were open to love anywhere they found it, and workers who joined a union because they believed they deserved better working conditions. The relief workers she portrays in each of the four stories are particularly poignant. The Depression has left an indelible mark on the minds of relief workers and those on relief as they call themselves.

The words and actions show both compassion and contempt for the poor. Because of the continued relevance of these feelings, reading *The Trouble I've Seen* is as important now as it was in the 1930s. In 1932, with the economy in a free fall, Herbert Hoover lost the presidency to Franklin Roosevelt who campaigned on a platform of stopping the country's descent into poverty. A relief administration of unprecedented scale was set up as soon as possible to aid the people who needed it most. It may have taken four months, but four million people have found employment again.

One of the earliest government jobs in the country was established by Harold Hopkins, a key component of Roosevelt's rescue effort. He recruited 16 authors and journalists including economists and novelists to conduct the interviews for him and receive their transcripts and notes. They visited every area in the country that had an exceptionally high rate of unemployment or poverty. They recorded their findings in detail and forwarded them to Hopkins. He wanted to put himself in the shoes of a man who had just lost his job, his money, and his home while watching his family spiral into poverty and despair. As the youngest member of Hopkins' team of detectives, Martha Gellhorn, uncovered a subject for his second book while conducting research for a report at Hopkins.

The Trouble I Have Seen is comprised of four short stories about people in the United States during the Great Depression who endured dire poverty, unemployment, and hopelessness. The Roosevelt administration employed a team of 16 reporters whose job was to uncover the human stories lurking behind the Depression-era data and report them accurately and confidentially to the president. Martha was the most recent addition. The financial toll of unexpected ruin is laid bare here.

One may also get a glimpse of the early writing style of the lady who is usually acknowledged to be the most talented war correspondent of this century. Martha Gellhorn's Great Depression anecdotes are a first-person description of the events she witnessed at that time. In the face of unexpected unemployment, appalling poverty, and pessimism, the stories reveal surprisingly the slow breakdown of the simple, homely sufficiency that formerly characterised American life. These pages make it quite evident how much it will cost to lose everything all at once. They perfectly portray the ambience of a generation that has been dragged into indifference as well as the mindset of young men who no longer trust in man or God, let alone private industry.

Gellhorn claims that she trained herself to be mentally tough since it was too vital, and she also learned not to cry while reporting and writes: "How to explain that I taught myself to be tough and indifferent, because it mattered too much and I learned not even to weep in my mind not to notice" (Moorehead, *Selected letters of Martha Gellhorn*, 119).

The Trouble I've Seen was written in 1936 as a collection of four short stories. It was re-released at the end of November by the travel books publisher *Eland*, with an "Introduction" by Moorehead. The stories follow the lives of five Americans who were impacted in various ways by the Great Depression, including soup factory workers Joe and Pete, who are laid off after a strike that results in marginal improvements in working conditions; Jim, a depressed young man who steals from the clothing store where he works as a delivery boy so that he can have Nic and Mrs. Maddison, a mother of grown children and staunch supporter of President Roosevelt, who loses her job as a result of the Depression.

Some of her best examples of this war reporting skill are the stories she tells about the shame of poverty, such as Pete selling shoelaces and gum on the street and being horrified when he discovers a blind man on a neighbouring corner doing the same thing, or Jim deciding that being unemployed was something to be ashamed of, as you'd be ashamed of a jobless person.

Mabel S. Ulrich praised the book for its realism,

saying that its four stories ring as realistic as an account from a relief worker's notebook and that it seems knitted not out of words but out of the very tissues of human beings. Thousands of people in the country have been inspired by stories of shovel-leaners and chisellers or by the nebulous belief that if a guy is ready to labour, he can definitely acquire anything (Arons, "Chronicling Poverty with Compassion and Rage").

Although *The Trouble I've Seen* was technically a work of fiction, its urgent documentary power was recognised, as we can infer from comments like these. Gellhorn's FERA assignment had a significant impact on the characters and events in her novels, and several of the plot-lines can be directly related to her reporting the Campbell's factory workers strike and amateur prostitution were bounties in the novel. Giving a brilliant idea to all the men out there for a beautiful New Year's resolution who run the world Gellhorn says: "On the night of New Year's Day, I thought of a wonderful New Year's resolution for the men who run the world: get to know the people who only live in it" (Gellhorn, *The Face of War* 98).

Either women were fired to make place for the returning soldiers, or they continued to work alongside men with lesser pay. The truth is that long before World War II's conclusion, many women had already refused to accept lower pay for work that men had traditionally done. Women who worked on London's buses and trams went on strike in 1918 to ask for equal pay with men. The London Underground and other South East cities joined the strike. In the United Kingdom, women have never organised, led or won a strike for equal pay.

The War Cabinet established a committee to investigate

the topic of equal pay when women began to advocate for it. After the war, the committee's final report was released and sent to the public report of the War Cabinet Committee on Women in Industry. This paper endorses the concept of equal compensation for equal labour. They reasoned that women's output would be less than men's because of their reduced strength and unique health concerns. Despite evidence that women had taken over men's tasks and executed them efficiently during the war, the popular and official view that women were less productive than men did not shift. Unions were assured that pay parity would be maintained even if women were shown to have entirely replaced talented men. However, it was made very apparent that these modifications were just temporary and would be reversed once the war was over and the troops returned. By the end of World War I, one million more women were working than in the summer of 1914. The vast majority of them had served in the armed forces before. An abundance of working-class women is nothing new; women from lower socioeconomic backgrounds have always had paid employment.

Women of all socioeconomic backgrounds helped keep the house fires burning during World War II by working in a variety of low-skilled and labour-intensive occupations, such as coal-heavers, railway porters, land-girls, carpenters, mechanics, postwomen, policewomen, and munitions workers. Women have proven themselves to be more than just passive bystanders during the battle. They contributed to the victory and changed the way people viewed traditional gender roles at the same time.

Several suggestions from the All-Party Speakers Conference were adopted into the Representation of the

People Act. The first bill giving women the power to vote was passed in the United Kingdom on February 6th, 1918. By the end of World War I, one million more women were working than in the summer of 1914. The vast majority of them had served in the armed forces before. The Act granted the franchise to women over the age of 30 who met one of the following criteria: they owned a home, were married to a homeowner, paid less than £5 per year in rent, or were graduates of a British university or were otherwise similarly qualified. Roughly 8.5 million women may have cast ballots in the 1918 midterm elections. At last, some women were able to participate in government.

Suffragist and suffragette candidates ran for the first time in this election, but none of them were successful in getting elected to parliament. The movement for women's suffrage was dismayed by the minimum age requirement. They expected that women above the age of twenty-one would be able to vote in elections just like males, but this was not the case. Two main factors caused the government to be reluctant to take this action. As a first step, if all women over the age of twenty-one had been granted the right to vote, they would have outnumbered male voters and formed the majority of the electorate. To add insult to injury, women under the age of thirty were considered too flighty and hence disenfranchised to vote for a member of parliament. Historians have spent a lot of time debating the significance of this landmark vote for women. Although expressing appreciation for their contributions to the war effort was crucial, it was not the only reason. Since women have made significant contributions to society, no nation could reasonably deny them the right to vote. There were several factors at play, including the war and the coalition government created in May 1915 which included several politicians who favoured women's suffrage, but many of the reasons against women's suffrage crumbled after the war ended. Asquith, who was opposed, was succeeded as prime minister in late 1916 by David Lloyd George, who had been the suffragette movement's most outspoken opponent for the first 10 years of his time as an MP. By 1917, Lloyd George had changed his tune, and he was more sympathetic to the campaign fighting for women's right to vote in the United Kingdom case. With time, women's right to vote gained more and more support. The first wave of women's suffrage led to several key steps toward lessening the vast inequities between men and women, and it was facilitated by the fact that women had played a significant role during World War II. This started as a slow but steady progression. In 1919, the Sex Disqualification Removal Act was passed, making it illegal for employers to discriminate against women based on their gender. This move made it possible for women to become lawyers and serve as solicitors, barristers, and magistrates. Eventually, most fields opened their doors to women, albeit tentatively in some, like the Civil Service. May Ying Welsh, an international crisis correspondent for Al Jazeera, claims in Barbara Kopple's 2005 documentary bearing witness on women war correspondents in Iraq following the Second Gulf War that her job put her in a dangerous situation. Mary Rogers, a photojournalist, argues that journalists are fair game in war zones because of their responsibility to report on the depth of human suffering amid military and political developments. Despite this, women continue to pack their bags and prepare for a journey straight into the centre of a human maelstrom, complete with laptops, satellite phones, notebooks, and pens. Hard-earned news has a shorter shelf life in the public consciousness and is pushed aside by celebrity updates and political tweeting ("Women's suffrage in the United Kingdom").

A journalist must put herself in the forefront to bring us the news of war, of how our warriors are doing in Iraq or Afghanistan or even on the Mexican border, at a time when they are under extreme scrutiny because of political rhetoric and manipulation. It was hoped that no young ladies would be swayed by this show and think that being a war journalist is a glamorous profession as a result of watching it. There is no greater danger for women in conflict zones than there is for men. However, in recent years, local citizen journalists, including many female reporters, have stepped in to fill the void left by the decline of foreign correspondents. In 1966, a young American journalist called Frances FitzGerald began covering the war in South Vietnam for magazines like the New York Times Magazine. When the reporting stopped being important to her, she stopped doing it. She came from a wealthy white household, making her the unlikeliest of war correspondents. Desmond FitzGerald's mother, Marietta Tree, was a liberal activist and socialite. Despite growing up in a home with servants and horses, FitzGerald had to fend off advances from famous people like Adlai Stevenson her mother's boyfriend and Henry Kissinger. Thanks to her family's connections, she was able to break into New York's feature journalism industry, but she was ultimately unable to pursue the work she was passionate about because of her gender. At the age of 25, she alone travelled to Saigon, just as the American war was intensifying, to get away from this glittering trap. Through their reporting on the Vietnam War, David Halberstam, Neil Sheehan, and Malcolm Browne became three of the most revered journalists of the 20th century. Every single person of them was a man. There was no shortage of coverage of lies and gaffes made by American politicians. FitzGerald looked at it from a unique perspective. She had a sheltered upbringing and was shocked to learn of the suffering endured by the Vietnamese people as a result of the American occupation, which included the loss of life and limbs as well as the dilution of their sense of national identity.

The politics of Buddhist students, the tragedies of refugees, the tactics of the Viet Cong, and the history and culture of Vietnam captivated her instead of the competition with her male colleagues, and she spent her time away from the office visiting hospitals, villages, and slums. When the United States assumed the role of colonial power previously played by the French, no politicians or journalists warned the American people that the war was hopeless. Someone in their twenties who had graduated from Radcliffe and had an interest in French ethnography and immersive reporting was the one who had to carry this horrible news home.

The Vietnam War had already generated some of the best journalism of the century, launching the careers of young journalists like David Halberstam, Neil Sheehan and Malcolm Browne. They were all men. All of them focused on the combat as well as the lies and failings of American officials. FitzGerald went after a different story. She had been sheltered her entire life and was deeply moved by the Vietnamese people's suffering—not merely their deaths, injuries, and displacement, but also their loss of identity under the crushing the weight of the Americans. Rather than competing with her male colleagues, she spent time in hospitals, villages, and slums, becoming immersed in Buddhist students' politics, refugee tragedy,

Viet Cong strategy, and Vietnamese history and culture. It took a Radcliffe graduate in his twenties with a flair for French ethnography and immersive reporting to break the awful news that no authorities or journalists were telling Americans that the war was futile because the US had taken the French imperialist role in Vietnam.

In *The Atlantic* describing Gellhorn, Elizabeth Becker remarked: "She was looking at things in a completely different optic like she was from a different country—a whole new meaning to the phrase foreign correspondent" (Becker, *You Don't Belong Here: How Three Women Rewrote the Story* 79). FitzGerald used her different optic and formidable intellect to pursue investigations that culminated in *Fire in the Lake*, published in 1972, one of the most important and decorated books of the war.

You Don't Belong Here tells the story of FitzGerald and two other women in Vietnam—the French photographer Catherine Leroy and the Australian correspondent Kate Webb. Becker is a former correspondent in Cambodia and the author of *When the War Was Over*. She was the first journalist to interview Pol Pot, and barely escaped the Khmer Rouge alive. Her theme in *You Don't Belong Here* conveyed with controlled anger in a riveting narrative using unpublished letters and diaries is that women reporters changed the way the war was covered. Before Vietnam, they had been barred from combat by the

U.S. government which didn't stop a few legendary writers from slipping past the barriers, such as Martha Gellhorn in World War II. Vietnam was an undeclared war. So the rules were never clear. Women journalists were still subjected to discrimination, harassment, and contempt, but they didn't have to ask permission to go where the men went, and often where the men didn't go. Vietnam became the first war in which women had a fighting chance as reporters. The difficulty of gaining acceptance forced them to find their way which led to ground-breaking work.

Becker, a former Cambodia correspondent, was the first journalist to interview Pol Pot and to survive the Khmer Rouge, both of which she chronicles in her book When the War Was Over. Her claim, presented in the riveting story "You Don't Belong Here", which makes use of previously unreleased letters and diaries, is that female reporters ushered in a new era in how the war was covered in the media. The United States government strictly forbade women from serving in the armed forces before Vietnam. However, some renowned authors, such as Martha Gellhorn and others managed to enlist support during World War II. Vietnam was an unofficial war, hence there were never any set ground rules for how combat would be conducted.

Women reporters were still the target of hostility and sexism, but they had access to all of the same venues as their male counterparts. Female war correspondents got their first real opportunity to contribute during the Vietnam War. They were forced to go their way, creating innovative breakthroughs since they couldn't get anyone to notice them.

Leroy came to Vietnam completely unprepared. She may have been short, but she was bold, and she earned respect by routinely surpassing the men. He stated this of the photographer who went into battle with the Marines. Few photographers got closer to soldiers than Leroy, who crawled in the mud alongside them if necessary, seeking for the eyes and slight shifts in expression. The soldiers hardly noticed her because of how quietly she moved.

There are now many female journalists, but they still face powerful stereotypes, and for some, the only way to be seen as legitimate is by being tougher than their male counterparts.

As Ms Lederer read aloud from *War Torn*, a 2004 book in which she and other female journalists from Vietnam describe their experiences, she was met with the ecstatic screams of a large group of children. A new generation of reporters, including many women, has changed the face of Ukraine's media. London-born Christiane Amanpour, CNN's chief international correspondent, has said that war reporting requires a sense of mission, a sense of purpose, and a sense of being able to tell a narrative, adding that it appears that women are particularly adept at this. CBS News correspondent Holly Williams, reporting from Istanbul, adds that it's also a matter of logic. The Gulf War in 1991, subsequent conflicts in the Middle East, and the tragic siege of Sarajevo from 1992 to 1996 during the war between Bosnia and Herzegovina are just a few of the conflicts she has covered throughout her career. Female-friendly profession has exploded in all forms of media, but Ms Amanpour noted that pay equality has not yet been achieved.

Female war correspondents of World War II didn't have time to worry about how their hair looked; they were too busy breaking ground for their co-workers in Afghanistan if it weren't for their reporting. Journalists of all sexes had to lobby for the right to cover World War II, as detailed in Judith Mackrell's book *The Correspondents: Six Women Writers on the Front Lines*.

Women journalists had a hard time finding work because they were not allowed into combat zones, and some editors received feedback from viewers that they didn't want to read tales written by women. The misogyny they've encountered may have its origins in their neighbourhood. Conversely, Gellhorn had no intention of disappointing anyone. During the time Hemingway and the other male correspondents were being herded aboard assault craft for the D-Day landings, she hitched a ride to an English port and convinced a policeman that she had authorization to interview American nurses on a hospital ship. She hid in the ship's lone WC until she heard the anchor being raised, safe from the other passengers' prying eyes. When she got to Omaha Beach in the morning, the beach had been turned into a bloodbath.

Despite Hemingway's prominence on the masthead, she contributed several noteworthy pieces on the subject of relocating dead bodies. Well-known women writers like dance critic and author Martha Gellhorn are smarter than the average person since they have to overcome more obstacles. In a few cases, they were reported on all across the world. After hearing that Hollingworth had made it to Tripoli with her T and T (toothbrush and typewriter), British commander Field Marshal Bernard Montgomery exclaimed that he would have no women journalists with his troops on the battlefield. The truth of his mother's previous existence only became clear to him after her death, when he found 60,000 negatives and prints in the attic: the woman he thought was crazy and embarrassing who fed his school friends cauliflower breasts coloured pink with tomato-tinted mayonnaise, actually saw the liberation of Paris and delivered some of the most gripping dispatches of World War II from her time in France. Similar to how female soldiers are routinely erased from history books, it appears that female reporters are similarly relegated to the sidelines. This omission is more than made up for by the six exceptional stories included in Mackrell's book.

Like their male counterparts, these female journalists found war to be intoxicating, making the transition back to civilian life particularly challenging. Reporting on the war left Gellhorn, who died at the age of 89 from cancer and melancholy, feeling shredded up within. Nothing about visiting the detention centres after the war ended was more shocking to them. Schultz first saw that the bodies in Buchenwald looked like piles of wood, while the survivors resembled emaciated corpses so malnourished that their ages could not be determined. Spending money is required for this kind of work. Gellhorn killed herself, and Miller hid her son's reaction to her war photos, long before PTSD was recognised as a mental health issue.

It's not just female foreign correspondents who have a lot of people to thank for what they've done. Mackrell has done all of us a tremendous favour by collecting their fascinating stories. Initially, she wished that she had included more of their work, but perhaps they are best served by leaving us with the desire to go and read first-hand how women experience war. She is not a fan of clichés. A woman wearing a Press badge on the front of her body armour stands amid the dust and turmoil of a warzone.

Some of the most prominent women journalists and writers in the industry share their experiences as frontline females exclusively with GQ Hype. Warren covered stories in Africa, Central America, Europe, and other regions for five years. Due to the delicate nature of the stories, she has covered in Rwanda and China, she has been the target of harassment, strict monitoring, and online insults. Warren said that being a woman doesn't give her any special advantages when reporting from abroad because there isn't much of a difference between men and women in the field. She agrees with Colvin that the reporter's unique perspective is more important to the credibility of the story than any other factor.

Because both her parents were war correspondents, Sulome Anderson spent most of her childhood in the company of male and female reporters covering conflicts. As she followed in her parent's footsteps, she was cognizant of the toll it may take on her psyche. She has made an effort to limit her exposure to violence because she knows it will have a terrible effect on her mental health. The macho attitude of stating we don't talk about our feelings because we are detached and we can manage anything is not a good one to fall into. Post-traumatic stress disorder is a serious problem among many journalists who have done this. It will only get worse if you disregard it. In his time working in the Middle East, Anderson was subjected to numerous unwanted sexual advances.

The overt sexualisation of children was dehumanising and objectifying. She said that she is not a prop as she reflected on her experiences with men who had spoken to or approached her with an air of entitlement. She now regrets the awkward encounters with men she had in her early days as a reporter. This incident occurred while she was doing a story in a Lebanese prison teeming with criminals and members of the Islamist mafia. She was lucky to escape that ordeal without any serious consequences. 'Her words are clear' which is a phrase many women find difficult to carry off, is another area where women journalists should improve. Sometimes we agree to things that make us feel bad because we want to make other people happy.

Those, on the other hand, are situations that could endanger someone's life. If you're not sure how comfortable you are with something, a good way to find out is to risk offending someone or losing access to something you need. Before joining *The New Yorker's* staff, Okeowo was a freelance journalist who covered Boko Haram and the Lord's Resistance Army. She is widely recognised as one of the most prominent foreign correspondents willing to risk life and limb to tell the stories of those fighting Islamic extremism across Africa. She avoids skirts, dresses, and anything that is too sexy. Being a woman can be disarming to your subjects, but it can also invite the kind of attention that can make your job more difficult than it needs to be. It was an arduous struggle.

There would be a lack of depth and breadth if only men told these tales. Callimachi has earned a reputation as a fearless reporter who has covered stories from all around the volatile Middle East. Not even the prospect of covering Isis for *The New York Times* deterred her from accepting the job. Given her background researching Islamic militants in Mali, she was eager to accept the position. Her in-depth reporting and choice of topics, such as Isis' sexual slavery of Yazidi women, raised crucial, even existential concerns. (Lippe, "Gendering War and Peace Reporting")

Sex is just one of many factors that can shed light on a predicament. She believes that telling stories from a woman's perspective is valuable because of the unique perspective afforded by her life experiences as both a girl and a woman. From 1914 to 1918, female reporters covered the major conflicts in Europe and the Middle East for both allied and neutral publications. Even though the front lines and their immediate surroundings were off-limits to journalists, several women were permitted access to them by the Allies and the Central Powers, and their firsthand descriptions and images were published in major publications throughout the war. Research on female war correspondents is still in its infancy, and female reporters have been mostly excluded from the most significant surveys of war correspondents. "Gendering War and Peace Reporting" by Lippe takes a global and comparative look at the various forms of women's war reporting during WWI. In February 1998, the *Irish Times* published an obituary for novelist and journalist Martha Gellhorn with the headline, First Female War Reporter Dies. Gellhorn reported on every major conflict of the twentieth century, including the Spanish Civil War, the Vietnam War, and the Arab-Israeli conflict.

The obituary states that women reporters have covered war since the 1930s. Journalists Margaret Fuller (1810-1850) and Jane Cazneau (1807-1878) covered the Mexican-American War (1846-1848) and the Italian War of Independence (1848-1849), respectively (1810-1850). This distinction of first woman war correspondent has since been bestowed upon several other women. According to Tim Luckhurst, women who covered the First World War were very uncommon outliers. This book seeks to debunk that claim. Many women, both enlisted and civilian, in neutral countries were able to visit the front lines between 1914 and 1918, writing about their experiences in newspapers and magazines.

Contrarily, scholarly investigations into this topic are uncommon. In the two most influential biographies of war correspondents, by Phillip Knightley (1929-2016) and Martin Farrar (1998), neither gender is represented. The contributions of women journalists to the war effort between 1914 and 1918 are rarely discussed or even mentioned at all. A new history of Americans in Europe during World War II includes a chapter on women and war reporting, although the emphasis is not on female war correspondents. Some research has been done on the topic of American war correspondents. This has led to a drastic reduction in our understanding of women war correspondents in other cultures.

Furthermore, the digitization of these newspapers has made it possible to conduct a full-text search for articles written by women in these newspapers. Almost all of these ladies wrote under their own names in newspapers and magazines, so we can trace their movements. The Austrian National Library's ANNO, the French National Library's Gallica, the United States Library of Congress's Chronicling America, the British Library's Papers Past and Australia's Trove, and the American and Canadian libraries' Gale Historical Newspapers and ProQuest Historical Newspapers are just some of the digital newspaper archives that allow full-text searching.

It's important to note that this is not a complete list. Additional reliable resources for biographies can be found in online encyclopaedias, dictionaries, biographies, and secondary texts. Books were written based on the diaries and newspaper articles of numerous women who served throughout the war. Before the advent of the internet, it was quite difficult to track down first-person accounts of the war that had been published throughout the battle (e.g. Internet Archive, HathiTrust). Alice Schalek (1874-1956), Nolle Roger (1874-1953), Peggy Hull (1889-1967), Mary Boyle O'Reilly (1873-1939), Helen Johns Kirtland

(1890-1979), and Alice Rohe (1890-1979) are just a few of the women photographers who have left behind personal archives or collections of their work (1876- 1957).

An annual magazine titled *Consequence* publishes a variety of works, including fiction, nonfiction, poetry, translations, and art, to foster a greater dialogue regarding the cultural and societal effects of war. Women authors and those who identify as women are severely underrepresented in works on war and conflict, with male veterans and service members dominating the field. *Consequence's* 2018 issue, commemorating the magazine's tenth anniversary, is devoted to women and people, delving into the complicated topic of violence, warfare, and the aftereffects of war.

Consequence is an anthology that explores the dark side of war in an effort to promote peace via moral and responsible behaviour. Six female reporters and documentarians from World War II paved the path for future female reporters and correspondents by covering the war from the front lines, breaking down boundaries, and standing up for what they believed in. These women broke new boundaries and displayed incredible bravery in their roles as reporters, photographers, and correspondents during and after World War I. Press credentials for Ruth Baldwin Cowan during World War II, seen at right.

Several European and Middle Eastern wars were documented by women from a wide variety of Western and non-Western countries who made their way to the front lines or quite close to them so far, but no female war journalists reporting from the Asian, Pacific or African war theatres could be identified. This book provides a detailed account of their lives and the different roles they performed in the struggle. The book claims that contrary to popular belief, female reporters covered the first global conflict from a unique and nuanced point of view.

There was a wide range of ethnicities, nationalities, battle zones, and media outlets represented in women's war reporting from 1914 to 1918. War journalists provide first-hand stories of military combat for distribution, as stated by the International Encyclopaedia of Communication because of the wide variety of media outlets and types of journalists that covered the war, determining who counts as a war correspondent is far from easy, as Kevin Williams puts it. But while some were able to get up close and personal with the action, others were kept at arm's length and unable to provide an accurate account.

Freelance writers and reporters without formal training or experience reporting wars and with tenuous affiliations to major news outlets have joined the ranks of mainstream media's credentialed journalists. In addition, several writers went to the front lines to cover the conflict and their accounts ultimately shaped the way the war was described in literature. This is especially true of the many female war reporters of the First World War who also happened to be accomplished writers. Similarly, the term 'war Correspondent' did not exist until much later. Journalists working independently to cover the fighting were sometimes referred to as war correspondents by the press. Concerning the American experience, Carolyn Edy wrote that women's war letters during World War I were mainly travelogues and personal essays that didn't mention combat operations.

According to the military's standards, many of these writers do not qualify as war journalists. Few women enlisted to serve in the military during World War I. They brought the most up-to-date information on the fight from wherever they were stationed (Edy, "Conditions of acceptance: The United States military, the press, And the woman war correspondent 1846-1945").

In some cases, officials authorised a visit to the battlefield. Some people were a long way from the front lines, but the battle nevertheless went on. They documented their time spent at field hospitals in their writings. Others were thinking about how the war was affecting people back home. Women's accounts of wartime experiences can appear in the form of travelogues, photo essays, or autobiographies. Dorothy and Carl Schneider distinguish between female war correspondents who were amateur and chance observers and those who were qualified journalists. This article classifies six different types of female combat correspondents. Six women's biographies will be used to illustrate the conclusions of the typology, each describing her unique path to and career in the news industry.

Reporters covering the war military authorities recognise Alice Schalek's expertise.

When it came to war reporting, only Austria-Hungary gave women the green light to apply for official accreditation. Seven women were among the 271 persons, both male and female, who were accredited by the military's primary propaganda organisation, the War Press Office (Kriegspressequartier), during World War II. One of the most well-known of these figures was Alice Schalek, a journalist, travel writer, photographer, and professor. Schalek, a Viennese Jew from a privileged family, published her first book in the early 1900s. Before World War I, she had visited North Africa, India, and Japan. From 1903 to 1935, she had her travelogues published in the feature sections of the Neue Freie Presse newspaper. The outbreak of war made it impossible for her to travel worldwide, putting her career in peril. Schalek was able to keep working as a journalist thanks to the personal connections she had established with the War Press Office, which ultimately led to her being granted accreditation in July 1915.

For the next two years, she reported from the Italian front as well as Galicia and Serbia, speaking with soldiers and officers and photographing the landscape. German mass-circulation weekly *Neue Freie Presse* and Berliner *Illustrirte Zeitung* carried multiple battle reports and photographic features. She also gave illustrated war lectures to an audience of 40,000 and released two books based on her war reporting Tirol in Waffen, Am Isonzo. Schalek probably did not participate in any actual combat in South Tyrol in 1915, when she went there with a group of war correspondents and personnel from the War Press Office. However, she observed real bombardment on the Isonzo River and the suffering of the soldiers during the spring and summer of 1916. She was free to go wherever she wanted and found herself in the thick of the fighting. Schalek had to go to combat zones at her own risk, unlike many of her male colleagues at the Conflict Press Office, who were rarely threatened by gunfire or mortars. When she saw the violence on the Isonzo for herself, her perspective shifted. She brought attention to the horrors of modern warfare by describing the destruction wreaked upon soldiers, people, and the landscape itself throughout her time spent in the conflict zones. Since her reporting was so forthrightly critical and honest, the War Press Office sacked her in September 1917 for fear that it would demoralise the public.

Yet Schalek maintained his popularity among the population all through the conflict. Misogynistic criticism of her essays, photos, and lectures didn't stop her from receiving widespread appreciation. In February 1917, the Viennese government awarded her a bravery medal. Her fame in Austria, where she had been a star since before World War I, faded after she left for the United States to escape Nazi persecution in 1939.

Austrian writer, journalist, and humorist Karl Kraus was Schalek's most vocal detractor (1874-1936).

This book is a devastating condemnation of the media's role in prolonging the war by moulding and misrepresenting popular perception of the conflict. Schalek has been given credit for up to eleven separate sequences. Kraus' severe assessment characterised Schalek's historical reputation for decades. These people were assigned to Cover War Stories for the Press Sofa Casanova. Many newspapers sent female reporters to the front lines to cover the battle. Even without formal military credentials, journalists were able to obtain access to the front lines and report on how the war was affecting soldiers and civilians.

Among the most famous of these was Sofa Casanova (1861-1958). She covers the Eastern Front for the esteemed Spanish newspaper *ABC* in Madrid. Galician-born writer, poet, playwright, traveller, journalist, and activist who wed a Polish philosopher and spent the remainder of her life in Poland. In 1915, she accepted an offer from ABC to work as the paper's Eastern European correspondent, a role she maintained until 1936. It was during this time that the conservative and pro-German backer Casanova became one of ABC's most popular columnists. She authored and published her writings after relocating to Minsk, Moscow and Saint Petersburg after evacuating with her family from Warsaw in 1915 due to the impending Red Army assault.

While a resident of St. Petersburg, she saw first-hand the horrors unleashed by the Russian Revolution. Casanova authored almost 220 articles in *ABC* detailing the struggle on the Eastern Front and attempting to create awareness and compassion for Poland's plight, despite Spain's indifference as a neutral country. She was an outspoken opponent of war and its associated violence and injustice. Her newspaper articles from the war were collected by Casanova into three books. Because of their position between the front lines and the home front, they witnessed first-hand the effects of early twentieth-century military methods. A lot of nurses have written or spoken publicly about their experiences in the field. They frequently shared stories of the bravery and resolve of the men they treated, as well as their ordeals with illness and injuries. A prime example is the Swiss novelist, playwright, journalist, and travel writer Nolle Roger, who enjoyed widespread renown in French-speaking Switzerland and France. Roger contributed to the front pages and feature pages of the Journal *de Genève* from the turn of the century until the 1940s with serialised novels and articles. Her essays have appeared in French newspapers and magazines, as well as the *Gazette de Lausanne*.

Not only did female war correspondents cover the front lines and the effects of the conflict on local civilians, but they also took a keen interest in the roles played by women at home. Due to the shortage of male labour, women were expected to take on additional responsibilities outside the home. Matilde Serao (1856-1927) is a notable figure in the study of the effects of World War I on the Italian people.

Serao's journalistic and literary accomplishments stem from his upbringing in Naples with his Greek mother and Neapolitan father. She wrote a column for and served as editor-in-chief of her newspaper, Il Giorno. During World War II, Serao worked as a journalist, covering the effects of the conflict on women at home, while maintaining a stance of neutrality and nonviolence.

However, some women were able to enter male-dominated spaces by dressing the part. As a result, American writers Mary Boyle O'Reilly and Dorothy Lawrence were able to enter Germany from Belgium by posing as peasant refugees. O'Reilly joined the Newspaper Enterprise Association as a foreign correspondent in 1913. After postings in Mexico and Russia, she was elevated to the position of London office manager. Her father was the famed Irish nationalist, poet, and writer John Boyle O'Reilly (1844-1890). O'Reilly was sent to Belgium at the start of the war to report on the plight of the civilian population there. She was able to get into German-occupied Louvain two days before her male colleagues and see the city being burned while disguised as a fleeing peasant. She went about her day in Belgium while in disguise, walking over German lines and making notes on her white shirt. She and her three male co-workers were taken prisoner by the Germans for spying on them, but they were eventually released to Holland. O'Reilly, pretending to be a Belgian soldier, also went back to London at the same time as the other three. To kick off her report, she made the following declaration: "Mary Boyle O'Reilly was expelled from Belgium by the Germans because of her work as a journalist" (Seul, "Women War Reporters").

Using a passport issued by the German consul in

Holland, she was allowed to return to Germany. If she had been working as a journalist, the Prussian army would have taken her into custody immediately. Therefore, she disguised herself as a normal Belgian refugee and made her way through the troops for several days. Indeed, the journey was one fraught with danger. For the next few months, O'Reilly reported from the Eastern Front of World War II which took him from France, through Norway and Sweden, through Russia (Saint Petersburg, Moscow), Lithuania (Warsaw), and beyond. Several American newspapers, including *the Boston Daily Advertiser, Boston Globe, Boston Pilot, Boston Herald, Seattle Star* and *The Day Book* printed O'Reilly's dispatches from the battlefield. She left Europe in February 1917 and returned to the United States on the final ship home before America entered the war. She spent the remainder of her life sharing her stories and insights from the conflict in writing and public speaking.

This classification has, up until now, featured women who have broken barriers in the field of combat reporting. Despite this, at least one female attempted to enter the area of freelance war reporting and was unsuccessful. Dorothy Lawrence (ca. 1896–1964), then 19 years old, gained notoriety in Britain as she crossed the English Channel to France disguised as a male soldier during World War I. Before 1914, Lawrence had had some of her lighter work published in the London Times and Pall Mall Magazine, but both newspapers and the British War Office were dismissive of her attempts to become a war correspondent. In the summer of 1915, she went to France to cover the war as a freelance war correspondent, and she tried to find a battle zone in the French sector. French officials arrested her and she was subsequently expelled from the nation. Therefore, she concluded that the only way to the front lines was to dress as a man. With the help of British soldiers, she was able to acquire a khaki uniform and forge identification documents to enter the British zone. Luckily, she was able to find work with a mine-laying outfit in Albert on the Somme. But because of her poor health and the fear of being identified as a woman by the commanding sergeant, Lawrence locked herself up after only ten days.

After being interrogated, French military officials, who believed Lawrence to be a spy, forced her to sign an affidavit. As soon as she returned to London, she found herself homeless and without a job. Although the War Office appreciated Lawrence's efforts to write a military tome, they demanded that she rework the first draught. Her work was heavily censored by the War Office after the war ended in 1919, and it received negative reviews in British newspapers. Due to her deteriorating mental state, Lawrence was institutionalised in 1925 and remained there until she died in 1964. Even though Lawrence's dreams of becoming a journalist were never realised, she still managed to embarrass the War Office by demonstrating the abilities of women in the workplace. She shouted with glee in her book. If war correspondents can't get out, then she tried her best to outdo them in every way: automobiles, credentials, and money. She did what she could do as a war reporter.

Lawrence, despite her time spent on the front lines, was unable to launch a successful career as a journalist. Cases like Schalek's, Casanova's, Roger and Serao and O'Reilly's, this one demonstrates that women who aspired to be war correspondents needed to have already achieved prominence in the media and literary worlds before the outbreak of hostilities. On the other side, Lawrence's exploits were widely celebrated by the American press.

Thriller was how the Yorkville Enquirer described her book. Miss Lawrence, the British journalist, became a national hero after the war's release of one of the most bizarre documents. It was unheard of until recently for a woman to enlist in the British Army. The working conditions for female reporters were drastically different from those for male reporters. For the Western Front, the Allied regime was the strictest. At the outbreak of World War I, all journalists were censored from entering the battlefields in France and Britain. Because of media and public objections, the Allies established a system of certified war correspondents under military supervision in the spring of 1915. Some journalists, especially women, were able to get to the front lines early in the war despite the restrictions placed on journalists in the fighting zone and write about their experiences.

Writer, poet, playwright, and criminologist F. Tennyson Jesse (1888-1958) was dispatched to Belgium in August 1914 to report on the German invasion. During the war, she travelled to Ghent, Termonde, the front, and Antwerp, but she was eventually forced to leave the city because of the Germans. Seven stories by her appeared in the *Daily Mail* between September 7 and October 9, 1914. After that, she went to France to cover the Red Cross there. Following that, the British Ministry of Information asked her to create an article about the Women's Army, which included groups like the Women's Auxiliary Army Corps (WAAC) and the Voluntary Aid Detachment (VAD). Her research was published in the *Daily Mail* in December 1915, and *The Sword of Deborah* was published the following year in 1919. *Collier's Weekly, Pall Mall Gazette,* and *Vogue* were just a few of the publications where she shared her stories as a female war correspondent.

The Australian author and poet Louise Mack (1870-1935) also reported on the German invasion of Belgium for British media. At the time of the German occupation, she was in Brussels and Antwerp. She claims that she left Antwerp on a fake passport while posing as a peasant. Sixty-two additional females served as nurses in World War I and wrote about their experiences in publications and tomes.

When World War I finally ended in Europe in November 1918, Peggy Hull was the first American woman to be officially recognised as a war correspondent. She kept covering the aftermath of the Russian Revolution and the arrival of American troops in Siberia. After being denied permission to write about her experiences in France for the *Chicago Tribune*, she published her stories in the *Newspaper Enterprise Association*, the *Chicago Tribune's* Paris Army edition, and the *El Paso Morning Times* in 1917. As Edy pointed out, without official accreditation from the United States military, no journalist is allowed near a conflict zone. Because of this, the American military provided facilities and lodging to a significant number of unaccredited combat correspondents. They were able to avoid interference from government censors and military authorities, allowing them more freedom in their careers and travels.

According to reports, the United States military welcomed as many as seventeen female war correspondents. Many American women, including Mary Boyle O'Reilly, Rheta Childe Dorr and Sophie Treadwell volunteered for the Red Cross and other organisations. Volunteering with the Red Cross in Belgium in 1915 was Mary Roberts Rinehart. She met soldiers from many other countries, including the United Kingdom, France and Belgium during her stay at the Western Front. She could see everything going on in the trenches, in the bombed-out villages, and in no man's land where she was standing. *Kings, Queens, and Pawns* is a collection of her short stories that were first published in periodicals like *The Saturday Evening Post, The Boston Globe* and *The Sphere.*

From the Eastern Front's Allies, there is limited information about the working conditions or attitudes of the military toward female journalists from neutral or ally countries who were only allowed to operate in Russia and Serbia. During the Russian Revolution in February 1917 and the Bolshevik Revolution in November 1917, several women from the United States and Canada reported on the events developing on the Eastern Front outside of Sofa Casanova of neutral Spain. Volunteer nurses in an American field hospital in Russia included Madeleine Zabriskie Doty, Louise Bryant of the *Bell Syndicate*, Bessie Beatty of the *San Francisco Bulletin*, and Rheta Childe Dorr of the *New York Evening Mail*, as well as *Harper*. They recorded not just the horrors of the revolutions but also the routines of ordinary Russians. The Women's Battalion of Death, founded and led by Russia's first female military leader, Maria Bochkareva, was another topic of study (1889-1920). Journalists covered the battalion's deployment to the front for a full week in July 1917.

An educator, writer, and ardent Catholic suffragist named Annie Christitch (1885- 1977) covered the war in Serbia for the British government between 1915 and 1918. A Serbian national with an Irish mother who was educated and primarily resided in the United Kingdom was sent to Serbia as a staff correspondent for the *Daily Express*. She established a relief centre in Valjevo and oversaw eight hospitals there while German and Austrian armies occupied Serbia. She was able to stay in the country because of her Serbian citizenship when everyone else had to leave. Her essays about the misery of Serbian war victims, originally published in the *Daily Express*, were reproduced in newspapers in Australia, New Zealand, and China. Her charitable activities in Serbia received substantial notice from British and international media due to her well-deserved reputation for generosity.

The Italian High Command also allowed women from nations who were neutral or allies to join the fight. Inez Milholland (1886-1916), a suffragist, lawyer, and socialist reformer, led a group of war correspondents from *the Chicago Daily Tribune, the Washington Post, the New York Tribune, McClure's,* and *Harper's* to the Italian front in the summer of 1915. However, the Italian government found fault with her anti-war writings and expelled her at the end of September 1915. The Italian government, according to the New York Times, considers the presentation of conflict from a pacifist standpoint to be not politically suitable.

Alice Rohe was a writer, photographer, and feminist who served as the first female overseas bureau head for United Press in Rome. Her tenure lasted from 1917 to 1919.

Instead of relying on native Italians to fill in the gaps in her knowledge, Rohe set out into rural Italy for the first time in her career. She covered the human toll of the war for publications like *National Geographic Magazine, Leslie's Weekly, Leslie's Newspaper, Leslie's Magazine,* and *the New York World.* Photojournalist Helen Kirtland of *Leslie's Weekly* was granted access to the front lines by the Italian High Command in 1917, after the surrender of 275,000 Italian soldiers at Caporetto. In the fall of 1918, photographer

Kirtland was given special permission to photograph Italian soldiers in the trenches. The acronym CPSU is what the world has come to know them as.

Even inside the Central Powers, working conditions for female combat reporters varied. At the onset of World War I, the Austro-Hungarian army made concerted efforts to keep all war correspondents away from the front lines. Then the War Press Office began arranging tours of the front lines, although not the actual battlegrounds for reporters from Austria-Hungary, Germany, and neutral countries. Austria-Hungary accredited several female journalists, including Alice Schalek Hede von Trapp and Maria Magda Rumbold from Austria, as well as Olga Fehér and Margit Vészi from Hungary. The front lines in the Alps, Galicia and Serbia were accessible to them often as part of a larger group of accredited war correspondents led by members of the War Press Office.

Female war reporters from belligerent and neutral countries were present in the major war theatres in Europe and the Middle East from 1914 to 1918. While the admission of journalists to the war zones was severely restricted by the Allies and Central Powers, a considerable number of women managed to access the frontlines or their vicinities and to publish their eyewitness accounts and photographs in well-known newspapers and magazines. Still, studies of female war reporters are rare and women are conspicuously absent from the leading surveys of war correspondents.

The Central Powers also welcomed women from neutral countries to visit Germany and Austria-Hungary. Madeleine Zabriskie Doty was an American lawyer, activist and pacifist who went to Germany after attending the Women's Peace Congress in 1915 in The Hague. She was a journalist who wrote for *the New York Tribune, the Chicago Tribune,* and *Good Housekeeping*. She witnessed the devastation the war wreaked on civilian life in Berlin and Hamburg first-hand.

Swedish poet and writer Annie Kerhielm (1869-1956) invited her newspaper publisher husband, Baron Dan Kerhielm (1863-1931), to Berlin in 1916. Annie was an opponent of women's suffrage and democracy who later became an admirer of Adolf Hitler. The book *Reporting War: Journalism in Wartime* is a compilation of the author Kerhielm's war reporting for the Swedish newspapers *Nya Dagligt Allehanda* and *Stockholm Dagblatt*. In addition, she wrote a lengthy article about life in Nazi Germany which was published in the *Leipzig Illustrirte Zeitung*. Despite the ongoing conflict, Berlin's cultural and social life carried on as if nothing had changed. In particular, German aristocratic women were praised for their alleged humility and dedication to the common good.

Popular American author and globetrotter Nellie Bly (1864–1922) was among the foreign male war correspondents officially recognised by the War Press Office in Austria-Hungary. She went to the Eastern Front in Poland, Galicia and Serbia for several weeks in the fall of 1914 to report on the situation for American newspapers. Between December 1914 and February 1915, the *New York Evening Journal* published twenty-one articles with the headline Nellie Bly on the Firing Line.

The German publication *Die Zeit* published an article by Bly as well. Bly's essay had been substantially modified, and it was after this that she decided to quit contributing to the German newspaper. She witnessed awful events at a Red Cross hospital and stated that that's quite hard to believe that this is happening. Hundreds upon hundreds of people are suffering and dying on the newly constructed roads and railroads since the war. Amidst their slaughter, thousands of other animals are being led to their violent deaths.

Do women have opinions about the war? Milly Buonanno has pointed out that it is a debatable and under-researched topic whether or not women war correspondents are willing and able to construct their gender-based agenda and convey their own point of view. Women's war reporting spanned a wide range of issues, including but not limited to military tactics, weapons, casualties, military strategy, and post-war recovery. Women worked in munitions factories, conscripted men worked in factories and farms, and women took care of their conscripted husbands at home.

Numerous publications coined the term the 'woman's angle' to refer to the coverage of the war from a female perspective by female journalists. Rheta Childe Dorr (1857-1948) and Gertrude Atherton (1857-1948) are two such women. Atherton, a writer and feminist, returned from France in 1916 and wrote a series of essays detailing the contributions women made to the war effort there, including aiding refugees and providing medical care to servicemen and civilians. Newspapers and female reporters all benefited financially from stories with a focus on women and their experiences since they reached a larger audience and could sell more ads.

However, many female reporters felt devalued when they were told they could only report on the woman's viewpoint of war. Women who dared report on wars fought by men were often ridiculed and degraded for doing so. Peggy Hull's male co-workers despised her proximity to the front and her writing style because her articles in the Paris edition of the *Chicago Tribune* in 1917 were well received by soldiers.

Females can and should be invested in the emotional growth of their male relatives, including brothers, fathers, husbands, and sons. They have changed their entire being while fighting by preventing any contact with their loved ones. This facet of the conflict is often overlooked by male war correspondents. Between 1914 and 1918, a large number of women served as war correspondents, writing about conflicts across Europe and the Middle East. The policies of the Allies and the Central Powers determined whether or not they were allowed entry into battle zones as accredited war correspondents on less formal assignments from their newspapers or as medics. Reporting from combat zones by women was as varied as the women's paths to those zones. Women's focus varied greatly, depending on a variety of factors, including their geographic location, access to the frontlines, assignments from their newspapers, and their own professional and personal interests. They ventured into hazardous areas, risking their lives. They published articles under their names in reputable periodicals detailing their eyewitness accounts:

> Here one has the perfect example of justice: The men have kept their women enslaved, stupid and limited and apart, for their male vanity and power; result the dull women bore the daylights out of the men. I wait every year for summer and it is usually good but it is never as good as the summer I am always waiting for. (Gellhorn, *The Face of War* 269).

These women war correspondents had their work published not only in their home countries but also in others around the world. German-born Thea Von Puttkamer wrote for the German, Austrian, Turkish, and German-American press while her Canadian counterpart, Florence MacLeod Harper, contributed to the American periodical *Leslie's Weekly*. Former employees of *Leslie's Weekly* include Margit Vészi, Alice Schalek, and Florence MacLeod Harper. Women journalists used a wide range of publications, from high- and low-quality newspapers to illustrated magazines and books.

Alice Schalek, Louise Mack, and Mary Boyle O'Reilly all lectured extensively after the war about their experiences as female veterans. They were able to strike up conversations with persons of varying socioeconomic backgrounds. They were members of the upper social strata, well-educated, financially secure, and well-known in their fields of journalism, travel writing, and photography. It was not uncommon for them to be suffragists, pacifists, and social reformers, all of which made them prominent political personalities. They began in their twenties and ended in their seventies and beyond. Women broke societal norms and entered traditionally male-dominated fields like travel, lecturing, journalism, photography, and war reporting even when they were expected to stay at home and raise children.

Because of this, a woman's chances of getting employed as a war correspondent greatly depended on her social standing and her career trajectory before the war. They kept contributing to their newspapers for decades after the war ended. However, Dorothy Lawrence's narrative demonstrates that a novice to the field of journalism without contacts was doomed to fail, even with her wartime expertise. It's interesting to note that female reporters didn't just cover the battle from the woman's standpoint. Nevertheless, women were determined to cover every aspect of warfare, including fighting on battlefields, soldiers' pain and suffering, the destruction of towns and villages, and the effects of war on civilians, especially women and children, even though their access to combat zones was often severely restricted.

Several female reporters reported and even broke some of the most important stories of the Second World War. These women not only displayed incredible bravery in the face of fire, but they also had to overcome numerous obstacles simply to be able to report from the frontlines. At that time, journalism was a male-dominated profession and many male correspondents including Ernest Hemingway felt arrogant and entitled and did not want women on the battlefield.

Women who opted to report from an active conflict zone had to overcome a ban on females on the frontlines that had been in force since the start of the war. In fact, until the end of the war, the British army refused to grant authorization to female journalists, stating that women, as the weaker sex, should not be placed in risky situations. There was also concern that women would cause sexual unrest among the soldiers, or that men on active service would act chivalrously by looking after the women rather than fighting the enemy. Surprisingly, one of the main objections was that women couldn't report from the front lines because they couldn't use the same latrines as males.

When America entered the war in December 1941, following the Japanese attack on Pearl Harbour, the authorities there proved to be considerably more open to women correspondents and let women closer to the action than the British did, but they were still reluctant to have them on the frontline. Some British women took advantage of this by being accredited to an American publication, allowing them to go to active conflict zones. Once there, they would use any gaps they could find or find policemen sympathetic to their cause to assist them; they were willing to go to nearly any length to get closer to the frontlines.

Female war correspondents received varied responses. Male journalists frequently believed that women had an advantage since they could use their 'feminine wiles' to flirt with officers and men to obtain stories that they might not have been able to obtain. However, the soldiers on the ground appreciated having the women present and were frequently eager to have a journalist with them who might document their tale if they were killed in combat. They also enjoyed the feminine companionship because they were lacking it during the war; many guys did not see their spouses or girlfriends for years on end.

Female war journalists of the First World War contributed to the breadth and depth of the coverage provided by male photographers by providing a unique perspective on the conflict. Six correspondents of World War II such as Lee Miller, Helen Kirkpatrick,

Martha Gellhorn, Sigrid Schultz, and Virginia Cowles—are followed by *The Correspondents*. Even the sections outlining the history of the war events read like a novel if you're not a huge fan of nonfiction! shattered glass ceilings and fought for their ideals, paving the path for future female war reporters. Their pioneering labour and bravery as journalists, photographers and correspondents throughout World War II and thereafter helped seal their place in history. Right, we see Ruth Baldwin Cowan's press pass from World War II. I shall elaborate on her in the following section. Before her untimely death in 1971, photojournalist Margaret Bourke-White (1904-1971) accomplished many ground-breaking feats. She was the first American woman to cover a combat zone and the first non-Soviet photographer to be included in the Soviet Union's official five-year photographic plan. As of 1936, Bourke-White was *Life Magazine's* first female photojournalist, having previously worked as an associate editor and staff photographer for *Fortune Magazine* in 1929.

When reporting on the battle, female reporters frequently seemed more subjective than men, attempting to convey a richer sense of location and time. By frequently writing their reports from the perspective of the troops rather than the commanders who were the traditional sources of information and attempting to place the person rather than divisions or brigades at the centre of their attention, they provided an alternative viewpoint to the conventional military accounts. The women felt that their deeper emotional response was an essential part of the story that would allow readers at home to experience more fully what it was like to be on the front lines with troops and what their men-folk were experiencing so far, despite the criticism they occasionally received for it.

However, regardless of their writing style, all correspondents had to report in a way that supported British morale and as a result, some stories and experiences could not be shared. Sometimes the censorship was official, but it was frequently self-censorship as they attempted to strike the difficult balance between accurate reporting and hiding some of the more unpleasant aspects of life and death on the front line. Many of these women were eventually able to speak more candidly about what they had seen and experienced until after the war when they could write a memoir without any restrictions.

Women reporting from combat zones saw a historical shift during the Second World War. Reporting from the front was all that was available to some people, giving them a sense of home and belonging. As a result, some people, like Clare Hollingworth, remained to report from combat areas long after the Second World War had ended. We regularly see on our TV screens a new generation of women reporting from the front line who stand on the shoulders of those who went before as war rages in Europe once more. In addition to new young women, who had paid the ultimate price for bringing the story to the public's attention, seasoned reporters like Lyse Doucet, Orla Guerin, Yalda Hakim, and Sarah Rainsford were reporting from Ukraine.

In 1941, when Germany broke the non-aggression pact, Margaret Bourke-White was the only foreign photographer in Moscow. Her portraits of Mahatma Gandhi and Dr. Bhimrao Ramji Ambedkar are also well-known in India and Pakistan. Candice Bergen portrays Gandhi in the film *Gandhi*. During World War II and the Vietnam War, Dickey Chapelle (1919–1965) worked as a photojournalist for National Geographic. Chapelle was wrongfully accused of espionage during the Hungarian Revolution of 1956 and spent two months in a Russian prison.

Dickey Chapelle earned the admiration of both the armed forces and her fellow journalists with a little help from his friends in the media. She was a member of the paratroopers, and she often went on missions with them. One of her many firsts is the tragic distinction of being the first female correspondent to be killed in battle. During her coverage of the Vietnam War, she was injured when shrapnel from a detonated land mine pierced her neck. When Dickey Chapelle passed away, she was given the kind of military burial that is unusual for a civilian.

Photographer and war correspondent Marjory Collins (1912-1985) is best known for her images from the American home front during World War II. That was how she described herself to others. She spent the 1930s in New York City, where she worked for PM and U.S. Camera. Collins, following World War II, combined her passions for writing and photography by travelling the world as a freelance photographer. She was a committed feminist and activist and launched the publication Prime Time for and by older women.

Ruth Baldwin Cowan (1901-1993) began her career at the San Antonio Evening News as a movie reviewer on the weekends but quickly advanced to the position of reporter.

After dropping her first name, Cowan began using the pen name Baldwin Cowan when contributing to the *Houston Chronicle* and the *United Press*. She was let go because she was working for a magazine that didn't allow women to be writers or editors.

Thankfully, she found fast employment with the Associate Press. Starting in 1942, she covered the war in Algiers for the Associated Press. Despite her employers' best attempts, she always found a way around him. She covered Washington D.C. during and after the war, including Eleanor Roosevelt's press conferences and a wide array of human-interest topics (Roosevelt, "My Day").

One of the best war correspondents of the twentieth century was Martha Gellhorn (1908-1998), an American journalist, novelist, and travel writer. While covering almost every major conflict in the world for more than 60 years, she covered events ranging from the Spanish Civil War through Hitler's ascent in Germany in the 1930s to World War II and the Vietnam War. She may be mostly remembered as Ernest Hemingway's third wife, but her achievements as a journalist considerably surpass this brief connection.

To get onto the Normandy invasion, Gellhorn hid in a hospital ship and pretended to be a stretcher carrier. Therefore, she was the only female service member to participate in the D-Day invasion in 1944. She was one of the first reporters to visit Dachau after it was liberated in 1945. From 1920 through 1966, Marguerite Higgins Hall covered conflicts in Europe, the Pacific, and the Middle East for the *New York Herald Tribune* and *Newsday*. She and her co-workers had been on the Hangang Bridge when it was bombed in Seoul, and they were unable to enter the U.S. military headquarters in Suwon, South Korea, via raft.

After a request from the General, the *Herald Tribune* received a telegram reading that the restriction on women correspondents in Korea had been abolished. Everyone has the utmost respect for Marguerite Higgins as a working professional. For all female war correspondents, this was a defining moment. Also in 1951, Higgins was awarded the first Pulitzer Prize for Foreign Correspondence by a woman for her coverage of the Korean War.

After being denied entry to the front lines along with other female journalists, Martha Gellhorn famously slipped away on a medical ship to cover the D-Day arrival in France during World War II. When war broke out in Korea in 1950, an American commander ordered Marguerite Higgins to leave the country. However, her protests were effective and the order was rescinded by General Douglas MacArthur.

The 1951 Pulitzer Prize committee acknowledged that Ms Higgins, as a woman was entitled to particular consideration because she had to work under unique circumstances. Denby Fawcett, the first war correspondent for the Honolulu Advertiser, had the opportunity to meet Edith M. Lederer, the first woman assigned full-time to the AP's Vietnam team when she arrived in 1972. Farrah Fawcett and many other women commanded an army of female troops who broke the gender barrier and gained equal access to the battlefield.

The Associated Press' main UN correspondent, Ms Lederer, called it a huge breakthrough:

Could women have made a difference in war reporting? Absolutely, Ms Lederer chimed in. It was evident to me that they were more interested in the war itself, which is the major reason they and I were there. However, I wrote several articles in Vietnam that I don't think my male colleagues would have done. For this reason, she also covered a clinic that specialises in reconstructive surgery for children, many of whom had been wounded in bombings or shootings. She said that was almost bowled her over since there were so many youngsters yelling with glee. Ms Lederer recited an excerpt from War Torn, a book published in 2004 in which she and other female journalists from Vietnam recount their experiences. A new generation of reporters, including many women, has altered the media scene in Ukraine. (Elber, "In Ukraine, female war reporters build on legacy of pioneers")

London-born Christiane Amanpour, CNN's top

foreign correspondent, has described war reporting as a sense of mission, a sense of purpose, a sense of being able to tell a tale. And it seems that women are especially gifted in this area. CBS News reporter in Istanbul, Holly Williams, says it's also a matter of logic. Reporting on crises in Asia, Europe, and the Middle East has made her painfully aware of the importance of including women's perspectives.

Ms Ward claims that the media has traditionally neglected to give adequate coverage to the perspectives of women who are directly affected by war. She makes an effort to integrate people's actual experiences as they exist in combat zones, the humanity behind the fiction. She emphasises that the military aspect is just as important to her. The visibility and audience of television news programmes give its reporters more sway.

A veteran reporter for ABC News Martha Raddatz, among others, has noted that many of their male colleagues also provide significant reporting to the newsroom. But Ms Raddatz claims that men love the equipment, and adored the planes in the past. Ms Ward and other female journalists owe a lot to their foremothers, especially Ms Fitz Gerald and Ms Gellhorn, who covered wars right from the Second World War to the U.S. invasion of Panama in 1989-90. People recognise Ms Amanpour as an innovator in her field. She has covered a wide spectrum of wars throughout her career, from the Gulf War in 1991 to following conflicts in the Middle East to the horrific siege of Sarajevo in the war between Bosnia and Herzegovina from 1992 to 1996. We may have been the last generation of female international correspondents, if not the only ones as said by Amanpour. The popularity of careers that welcome women has exploded in the press.

However, Ms Amanpour pointed out that gender-waged parity has not been realised just yet.

Ms Ward claims that this is the case across the board in the media. Ms Ward remarked journalism as a very male-dominated profession in general, notwithstanding the growing number of women in TV journalism. Only one person can be seen on camera at any given time. A television crew consists of four people and most of them are still guys then and two of them operate the cameras in front of and one behind the presenters. There are still more men than women working in the media industry, despite recent changes.

Regarding the missing perspectives of women in the news, a report from the Bill & Melinda Gates Foundation is set to be released in 2020.

The report acknowledges that the majority of journalists in newsrooms around the world are men even though progress has been achieved. Ms Amanpour claims that female reporters face unique challenges in non-democratic regions and countries. A lot of societal pressure is put on them, especially in the Islamic world and other parts of what she calls the patriarchy. Men are required to stay and safeguard their towns in Ukraine, but women and children are free to leave at will. Fox News Channel's senior producer is well-versed in the nuances of opposing viewpoints. Originally from Jerusalem, he has also worked in Ukraine with correspondent Trey Yingst. In 2004, she was working as a foreign journalist for an Israeli TV network when she requested a promotion to field producer.

What she was remembered by others was that it's a man's responsibility and only men can achieve it. Her next stop was at Fox, the television network in 2005. Ms Friling had a rough time in Ukraine. Her grandparents' departure from Nazism and the Soviet Union in the 1940s brought to mind the current exodus of migrants from Kyiv. She saw women and children, and even recognised the faces of her own grandparents; which had a profound effect on the next generation. Ms Raddatz, a seasoned reporter who covered the initial refugee evacuations and who returned to Ukraine this past Friday, has seen a lot of change in the country in the last two years.

The top foreign affairs journalist for ABC News Stephen Dziedzic has shifted his attention from the Bosnian crisis he covered in the late 90s' to the wars in Iraq and Afghanistan. Initially, he was concerned that if something were to happen to him in Iraq, people would wonder how could he do that, go over there, when he has two children.

However, he clarified that they would never speak to a man in such a manner. His scepticism is high that they would behave in such a way. Covering a conflict as a journalist is difficult enough without having to constantly fear for your own safety. NBC News correspondent Erin McLaughlin said that her parents were more worried about her safety in Ukraine than they had been about any of her previous assignments, including one in Iraq.

Because they were so worried, Ms McLaughlin's brother remained with them all weekend even though it was challenging, they understood that this was his calling. This essential task must be performed by someone. Ms Ward, a wife and mother of two, has two children and says her career is stressful. At the end of yet another long day in Ukraine, Ms Ward spoke passionately that it is been very difficult to be away from home on his son's fourth birthday.

It's possible that her co-workers wouldn't be

sitting on the hotel balcony worrying about their hair if it weren't for the ground-breaking work done by women war correspondents during World War II. If that hadn't happened, they might not even be in Afghanistan, and if they were certainly wouldn't have been there. The book *The Correspondents: Six Women Writers on the Front Lines of World Conflict II* by Judith Mackrell details the struggles faced by female journalists as they attempt to gain access to the warzone. Women journalists had a hard time finding work because they were not allowed into combat zones, and some editors received feedback from viewers that they didn't want to read tales written by women.

Hemingway and the other male correspondents were hustled onboard assault craft for the D-Day landings, but she managed to hitch a ride to an English port and convince a policeman that she had the authority to interview American nurses on a hospital ship. Afraid that they wouldn't be able to find her once they were on board, she hid in a stall and waited for the sound of the anchor being raised before emerging. When morning finally came, she found Omaha Beach to be a bloody bloodbath. Despite Hemingway's prominence on the masthead, she contributed several noteworthy pieces on the subject of relocating dead bodies. Women like dance critics and author of several prior nonfiction books, Gellhorn, are smarter than males because of the obstacles they must overcome. In a few cases, they reported all across the world. In the latter half of the 1990s, Martha became aware of an elderly woman who was seated next to the editor and society columnist of The Sunday Telegraph. She had worked as a correspondent for a foreign country at one point. After some time had passed, she went online to search for her.

British reporter Clare Hollingworth has a good claim on the title of Scoop of the Century. For the 20th century, that is. Because it was Hollingworth who broke the story of World War II. Hollingworth died Tuesday in Hong Kong, where she had lived for the last four decades of her life. In August 1939, Hollingworth was in Poland as an aid worker, but then switched careers and turned to journalism. She landed a job with Britain's Daily Telegraph newspaper. Tensions were mounting with Germany, which had just closed border areas to non-residents. The only exception was for diplomats. Hollingworth followed her instincts and convinced a British diplomat friend to lend her his car. She drove, alone, to the frontier, and crossed into Germany. It was her first week on the job.

There in the fields, she saw endless rows of large objects under burlap sacks. When the wind blew, she saw tanks. (Woolf, "Remembering Clare Hollingworth, the journalist who broke the news of World War II")

The German invasion of Poland — the beginning of World War II — began just before dawn on Sept. 1, 1939. Hollingworth was again close to the frontier. She called the British Embassy, which at first refused to believe her. She said, well, listen to this, and thrust the phone out of the window as German tanks roared past. It was the first confirmation of the invasion that the British government received. Once again, thanks to Hollingworth, the Telegraph was first with the story. It was the start of a long career as a war correspondent that took Hollingworth through World War II. After the war, she always seemed to be in the right place at the right time, in the words of one colleague. She followed conflicts throughout the Middle East, Algeria and Vietnam.

Hollingworth also played a role in saving many people's lives. Before the war, as an aid worker, she helped thousands of people, mostly Jews, obtain British visas. This allowed them to get out of Eastern Europe ahead of the Nazi storm. She continued to help refugees and displaced people after she became a reporter. In her mid-90s, Hollingworth fell victim to a scammer, a much younger man who managed to persuade her to give him control of her estate. He emptied her accounts. Hollingworth sued and he promised to repay the money. But much of it is still outstanding. (Woolf, "Remembering Clare Hollingworth, the journalist who broke the news of World War II")

Virginia Cowles, a former society girl who went off to the fight in high heels, was one of the few journalists to cover both sides of the Spanish Civil War. Sigrid Schultz, the German correspondent for the *Chicago Tribune*, was one of the most courageous journalists of her day because she risked death threats and surveillance to expose Germany's march into fascism while also hiding her Jewish background. When enemy fighter planes began strafing the cliffs of Dover, all the soldiers evacuated except for Cowles and Kirkpatrick, who were left to count the aircraft. However, they were not precisely a group of sisters. They were intensely competitive, maybe as a result of their tough circumstances. Even though General Eisenhower provided Kirkpatrick equal access to military information as the United States entered the war, she was always last in line for interviews. On the left jacket pocket of the uniforms of the few other female journalists who were granted permission to wear them, the words War Correspondent were sewn in. The appeal of a woman, on the other hand, opened up a world of opportunities.

Virginia Cowels appears to have encountered a large number of people who were willing to give her rides in their planes and cars, as well as those who asked her to tea with Hitler, a lunch in honour of Churchill, and an interview with Mussolini. The female reporters, like their male counterparts, had a difficult time adjusting to life back home in peacetime.

Gellhorn, who died at 89 from cancer and melancholy, stated in her farewell interview that covering the conflict had left her feeling shredded up within. Nothing about arriving at the detention centres after the war's end was less than shocking. Schultz initially mistook the piles of dead at Buchenwald for timber, and the survivors for skeletons so emaciated that they could not be dated. A financial outlay is typical for this sort of work. Gellhorn killed himself, and Miller hid her son's reaction to her war photos, long before PTSD was recognised as a mental health issue. Not just foreign correspondents owe these women a debt of gratitude, but the entire world. By collecting their fascinating tales in one place, Mackrell has done us all a great service.

A woman amid the dust and chaos of a warzone proudly displays her Press badge on the front of her body armour. It's likely that your mental image of American journalist Marie Colvin, who was known for her dogged determination to write what she called the first draught of history, includes an eyepatch (she lost an eye to shrapnel in Sri Lanka and largely shrugged it off) and a nearly illegible reporter's notebook. Despite her many successes, Colvin was a woman who operated in a male-dominated field. She talked about her time working in some of the most dangerous places on Earth on the frontlines where macho-centric norms prevailed and any meaningful display of femininity was seen as an extra weight. In an opinion piece titled "Courage has no Gender", Colvin once wrote that she bristled with the thought that her sexuality would make her stand out from her masculine co-workers. She was famous for wearing her most expensive La Perla panties even when she was in potentially dangerous situations. She insisted that both male and female reporters had the same responsibilities. They wore the same clothing for days, endured shelling, and listened to the cries of the helpless. Grime and body odour adhered to the skin of both sexes, and the smell of fear and death permeated the air. Colvin, who was never fearless because he knew the brutal reality of war, said that fear was a tremendous equaliser. Being a woman on the front lines presents unique dangers that men rarely face. This calls for a special sort of fortitude that men typically lack.

Reporters, especially women, are vulnerable to sexual assault, suffocation, and mutilation even in seemingly safe environments. Alexis Okeowo, a staff writer at *The New Yorker*, says that Wall's death in Copenhagen made her reevaluate the dangers that female journalists face and whether or not she wants to continue in the profession possessing any degree of confidence in subjects. Security is knowing that a person will not harm you if you visit their house or another site while conducting fieldwork. Elaborating on the incidents of having faced sexual attacks while reporting on war, Martha Gellhorn explains in *The Trouble I Have Seen*:

As a woman serving on the front lines, you are frequently put in the position of having to manage circumstances where sexual assault or rape is a real possibility. I was once told that if I were ever the victim of a sexual attack while working as a female reporter, donning a bathing suit might buy me some time. There is an unspoken expectation that you should become close with the local males around you in order to secure their services as a fixer or translators. For some, this news may come as a shock. I have been cautioned that reacting angrily to them or rejecting their sexual advances too forcibly could result in a tense or even violent situation. Even the best security methods have their limits. As one example, in 2017, Swedish journalist Kim Wall was murdered by a man she had previously tracked down for an interview. (Gellhorn 92)

If you choose to overlook the problem, it will only get worse. While working in the Middle East, Anderson was subjected to numerous unwanted sexual advances. The overt sexualisation of children was dehumanising and objectifying. She did regret the unpleasant encounters with males she had in her early days as a reporter.

One instance occurred while reporting in a Lebanese prison teeming with criminals and members of the Islamist mafia. Anderson got out of that situation unscathed because of her good fortune. Another area where female journalists may need some work is in learning how to properly say no and her words are unequivocal on that point. She was one of the most well-known foreign correspondents, and she risked her life to report on the fights against Islamic extremism in Africa. On the occasions when she had an appointment, she left on her own. Sometimes she waited for an editor's approval before taking action.

Okeowo, like many other women in the media, struggled as a freelance journalist to balance her gender with the expectations of her industry. When asked why she never wears skirts or dresses, she responds. She notes that while a woman's femininity may be disarming to your subjects it can also invite the kind of behaviour, they think they can get away with. There's an old proverb that reads 'Be careful, for it has two blades.' The need for more women to fill roles traditionally held by white men is highlighted by her calm and considerate response. Despite the challenges of being a woman in journalism or working abroad, hearing women's perspectives is crucial. Female reporters rarely have the interpersonal skills of their male counterparts. The stories would be flat and one-dimensional if only men told them.

Callimachi is widely recognised as a top journalist in the Middle East since she has often risked her life to cover stories there. She wasn't put off by the dangers of her new job as *The New York Times'* Isis reporter. For this reason, and because of her prior research on Islamic terrorists in Mali, she was excited to accept the position. She exclaimed that she was ecstatic. Her in-depth reporting and choice of topics, such as Isis' sexual slavery of Yazidi women, raised critical, even existential, concerns. In this connection, Gellhorn wrote in *The Trouble I Have Seen*:

At this point in my career as a journalist, I started to wonder whether or not I was making a difference in the world. The following is an example of her assertions: When I took these horrifying charges of abuse and published them on the front page of the New York Times, I asked myself, "What kind of public service was I performing?" What steps can I take to be of assistance to these women? I've always been aware that the work that I do is significant; nevertheless, when you witness such devastation on a daily basis, you have to ask if what you're doing is enough. Nevertheless, the coverage had a significant impact. The genocide of the Yazidi people is now officially recognised as a crime against humanity by the international community. And if the gender issue hadn't been dealt with, this shift never would have happened. The Yazidi crisis was not first seen as a terrorism- related issue by the editors of *The New York Times*: She goes on to say that it was hard for her to persuade her editor that covering the rape of Yazidi women was relevant to her job as a terrorist correspondent. (74)

Gender is just one of several factors that can shed light on an issue. A woman's viewpoint of the world, shaped by her time spent both as a girl and a woman, is invaluable, in her view, for storytelling. The major conflicts in Europe and the Middle East from 1914 to 1918 were reported by female war correspondents from both sides and neutral countries. Though the front lines and their environs were off-limits to journalists, several women were granted access to them by the Allies and the Central Powers, and their first-hand accounts and photographs were published in prominent publications throughout the war.

Women are underrepresented in the most prominent surveys of war correspondents, and research on female war reporters is relatively uncommon. In this chapter, we explore the varied experiences of women who covered the First World War for a variety of media outlets from a transnational and comparative perspective. Many nurses have gone public with their experiences in print media. Despite their hardships, they frequently reported on the courage and resilience of the soldiers they treated.

Roger contributed to the front and feature pages of the Journal *de Genève* from the turn of the century through the 1940s with serial novels and articles. Her essays also appeared in French newspapers and magazines, as well as the *Gazette de Lausanne*. During World War II, Roger worked as a nurse at a hospital in Lyon, France. They were all collected and released at the same time. Although Roger asserted that she had released the memoirs of a recently deceased, unidentified nurse, we have no way of knowing whether or not the content was based on the nurse's actual experiences or merely the product of her vivid imagination. The brave soldiers' plight is vividly depicted across all six tales, and the nurses' kindness and skill are praised throughout. They detail battles fought, injuries sustained, and care received by the troops. The articles were published in French newspapers, so they quickly gained widespread attention there.

The Revue des deux Mondes, a French journal considered Roger's *Les Carnets Roger* her best work describing it as having a perfume of heroism despite its recounting of all the hardships Roger had experienced. Roger had numerous conversations relating to Les Carnets. Roger's other writings about the war demonstrate her neutral Swiss citizenship and her compassion for the civilian victims of the battle.

Most of these essays first appeared in periodicals like the *Journal de Genève* and the *Revue des deux Mondes* before being collected into books. Two volumes such as *Evacuees Make it Through Switzerland's Passage* and *The Journey of Emigrants through Switzerland* detail the journey of Belgian war refugees and civil internees evacuated from German-occupied territory through Switzerland, while *Le Train des Grands Blessés* describes the exchange of injured French and German soldiers on neutral Swiss territory.

From 1914 to 1918, female war reporters from both

combatant and neutral nations were present in the main battle zones in Europe and the Middle East. While the Allies and Central Powers severely limited the entry of journalists into the war zones, a sizable number of women were able to reach the frontlines or their environs and publish their eyewitness stories and images in renowned newspapers and magazines. However, research on female war reporters is scarce, and women are conspicuously underrepresented in the top studies of war correspondents. From a comparative and global standpoint, this article describes the diversity of female war reporting during the First World War.

As a historian of the war's impact on the Italian people, Matilde Serao (1856-1927) stands remarkable. Serao was raised in Naples by his Greek mother and Neapolitan father, and she eventually became a journalist and author. She was also the editor-in-chief and writer for her newspaper, *Il Giorno*. Throughout World War II, Serao worked as a journalist, covering topics including the war's effect on women's lives at home while maintaining a stance of neutrality and nonviolence:

Thus, the Italian country ladies in summer and fall have doubled and tripled their daily jobs: the heaviest, hardest, most extenuating work of males. Italian rural women, who will sing your pure and simple glories? as an example. During World War II, many Italian women in rural areas found themselves shouldering the traditional male roles of breadwinner, housekeeper, and caretaker of domesticated animals alone (Seul, "Women War Reporters").

The fact that Serao spoke to a middle-class female audience who shared her experiences and opinions makes her journalism particularly notable. However, some women were able to enter male-dominated spaces by dressing the part. Thus, American writers and journalists Mary Boyle O'Reilly and Dorothy Lawrence were able to enter Germany via Belgium by posing as peasant refugees. O'Reilly joined the Newspaper *Enterprise Association* as a foreign correspondent in 1913 and then after postings in Mexico and Russia, she was elevated to the position of London office manager. Her father was the famed Irish nationalist, poet, and writer John Boyle O'Reilly (1844-1890).

O'Reilly was sent to Belgium at the start of the war to record the plight of the civilians there. She was the first American journalist to witness the Germans burning down Louvain, and she did so two days before her male colleagues did so by infiltrating the city disguised as peasant refugees. She went about her day in Belgium while undercover, examining German lines and making notes on her white shirt. She and her three male co-workers were arrested for spying on the Germans but were eventually released to Holland.

When the other three returned to London, O'Reilly followed them disguised as a Belgian soldier. The following was included in the summary of her findings: Mary Boyle O'Reilly was expelled by the Germans from Belgium because she was a journalist. Using a passport issued by the German consul in Holland, she was able to return to Germany. If she had been working as a journalist, the Prussian army would have taken her into custody immediately. As a result, she posed as a common Belgian refugee and travelled for days through the army.

In reality, it was a dangerous journey of faith. For the ensuing months and years, O'Reilly would journey from France to the Eastern Front of World War II, stopping in

Norway, Sweden, Russia (Saint Petersburg, Moscow), Lithuania (Warsaw), and beyond. Several American newspapers, including the *Boston Daily Advertiser*, *Boston Globe*, *Boston Pilot*, *Boston Herald*, *Seattle Star*, and The *Day Book*, printed O'Reilly's dispatches from the battlefield. Back in the United States in February 1917, she caught the final ship home before America entered the war. She spent the remainder of her life sharing her wartime memories through writing and public speaking.

However, at least one female named Dorothy Lawrence tried entering the area of freelance war reporting and was unsuccessful. Dorothy Lawrence (1896–1964), then 19 years old, gained notoriety in Britain as she crossed the English Channel to France disguised as a male soldier during World War I. Some of Lawrence's lighter work had been published in the *London Times* and *Pall Mall Magazine* before 1914, but both newspapers and the British War Office ridiculed and rejected her attempts to become a war correspondent. She was a freelance war correspondent working in France during the summer of 1915 when she was arrested by French officials for trying to enter a combat zone in the French sector and told to leave the country. She concluded that the only way to the front lines was to dress as a man. With the help of British soldiers, she was able to obtain a khaki uniform and forge identification documents to enter the British zone. She found work with a company in Albert on the Somme that specialised in laying mines. However, due to her poor health and the fear of being identified as a woman by the commanding sergeant, Lawrence was locked up after only ten days. After interrogation, French military officials, who believed Lawrence to be a spy, forced her to sign an affidavit. They shipped her back to London, where she promptly became homeless and jobless.

The War Office requested that Lawrence rework her draft of the war book she had written which Lawrence did. After the war ended in 1919, the War Office heavily censored her book which was met with widespread criticism in British newspapers and failed to sell well. Due to her deteriorating mental state, Lawrence was institutionalised in 1925 and stayed there until she died in 1964.

Lawrence's ambitions to become a journalist were ultimately dashed, but she still managed to embarrass the War Office by proving that women can do just as much as men in the workplace. If war correspondents are unable to leave the country, she will attempt to do so using her superior resources like cars, credentials and cash. Lawrence was unable to launch a successful journalism career despite her time spent on the Western Front. Cases like Schalek's, Casanova's, Roger's, Serao's and O'Reilly's and this one demonstrate that women who aspired to be war correspondents needed to have already achieved prominence in the media and literary worlds before the outbreak of hostilities.

On the other side, Lawrence's exploits were widely celebrated by the American media. Her book was called a thriller by the Yorkville Enquirer. An odd document from World War I has catapulted a British newspaperwoman named Miss Lawrence to the ranks of national heroes. There have never been any British women in the active fighting forces of the British Army before today. It was very different for female reporters and journalists covering the Allied forces on the Western front to work in and gain access to war zones than it was for male reporters and journalists.

The Western Front regime imposed by the Allies was the strictest. At the outset of World War I, all journalists were banned from entering the battlefields in France and Great Britain. After receiving concerns from the media and the public, the Allies established a system of certified war correspondents under military supervision in the spring of 1915. Several journalists, including women, were able to get to the frontlines early in the war and write their firsthand accounts of the battle despite the restrictions placed on media in the conflict zone.

F. Tennyson Jesse (1888-1958), an English author, poet, playwright, and criminologist, was dispatched to Belgium in August 1914 to report on the German invasion. During the war, she travelled to Antwerp, Ghent, Termonde, and the front, but she was eventually forced to leave after the Germans arrived. From the 7th of September through the 9th of October of 1914, she contributed six articles to the *Daily Mail*. Later, during reporting visits to France, she covered the work of the Red Cross. After that, the British Ministry of Information asked her to create an article about the Women's Army which included groups like the Women's Auxiliary Army Corps (WAAC) and the Voluntary Aid Detachment (VAD). She first published her results in the *Daily Mail* in December 1915, and then again in 1919 with the publication of *The Sword of Deborah*.

Writing for publications like *Collier's Weekly*, *Pall Mall Gazette*, and *Vogue*, she devoted her time as a female war correspondent during World War I. The Australian author and poet Louise Mack (1870-1935) also reported on the German invasion of Belgium for British media (*The Daily Mail*, *Evening News*, and *The Sphere*). During the German occupation, she was in Brussels and Antwerp. She claims that she left Antwerp using a fake passport and a rural persona. Sixty-two more women than the previous count served as nurses during World War I, and many of them later chronicled their experiences in print.

Olive Dent (1884-1930), a British VAD nurse, served in a military hospital in Rouen, France, during the years 1915 and 1916. *The Daily Mail, The Lady,* and *The War I* illustrated all of her published as a war correspondent, as did the *Yorkshire Evening Post* and *Evening News*. When American war journalists first arrived in France in the summer of 1917, they were met with rigorous regulations and a ban on female reporters from operating under official cover.

When World War I in Europe finally ended in November 1918, Peggy Hull was the first American woman to be officially recognised as a war correspondent. After being denied permission to write for the *Chicago Tribune,* she published her stories on her time in France in 1917 for the *Newspaper Enterprise Association* and the *Chicago Tribune's* Paris Army edition, as well as the *El Paso Morning Times*. Edy pointed out that journalists needed accreditation from the U.S. military to enter or approach a fighting zone.

This meant that the American military provided facilities and lodging to a significant number of journalists who were not officially recognised as war correspondents. They were able to avoid interference from government censors and military officials, allowing them more freedom in their careers and travels.

As many as seventeen women were given official designation as visiting war correspondents by the American military, according to historical records. Three American women made significant contributions to the Red Cross and other volunteer organisations: Rheta Childe Dorr (1866-1948), Sophie Treadwell (1885-1970), and Mary Boyle O'Reilly. In 1915, Mary Roberts Rinehart (1876-1958) visited the Western Front as a Red Cross volunteer in Belgium where she spoke with soldiers from Belgium, France, and Britain. From where she was, she could see the trenches, the bombed-out villages, and no man's land. Her articles from the Saturday Evening Post, the Boston Globe, and The Sphere were collected into a book titled *Kings, Queens and Pawns*.

The Allies on the Eastern Front Little is known regarding the working circumstances or military attitudes toward women journalists from neutral or allied nations in only Russia and Serbia. Excluding Sofa Casanova of neutral Spain, several women from the United States and Canada covered the Eastern Front, reporting on events such as the Russian Revolution in February 1917 and the Bolshevik Revolution in November 1917.

In the years between 1915 and 1918, Catholic suffragist, educator, and novelist Annie Chrisitch (1885-1977) chronicled the war in Serbia for the British government. During her time with the *Daily Express*, she was assigned to cover events in Serbia as a staff correspondent. Although she was born in Serbia, her mother was Irish, and she spent most of her life in Britain. During the German and Austrian occupation of Serbia, she set up a relief centre and administered eight hospitals in Valjevo. Having Serbian citizenship gave her the privilege of staying when everyone else was expelled. Her pieces for the *Daily Express* on the misery of Serbian war victims were reproduced in publications in Australia, New Zealand, and China. Her humanitarian work in Serbia received a lot of attention from British and worldwide media. The Friends of the Italian Front Flavia Steno (1877-1946), a journalist, Stefania Türr (1885-1940), the writer, founder, and editor of the monthly

La Madre Italiana, Ester Danesi Traversari (1878-1965), and Annie Vivanti (1868-1942), a poet, playwright, and theatre artist, were all recognised by the Italian High Command on the Italian front (1877-1968). Steno was permitted to travel as far as four kilometres away from the battlefield to reach military hospitals on Mount Krn. Her writings about the experience appeared in *Il Secolo XIX*. British journalist Barbara Allason (of La Donna, La Lettura, and Gazzetta del Popolo renown) travelled to Italy's defence lines as a war correspondent for several British publications and became fast friends with Anglo-Italian journalist Annie Vivanti (e.g., The Times, Westminster Gazette, The Nineteenth Century and After). Both ladies had access to Italian military facilities, including border stations and the Udine military headquarters.

Stefania Türr travelled to the Italian front, including the trenches. Her accounts of life on the front lines, in the devastated towns outside of the fighting, and the immense organisation of military supplies can be found in *La Madre Italiana* and her book *Alle trinceed'Italia*. It, like Alice Schalek's other books, was filled with photos of World War II soldiers and battlefields.

In addition to women from Italy, the Italian High Command allowed women from neutral and ally countries to serve on the front lines. Inez Milholland (1886-1916), a suffragist, lawyer, and socialist reformer, led a group of war correspondents from the *Chicago Daily Tribune,* the *Washington Post,* the *New York Tribune, McClure's,* and *Harper's* to the Italian front in the summer of 1915. It was because of her anti-war writings that the Italian government expelled her at the end of September 1915.

Leslie's Weekly's photographer Helen Kirtland was

granted access to the front lines in 1917 by the Italian High Command after the capture of 275,000 Italian soldiers at Caporetto. In the fall of 1918, Kirtland, the photographer, was given special permission to photograph Italian soldiers in the trenches. The CPSU is what they go by. Conditions for female war correspondents varied widely across the Central Powers.

War correspondents from Austria-Hungary, Germany, and neutral countries were given escorted tours to the frontlines by the War Press Office after the Austro-Hungarian military first attempted to bar them from the battlefield in the early stages of World War I. Austria-Hungary accredited several female journalists, including Alice Schalek, Hede Von Trapp, Maria Magda Rumbold from Austria, and Olga Fehér and Margit Vészi from Hungary.

Accredited war correspondents were occasionally allowed to travel to the front lines in the Alps, Galicia and Serbia, accompanied by guides from the War Press Office. There is a scarcity of data about female German journalists. The German Empire instituted strict censorship of the media and prevented any reporters from reaching the front lines. In contrast, German ambulance corps member Thea von Puttkamer (1882-1952) stationed in Constantinople was linked with the Turkish army and published her accounts in German, Hungarian, and Turkish media sources also covered the Gallipoli campaign. British and Australian troops who had been forced to evacuate their stations after their armies were routed commended the Ottoman soldiers for their bravery and valour at the time.

The South Carolina Union Times reported in August 1917 that Von Puttkamer was linked to the Turkish forces operating in Mesopotamia and was thus the only lady war correspondent officially acknowledged by the German government. She is not included on the (imperfect) official German list of war correspondents. Novelist and journalist Friedel Merzenich (1879-1956) served as an editor for the German soldiers' newspaper *Liller Kriegszeitung* from its launch in the spring of 1915 until the war's end in 1918.

Other than her role as editor, Merzenich contributed to several German war newspapers, including the *Liller Kriegszeitung, Berliner Tageblatt, Magdeburger Zeitung, Illustrirte Zeitung,* and *Die Woche.* The compilation of her 1918 contributions to the *Liller Kriegszeitung* was released as a book. The Central Powers also encouraged women from neutral nations to visit Germany and Austria-Hungary. After participating in the Women's Peace Congress in 1915 at The Hague, the American lawyer, activist, and pacifist Madeleine Zabriskie Doty travelled to Germany. She was a correspondent for the *New York Tribune,* the *Chicago Tribune,* and the *Good Housekeeping.* She witnessed the war's effects on civilian life in Germany, especially in Berlin and Hamburg, first-hand.

In Berlin, normal levels of cultural and social activity were maintained even though the war was still going on. In particular, upper-class German women were held up as models of virtue due to the perception that they had low self-esteem and were dedicated to the general good. In August of 1914, Carmen de Burgos Segui (1867-1932) contributed several articles about the war to *El Heraldo de Madrid* under the pen name Colombine.

These articles were later compiled into the book *Mis viajespor Europa.* Famous American author and world traveller Nellie Bly (1864–1922) was among the foreign (male) war correspondents officially recognised by the War

Press Office in Austria-Hungary. She spent several weeks in the fall of 1914 reporting from the Eastern Front for American newspapers in Poland, Galicia, and Serbia.

Between December 1914 and February 1915, the New York Evening Journal published twenty-one articles with the heading "Nellie Bly on the Firing Line." Bly also had an article published in *Die Zeit*. Bly decided to stop contributing to the German newspaper after this, after discovering how extensively her essay had been revised. She visited a Red Cross hospital and saw awful events which she described as impossible to believe in one of her articles.

In the wake of the war, hundreds upon hundreds of people have been killed on the roads and in the trains that have grown up to accommodate the masses. Thousands of other animals are being led into the same brutality as they perish. Milly Buonanno has remarked that the question of whether or not women war correspondents are willing and able to construct their own gender-based agenda and present their own point of view is controversial and poorly researched.

Women reporters covered all aspects of war, from the fighting and weapons used by soldiers to the military strategy and tactics used by commanders and the civilians affected by the conflict. The work done by women in munitions factories, the work done by men who were drafted in factories and farms, and the work done by women who cared for their conscripted husbands and fathers at home are all examples. Numerous magazines developed the term 'women angles' to describe the coverage of the war from a female perspective by female journalists. To cite only two examples, consider Rheta Childe Dorr (1857-1948) and Gertrude Atherton (1857-1948). A novelist and feminist, Atherton returned from France in 1916 and wrote a series of reports on women's war labour, including caring for refugee troops and residents.

Publishing companies and female reporters all benefited financially from stories with a female focus since they attracted a larger audience and could sell more products to that audience. *Saturday Evening Post* editor George Lorimer (1867-1937) stated in 1915 when he dispatched four women to cover the war in Europe that there is seldom a tremendous narrative in the front of the struggle. It's in the doctor's office, your living room, and even your bed. Women have a better understanding of the big picture and the myriad nuances involved in waging war than men do.

However many female reporters felt devalued when they were told they could only report on the woman's viewpoint of war. It was common practice for women to be ridiculed and degraded when they dared to report on wars fought by males. Peggy Hull's male employees loathed her proximity to the front and disliked her writing style because of her articles in the Paris edition of the *Chicago Tribune* in 1917 that were highly welcomed by soldiers.

After Alice Schalek began covering the war, male journalists and military officials questioned her credibility. For instance, in the Arbeiter-Zeitung on November 26, 1915, she argued that women shouldn't cover wars because they don't understand the psychology of war and because being a woman and writing from a female perspective are the ideal qualities for being a war correspondent. It's not unfeminine for a woman to be curious about her brothers, fathers, husbands, and sons' inner lives.

They have been able to undergo a profound

transformation of their inner lives because, while in combat, they have completely shut out any thoughts of their homes and families. War correspondents who are male tend to brush over this facet of the battle. Gellhorn, unlike Hemingway, was not given formal permission to accompany the Allied invasion of Normandy on June 6, 1944, but she nonetheless sneaked onto a medical ship and barricaded herself in a lavatory until it started sailing across the English Channel. Gellhorn, who was posing as a stretcher-bearer, was the first female reporter on the scene when they arrived at Omaha Beach. She waded to the beach to gather injured and aid medical teams, arriving in Normandy before Hemingway. In her report for *Collier's*, she observed:

Everyone was violently busy on that crowded, dangerous shore. The pebbles were the size of apples and feet deep, and we stumbled up a road that a huge road shovel was scooping out. We walked with the utmost care between the narrowly placed white tape lines that marked the mine-cleared path, and headed for a tent marked with a red cross.... Everyone agreed that the beach was a stinker and that it would be a great pleasure to get the hell out of here sometime. (Lancaster, "D-day: Martha Gellhorn goes Rogue to get her Story")

Between 1914 and 1918, many women served as war correspondents, writing about conflicts across Europe and the Middle East. The policy of the Allies and the Central Powers determined whether or not they would be allowed entry into combat zones as accredited war journalists, on less formal assignments from their newspapers, or as nurses. It was as varied as the women who reported from war zones. Location, proximity to the action, editorial mandates, and personal and professional interests all had a role in shaping the women journalists' areas of interest. They crossed over into enemy territory, putting their lives in danger. In renowned publications, often using only their first names, they described what they saw as eyewitnesses.

These women war journalists had their work published not just in their home countries but also in others around the world. Florence MacLeod Harper, a Canadian, contributed to *Leslie's Weekly*, an American publication; Thea Von Puttkamer, a German, wrote for the German, Austrian, Turkish, and German-American press. Florence MacLeod Harper, Margit Vészi, and Alice Schalek all contributed to *Leslie's Weekly*.

Women reporters used a wide range of print and visual media, from high-low-circulation periodicals to illustrated magazines and books. The three women veterans Alice Schalek, Louise Mack and Mary Boyle O'Reilly frequently spoke to groups about their wartime experiences after returning home. They were able to form relationships with people of diverse socioeconomic backgrounds. Except for Dorothy Lawrence, who was only 19 at the time, all of the other participants were prominent members of the upper class who were either journalists, photographers, or both. They shared a common political background as suffragists, pacifists, and social reformers. They started in their twenties and went well into their sixties and beyond.

Even though women were socially expected to stay at home and raise children, many broke the mould and sought traditionally male-dominated professions including lecturing, journalism, photography and war reporting. Because of this, a woman's chances of getting employed as a war correspondent greatly depended on her social standing and her career trajectory before the war. They kept contributing to their newspapers for decades after the war ended. However, Dorothy Lawrence's narrative demonstrates that a novice to the business of journalism without contacts is doomed to fail, even with her wartime experiences.

Intriguingly, the women's aspect was not the only perspective covered by female combat correspondents. Nevertheless, women were determined to cover every aspect of warfare, including fighting on battlefields, soldiers' pain and suffering, the destruction of towns and villages and the effects of war on civilians, especially women and children, despite the fact that their access to combat zones was often severely restricted.

Male photographer's perspectives were broadened and enriched by the female war correspondents' varied reporting during World War I. During World War II, these six women namely Martha Gellhorn, Lee Miller, Sigrid Schultz, Virginia Cowles, Clare Hollingworth, and Helen Kirkpatrick blazed a trail for future female war reporters by challenging stereotypes and standing up for what they believed in. Their groundbreaking work and bravery as wartime and post-war journalists, photographers, and correspondents helped secure their place in history. Before her untimely death in 1971, photojournalist Margaret Bourke-White (1904-1971) accomplished many groundbreaking feats. She not only broke new ground as the first female American war correspondent, but she also broke new ground as the first non-Soviet photographer to gain access to the Soviet five-year plan for photography (Mc Euen, "Seeing America: Women Photographers between the Wars").

In 1929, Margaret Bourke-White worked as an associate editor and staff photographer for *Fortune* and in 1936, she became the first female photojournalist for *Life*. She was the only foreign photographer in Moscow when the Germans invaded in 1941 after Germany had broken the terms of its non-aggression treaty. Her portraits of Mahatma Gandhi and Dr Bhimrao Ramji Ambedkar are also well-known in India and Pakistan.

Dickey Chapelle (1919-1965) was a photojournalist for National Geographic who covered both World War II and the Vietnam War. During the Hungarian Revolution of 1956, Chapelle was wrongfully accused of spying and imprisoned by the Russians for two months. Chapelle earned the respect of the military with the assistance of his fellow journalists. She was a member of the paratroopers and often went on missions with them. One of her firsts is the tragic distinction of being the first female correspondent to be killed in battle. She was covering the Vietnam War when a land mine went off and shrapnel hit her in the neck.

Full military honours were accorded to Dickey Chapelle's burial, which is unusual for a civilian. Among the many accomplishments of photojournalist Marjory Collins (1912-1985), her reportage of the American home front during World War II is particularly well known. She described herself in those terms. She was an editor at U.S. *Camera* magazine during the 1930s in New York City. Collins, after WWII, combined her passions for writing and photography by travelling the world as a freelance photographer. Ruth Baldwin Cowan (1901-1993) started as a movie reviewer for the San Antonio Evening News on the weekends, but she quickly moved through the ranks to become a reporter.

Cowan's pen name for the Houston Chronicle and the United Press was Baldwin Cowan after she stopped using her given name in her work. After it was discovered that she was working for a magazine that explicitly forbids the hiring of women, she was fired. The good news is that the Associate Press didn't hesitate to hire her. She began her career as an AP reporter in 1942 when she was sent to Algiers to cover the war there. It didn't matter how hard her supervisor tried to stop her, she always managed to evade him. She covered the capital city of the United States during and after World War II, focusing on human-interest stories and events like Eleanor Roosevelt's press conferences.

American journalist, novelist, and travel writer Martha Gellhorn is widely regarded as one of the finest war correspondents of the twentieth century. She spent more than 60 years covering the world's major conflicts, including the Spanish Civil War, Hitler's rise to power in the 1930s, World War II and the Vietnam War. While she will always be remembered as Ernest Hemingway's third wife, her work as a journalist far outshines their brief marriage.

To participate in the invasion of Normandy, she hid in the toilet of a hospital ship and pretended to be a stretcher carrier. She was the only female member of the armed forces to take part in the D-Day invasion that took place in 1944. She submitted one of the earliest reports from Dachau in 1945, shortly after the camp was freed from its Nazi occupation. From 1920 through 1966, American journalist and war correspondent Marguerite Higgins Hall covered conflicts in Europe, the Pacific, and the Middle East for the *New York Herald Tribune* and *Newsday*. She and her co-workers had just rowed from Seoul to Suwon, South

Korea to see the U.S. military headquarters there when they heard about the bombing of the Hangang Bridge.

The limitation on women correspondents in Korea has been repealed after a plea by the general was sent to the *Herald Tribune*. Everyone has the utmost respect for Marguerite Higgins as a working professional. For all female war correspondents, this was a defining moment. For her reportage of the Korean War, Higgins became the first woman to win the Pulitzer Prize for Foreign Correspondence in 1951.

Gellhorn, who was always sceptical of politicians, passionately championed the cause of the oppressed. Her short stories and novellas, known for their sparse style, include *The Weather in Africa* (1978), *The Novellas of Martha Gellhorn* (1993) *What Mad Pursuit* (1934) *The Trouble I've Seen* (1936) *The Heart of Another* (1941) *Liana* (1944) *The Wine of Astonishment* (1948) or *Point of no Return* (1948).

Martha Gellhorn was a courageous war correspondent who covered practically every major conflict during a time when female journalists were in little supply. Her debut novel was not a success. Critics generally disliked *What Mad Pursuit*, if it received any notice at all. One described it as palpable juvenilia while another described it as a rather futile book. Three college buddies seeking fulfilment, significance, and sexual experience are met with disappointment as the story moves. Gellhorn was dissatisfied with the book's reception. It was never reissued, and she only sometimes named it as one of her published works. She didn't dwell on the books' failure, any more than she did on her brief failed marriage to Ernest Hemingway. She proceeded to write several books — fiction, nonfiction, and memoir — while also reporting courageously from combat zones. This initial review of *What Mad Pursuit* by Martha Gellhorn in the *Brooklyn Daily Eagle*, November 18, 1934, is typical of the book's reception. The prologue and core theme of Miss Gellhorn's books is that nothing unpleasant ever occurs to daring individuals.

Frederick thus writes in his piece "Three Modern Girls: What Mad Pursuit": "Nothing ever happens to the brave, prefaces Miss Gellhorn's novel and serves as its theme. Hemingway still has much to answer for. *What Mad Pursuit* is a brash, incredibly youthful story of three girls who leave college precipitately and hurl themselves headlong upon the pricklier thorns of life" (Stokes, "Three Modern Girls").

What Mad Pursuit is the story of three girls in the same boat. The opening chapter shows them at college. The rumblings of the fast-approaching storm of discontent grow louder, as the pages turn. For the climax, the heroines leave college, one under expulsion, one in protest at the other's summary dismissal, and the third, for no good reason, leads on the bandwagon that leads to nowhere. The exploits of the three fill the major portion of the book. All are driven on by an insatiable desire for an elusive piece of the mind and soul, each in her own tortured, tortuous way. Tawdry death by murder in the rooms of her paramour comes to one, affliction with a social disease faces another, and third — in mind, the least striving but most deserving —finds security. This book is definitely amateurish.

Like the futile lapping of a surgeless lake, the procession and recession of climax and anti-climax, fraught with emptiness, leave the reader with an uneasy, dissatisfied mind.

The four interconnected stories in *The Trouble I Have*

Seen capture Martha Gellhorn's first-hand experience of the Great Depression. They convincingly depict the slow spiritual collapse of the simple, homely adequacy of American life in the face of abrupt unemployment, acute poverty and pessimism. Here the fiction is fashioned with documentary truth. They capture the spirit of a generation drawn into apathy, as well as young men who no longer believe in man or God, let alone private industry. Gellhorn was the youngest of sixteen handpicked reporters who were paid to deliver accurate, secret reports on the human tales behind the Depression statistics directly to Roosevelt's White House. In these pages, we learn about the true cost of widespread destitution. Narrating the painful situations while reporting those wars live from the frontline, she observed that "we can taste the dust in our mouths, smell the disease and feel the hopelessness and the despair" (Gellhorn, *The Trouble I Have Seen* 248).

And we can hear the first cadences of a writer's voice here, who went on to become, possibly, the greatest female war reporter of the twentieth century. In 1934, Washington New Dealer Harry Hopkins assigned cub reporter Martha Gellhorn, who had just returned from Europe, to report on the effects of the Depression on the textile communities of North Carolina and New England. She wandered around slums and shacks, dressed in couture from Paris, to interview men and women afflicted by starvation, disease and despair. She discovered her lifetime writing voice while writing these reports. One of her finest works is *The Trouble I've Seen*, a quartet of short stories inspired by her experiences.

The Heart of Another is a collection of short stories that are clearly the result of her own and her companions' experiences in wartime Europe, Spain during the Civil War, France during the occupation, the front in Finland, the Mannerheim Line, the air base, Corsica, the Tyrol, and so on. The stories are more austere in their emotional and human qualities than her earlier writings and are more tuned to the agonies of unspoken emotion that this war seems to engender. The greatest of the bunch is *A Portrait of a Lady*, about a woman journalist who uses her sensuality to acquire her story and Luigi's House, about a Corsican vineyard hand who risked everything to keep what he considered his own.

Liana, like Gellhorn's debut novel *What Mad Pursuit*, is difficult to find. It would be fascinating to investigate whether a modern interpretation of it might come across as racist or sexist. Having studied Gellhorn and her deep belief in humanity and women's equality, it's difficult to see her consciously or dishonestly writing a book with a biased slant. Copies of *Liana* are difficult to come by. Gellhorn is regarded as one of the twentieth century's outstanding war correspondents. It's a fitting legacy, but she also wrote some excellent fiction. Her firsthand experiences as a World War II correspondent inspired *The Wine of Astonishment*.

"The Feminine View on War", a review of Martha Gellhorn's *The Wine of Astonishment* was published in *The Daily Oklahoman* on November 7, 1948, which asserted that women were typically denied the experience of writing personally and realistically of males in conflict until World War II. This is demonstrated in Martha Gellhorn's story about soldiers during the Battle of the Bulge and the Allied invasion of Germany.

Gellhorn's novel is set against the backdrop of her nine years working as a war journalist covering the war in Spain, the Russo-Finish War, the Sino-Japanese conflict before Pearl Harbour, World War II in Europe and finally, the post-war combat in Java. Miss Gellhorn's portrayal of troops can be as tough-minded as early Dos Passos or Norman Mailer, or as sensitive as Ernest Hemingway's love story set in a fighting scene in *A Farewell to Arms*. In truth, Miss Gellhorn is comparable to Hemmingway due to the uniqueness of her characters and her delicately modulated manner. Beginning with the combat in Belgium, this tale follows two soldiers- Lieutenant Colonel Smithers, a Georgian battalion commander, and his jeep driver, Jacob Levy, a gorgeous Jewish teenager from St. Louis as they reached Luxembourg for a two-week vacation.

In an affair with a disillusioned Red Cross girl, Smithers seeks love and an understanding of the meaning of human existence; and Levy discovers what Smithers fails to explore in his love for a gentle and lovely country girl. The novel culminates with an irrational act of violence perpetrated by Levy following a visit to the Dachau crematory when he first realizes the tragedy and immensity of the Nazi rejection of humanity.

Miss Gellhorn's treatment of her interconnected topics is deft, her characterization is sympathetic and convincing, and her language is adaptable and perceptive. *The Wine of Astonishment* is unquestionably one of the best World War II novels.

Although Martha Gellhorn is mostly recognized for her outstanding journalism, *The Novellas of Martha Gellhorn* illustrates her formidable skills as an observer of social manners and cultural variations in settings, ranging from the United States through England and Italy to Africa. *The Novellas of Martha Gellhorn* includes some of her best literature, ranging from her Depression-era piece, *The Trouble I've Seen* to the three novellas collected in *The Weather in Africa* (1978). Gellhorn's obsession for travel, and her desire to see how other people live, inspired the novel. *The Trouble I've Seen* novellas are firsthand descriptions of persons she encountered while working for President Franklin D. Roosevelt's Federal Emergency Relief Administration. The manner in which these individuals thought and dressed is noted with exquisite detail and sympathy but with remarkably little of the sentimentality that often mars the proletarian fiction of the 1930s.

The Wine of Astonishment examines the horrors of war and the issues of personal responsibility that still resonate today. When it was first published, it was a *New York Times* bestseller. It was long out of print and was reissued in 2016 as *Point of No Return* in paperback and as an e-book. Describing her own memorable experience of reporting in Dachau, Gellhorn writes:

Dachau has been my lifelong point of no return. From the moment when I walked through the gate of that prison, with its infamous motto, 'Arbeit Macht Frei,' and when I walked out at the end of a day that had no ordinary scale of hours, I was changed, and how I looked at the human condition, the world we live in, changed ... Years of war had taught me a great deal, but war was nothing like Dachau. Compared to Dachau, war was clean. (Gellhorn *Point of no Return* 233)

Gellhorn's later writing frequently deals with the issue of marriage; notably, the titles of her four stories in her second book of novellas, *Two by Two* (1958), are taken from the marriage service: *For Better for Worse, For Richer or Poorer, In Sickness and in Health* and *Till Death Us Do*

Part. She demonstrates a superb ear for dialogue in this scene, conveying the joys and stresses of courting and marriage through the exchanges of lovers who frequently misinterpret the meaning of each other's words. *Pretty Tales for Tired People* (1956) has three novellas that reflect her continued fascination with the vagaries of marriage.

The titles of her novella collection, *The Weather in Africa*, allude to the impact of climate and geography on human character; *On the Mountain, By the Sea* and *In the Highlands*. Gellhorn lived many different lives in her well-travelled career, but it is a tribute to her imagination that she was able to create whole worlds and independent personalities that transcend their roots in her biography. Although Gellhorn does not adopt an explicitly feminist stance, her delicate depictions of men and women invariably bring out concerns and problems concerning women. Her male and female characters repeatedly circle around the problem of commitment to each other. There are happily married couples in her fiction, but they are a rarity, serving only as fixed points in an unstable marital universe in which the most urbane couples take lovers and treat marriage as a form of convenience, as a necessary and comfortable institution, but rarely as a permanently romantic or inviolable union.

Women in Gellhorn's fiction frequently find themselves alone, having been rejected and occasionally tricked by their male lovers and husbands. However, males are not necessarily villains, and women can be fools. Gellhorn's depiction of the sexes is devoid of sentimentality. Women are alone because marriage, in her opinion, is a tough institution to maintain. Her ladies can be lost both inside and outside of marriage since it can disclose or worsen their flaws, but it is not a cause of human failing. *By the Sea*, one of three novellas set in Africa is perhaps her most moving. Mrs. Jamieson makes a motor drive to get away from her failed marriage and the death of her small kid while on vacation.

Praising the sheer talent and intelligence of Martha Gellhorn for her daring war reporting, Nava Atlas writes in his article: "I do not know whether or not Martha Gellhorn is a novice in the field of fiction. I do know that her genius is obviously, still in the embryo and will require more development, if *What Mad Pursuit* is to be taken as a sample of her talent" (Atlas, "What Mad Pursuit: Martha Gellhorn's Lost 1934 Novel").

Gellhorn's major impact has been seen as a journalist. Her superb war reportage, reprinted in *The Face of War* and her articles on social and political issues, reprinted in *The View from the Ground* have won her considerable acclaim. Her nonfiction has appeared at regular intervals both in book form and in mass-circulation magazines. Her body of fiction, on the other hand, is small and has appeared irregularly. She said that she found fiction difficult to write, even though she often preferred it to her journalism which she wrote rapidly and without much revision. Moreover, her brand of fiction, a kind of novel-of-manners approach, has seemed unremarkable when juxtaposed against the experimental and innovative fiction of the twentieth century. She has been classed as a minor writer of fiction, continuing the tradition established by Henry James and Edith Wharton.

Nevertheless, interest in Gellhorn's fiction has steadily increased. *The Novellas of Martha Gellhorn* is only one effort by publishers to reprint her best work. Virago

Press, which specializes in reviving important work that deals directly with women's issues, has issued paperback editions of *A Stricken Field* and *Liana*, two novels that centre on women striving to survive in male-dominated societies. The women in these novels are victimized by men, though the female reporter in *A Stricken Field* has an unquenchable ambition that makes her more than a match for the male journalists who admire her but cannot resist the temptation also to belittle her. Narrating her struggling days of war reporting, Martha explains: "All amateur travellers have experienced horror journeys, long or short, sooner or later, one way or another. As a student of disaster, I note that we react alike to our tribulations: frayed and bitter at the time, proud afterwards. Nothing is better for self-esteem than survival" (qtd. in Introduction *Travel with myself and Another*).

Gellhorn has never been a programmatic writer. Her values are derived from her precise observations of people and events. She can be as hard on her female as on her male characters. She has spent little time decrying the unfairness of male privilege, instead preferring to fight for her place in traditionally male preserves. As her novellas reveal, Gellhorn's passion is social justice. If human beings are treated decently, she implies, such issues as the relationship between the sexes and women's rights will receive their fair share of attention. The protagonist of the novel *Point of No Return*, Jacob Levy, witnessed the liberation of the Dachau concentration camp, and the shock of the experience changed everything. Quoting Martha Gellhorn talking about people's fear of old age, Taylor Jasmine writes in her article: "Why do people talk of the horrors of old age? It's great. I feel like a fine old car with the parts gradually wearing out, but I'm not complaining, ...

Those who find growing old terrible are people who haven't done what they wanted with their lives" (qtd. in Jasmine "Martha Gellhorn: Quotes by a Courageous Woman").

Praising Martha Gellhorn for her Courageous nature as frontline correspondence, Rick Lyman writes in the magazine *The New York Times*: "Reading Martha Gellhorn for the first time is a staggering experience. She is not a travel writer or a journalist or a novelist: she is all of these, and one of the most eloquent witnesses of the twentieth century" (qtd. in Lyman "Martha Gellhorn, Daring Writer, Dies at 89"). Asserting that people would rather swallow lies than the truth as though the lies were comforting and appetising, Gellhorn writes: "Gradually I came to realize that people will more readily swallow lies than truth, as if the taste of lies was homey, appetizing: a habit" (Gellhorn, *The Novellas of Martha Gellhorn* 314).

CHAPTER V

Conclusion

Despite journalism's long history of use, the term itself remains undefined. The term 'journalism' is commonly used to describe the process of disseminating information to the general public. Journalists are those who actively seek out and report on news and other informational developments while the media are the vehicles through which this information is disseminated.

When it comes to covering war, journalism has been at rock bottom. In contrast, journalists do not enjoy an Olympian vantage point from which to assess the causes and effects of a violent incident. Reporters' viewpoints are limited and distorted by propaganda and the generals' perspective just as distant readers' perspectives are limited and distorted by prejudice and ignorance. The truth is masked by partisanship and censorship.

Reporters covering conflicts may feel that they are profiting off of the pain they witness. Cynicism is a common theme in works about war that have been written throughout time. The tone was set by Samuel Johnson in 1758 about the loss of the love of truth being one of the war's greatest tragedies when desire leads and credulity feeds falsehoods. A large number of soldiers and scribblers, who are accustomed to robbing and lying even in times of peace, populate the streets and the garrets.

Gellhorn eagerly followed the conflict, causing her marriage to a prominent man who preferred to have her at home to fall apart. She used her in-depth understanding of the war's wider picture to provide context for regular battle scenes as she chronicled the liberation of Paris and Dachau for *Town and Country* Magazine.

Martha Gellhorn's most important contribution to the world was as a relator of disputes which she did meticulously. Neither her demeanour nor her looks was considered saintly. As a veteran, she could appreciate the fascination with war stories. She had been married to Ernest Hemingway for the last five years of his life. According to Caroline Morehead's outstanding biography from 2003 'Apocrypha', a term Gellhorn created to identify the authors of such works, was no accident.

After the war, Gellhorn divorced Hemingway and lived for a time in Cuernavaca, Mexico. She continued to write for *The Saturday Evening Post*, first to explore the toll of the war on the street children of Rome, then to document her adoption of an Italian orphan:

I knew those children in the war. I saw them scraping an existence for themselves in the rubble of Naples; I saw them brought in, bleeding and wild, to battalion aid stations because they'd walked on mines like any soldier; I saw them dumped into trucks and moved, they didn't know where. I thought them the bravest people possible, and beautiful and quick and cheerful in the centre of hell, where they lived…. They ought to declare war on grownups, I thought furiously, who killed their childhood. (Gellhorn)

In the introduction to *The Face of War*, her most well-known compilation of reports, she admitted that she was a special sort of war profiteer. The book was published in 1959. As a war correspondent, Martha Ellis Gellhorn was among the 20th century's finest. Her reports have comprehensively covered nearly every significant international event over the last 60 years. While working as a war correspondent in Spain during the Spanish Civil War, Gellhorn penned this book.

Gellhorn's impact on the evolution of war reporting is dissected. Gellhorn's writings centre on everyday people rather than on military conflicts. She told the account of the war using literary devices and methods and thus can be seen as a forerunner of literary journalism in the 1960s. Here, we see a war correspondent portrayed as a famous and courageous explorer from the era depicted. This book has examined her *Collier's* Weekly pieces, correspondence with literary and political heavyweights, diaries stored in her archive at Boston University, and fiction to learn more about her participation as a writer and activist in the Spanish conflict. Gellhorn's political and professional activity during the Spanish Civil War was intricately intertwined with her relationships with two notable people.

Eleanor Roosevelt was the first to have a fruitful, nearly three-decade-long relationship with Gellhorn as a go-between for Franklin Delano Roosevelt and republican administration officials and sympathisers alike. A journey to Spain in 1940 led to the marriage of Hemingway and Gellhorn. Their professional rivalry led to their divorce in 1945 while they were both foreign correspondents for the same newspaper. During their time together in Spain, Gellhorn's early works were profoundly influenced by Hemingway's writing.

Most war correspondents were burly, booze-soaked men before World War II. Women were not deemed qualified to report on such a macho subject as war in the early 20th century when English-speaking countries restricted war reporting to combat reports. It's not surprising that English-speaking allies during WWII looked down on female journalists. It is without a doubt because professors have paid little attention to women's war reporting during World War II.

While studies of women's and minorities' pasts in the twenty-first century have been done, they have mostly focused on the national level. This book argues that the journalism produced by women during World War II is essential to our comprehension of that struggle. There was a striking lack of female war correspondents from English-speaking Allied countries in the Soviet Union. Every major conflict between the Spanish Civil War and the conclusion of the Cold War was covered by Martha Gellhorn.

Writing letters to her close ones, as mentioned in *Selected Letters of Martha Gellhorn,* she wrote: "Life is not long at all, never long enough, but days are very long indeed" (Moorehead 234). Gellhorn's letters are just as interesting and enlightening as her battle dispatches. By reading her letters, we get a glimpse into Gellhorn's personal life and her marriage to Hemingway, humanising the often-elusive journalist. A young American woman who risked her life covering the Spanish Civil War and the Great Depression, Martha Gellhorn is revered as a hero in the United States.

Despite her notoriety as a result of her eyewitness tales from the front lines, her private life was tumultuous and difficult. Due to her work as a war correspondent, Ernest Hemingway's marriage with her ended in divorce.

In this fascinating account of a woman's life, Moorehead describes how fiercely Martha fought against injustice and how earnestly she tried to tell the human tale.

From 1937 until 1959, Gellhorn reported openly and honestly on crises in the Middle East and Central America, demonstrating an open and sensitive conscience and genuine empathy for people of all political persuasions. She felt obliged to write rapidly out of concern that she would soon forget the unique sights, sounds, phrases and gestures of that time and place. She was relentless no matter how far she travelled.

In 1937, while living in Spain, Martha Gellhorn decided to become a war journalist and later published her observations and reporting in the 1938 book *The Face of War*. The term 'interim' was commonly used to designate different wartime peace initiatives, including those in Spain, Finland, Europe, Java, Vietnam and the Middle East during World War II.

Each chapter is prefaced with an autobiographical preface written by Gellhorn in which she discusses how she came to cover these fights and what she thinks about combat and the writing process. Gellhorn prioritises her career as a war correspondent over her identity as a writer. And that means she'll have to contend with gender norms in this predominantly male nation that discourage women from covering wars from the front lines.

During World War II, she had a hard time keeping secret the D-Day landings on Normandy beaches and the Allied effort in Italy. Mary Douglas, an American reporter, is adored by her fellow international correspondents at a Prague hotel, where they inform her that the story of Czechoslovakia is already gone. Mary can't report on the findings of other reporters who have visited concentration camps and documented proof of torture due to official censorship. Journalists have taken sanctuary in the hotel after their Czechoslovak driver was detained and they were warned by German guards that their press credentials would not protect them the next time. Mary's male employees regard her tardy arrival in Prague as evidence that she is unable to let go of the past and move on from Spain, but they also see it as a chance to acquire a story for their newspaper.

To rephrase, airships are crucial to the plot at all times. Mary relates her experience as if she were a reporter, beginning with a naive curiosity and developing into a profound commitment. As she learns more about the issue at hand, her ability to empathise with those affected by it decreases. This woman has a lot of clout due to her status as an American journalist, her wealth, and her ability to travel freely across the world. Nearby Czechs and Sudeten Germans are helpless to stop what she's going through. Mary is in a position of authority that few others can match due to her individuality, nationality, and occupation. But she just can't seem to grasp anything, no matter how hard she tries. She is unable to save her friends or even locate them. Explaining how Citizenship is a difficult job that requires the citizen to create his or her own informed opinion and abide by it Gellhorn contends: "Citizenship is a tough occupation which obliges the citizen to make his own informed opinion and stand by it" (Moorehead, *Selected Letters of Martha Gellhorn* 252).

Mary's narrative seeks to find a modicum of strength in the face of insurmountable adversity, even if there is no escape and no hope. Mary's interest in and concern for the refugees grows throughout A *Stricken Field* as Gellhorn presents a horrifying and vivid picture of their sufferings:

If there is a war, then all of the things most of us do won't matter anymore. I have a feeling that one has to work all day and all night and live too, and swim and get the sun one's hair and laugh and love as many people as one can find around and do this all terribly fast, because the time getting shorter and shorter every Day. (Moorehead, *Selected Letters of Martha Gellhorn* 263)

The Trouble I've Seen by Martha Gellhorn is a novel set during the Great Depression. This is a fascinating picture of the slow but sure demise of the simple, everyday parts of American life, and it should give pause to those who doubt that things can get any worse in the United States. These men represent an entire generation that has lost faith in humanity and the free market.

President Franklin D. Roosevelt urged Martha to give him reliable, confidential reports on the anecdotes that back up the Great Depression's statistics, and she agreed to do so. The true price of pervasive poverty is revealed in these pages. Even though we can't see it, death and despair infuse our bodies with a dreadful odour. I believe she went on to become one of the most influential women war correspondents of the 20th century.

Martha has moved to pen four novellas on the Great Depression after witnessing the suffering of others around her. Gellhorn obviously cares very much about the people she meets. Gellhorn, inspired by her childhood reporting to the Roosevelt White House, composed four short stories set during the Great Depression. She writes with a critical yet sympathetic view about those who endure filth, hunger and disease. *The Trouble I have seen* concludes with a story about a little girl named Ruby who, at the age of eleven, turns to prostitution to earn money for roller skates.

Motivated by the atrocities committed by fascist regimes in Spain and Germany and by the ongoing tragedy in Central America where people are choosing to maintain their dignity in the face of government brutality, Martha Gellhorn wrote *The View from the Ground* spanning her life and travels from the 1930s through the 1980s. Numerous essays in this anthology provide descriptions of these zones. *The View from the Ground* has everything: a heinous crime, a crumbling civilisation, and a happy ending for the novel's least admirable protagonist. There are no exciting moments in this piece of work that make the reader feel anything other than exhausted, like the worthless lapping of an empty lake in a river that has no water in it. To Gellhorn, it was deeply upsetting when readers rejected her novel. She barely mentioned that it was a book at all. Her first novel *What Mad Pursuit*, was met with mixed reviews from critics. It's been termed everything from palpable juvenilia to a totally worthless endeavour. It's hardly often that a correspondent makes as effective use of citations from other texts as she does in *What Mad Pursuit*. The meticulously created scenarios on which her opinions are based should be presented to as many individuals as possible.

According to Merle Rubin of The Christian Science Monitor, Martha Gellhorn avoids geopolitical abstraction and ideological indoctrination by placing the reader amid the disaster. She has covered numerous wars, including the Spanish Civil War, World War II, the Eichmann trial, the Arab-Israeli conflict, and the Vietnam War, all of which have frustrated and angered her. She is dedicated to reporting the truth no matter how difficult it may be.

According to Martin Northway's article, Martha Gellhorn's *A Stricken Field* exemplifies the usefulness of fiction as evidence. According to Marianne Hauser in the Saturday Review of Literature, Miss Gellhorn excels whether she is capturing everyday situations or pulling out the political background. In her performances, she can evoke the chaos of a mob and the hopelessness of a refugee camp. *A Stricken Field* is a highly precarious environment. Mary Douglas has developed an exceptional capacity for empathy as a result of her experiences. The Boston Transcript's Pamela Taylor says that Gellhorn's story is told with speed, passion, and vivid, unmistakable emphasis.

Miss Gellhorn is well-known for her expertise as a journalist. Using her knowledge, sympathy and sharp eye, she crafts innovative writing that is gentle on the reader. Alida Becker of the Philadelphia Inquirer writes that these items show that Gellhorn was a ground-breaking lady for her day. *San Francisco Chronicle* contributor Jeffrey Rodgers calls Gellhorn a master of short, dramatic, and evocative pieces, adding that her writing is always anchored in the sentiments she was experiencing at the moment. In her spare time, she likes to learn more about issues of social justice and human rights. *Granta* contributor Bill Buford claims that novelist, journalist, and travel writer Martha Gellhorn does not fall under any of these categories. She can get her hands on anything imaginable, and much more besides "Martha Gellhorn: A Furious Footnote in History").

While she was in Czechoslovakia and writing *A Stricken Field,* World War II erupted (1940). Before the Munich Agreement, Gellhorn witnessed Prague's transformation from a proud democracy into a country ruled by German troops. After the communists took power, the journalist went back to Prague to help refugees and attract attention to the country's plight, but she was unsuccessful. The fascinating portrayal of the Gestapo's suppression of a town is one of Gellhorn's finest works.

A Stricken Field, Martha Gellhorn's 1940 novel on the final solution is often regarded as her best work. The scenario became more problematic due to her lack of comprehension. *A Stricken Field* takes place in the middle of historic Prague for a full week. Because of appeasement and humility on the part of Neville Chamberlain and Edvard Benes, Hitler's army was able to take over the Sudetenland without a battle in the end. Czech immigrants were unpopular in Germany ever since Hitler came to power in 1933, but anti-fascist and liberal German refugees were able to depart the country ahead of some of them. Everything has been returned to its proper location.

The concept of a concentration camp is horrifying, yet it strikes a different chord of horror in different people. Although the Gestapo's existence has been officially denied, it is quite likely. Because they all have Western passports, Mary Douglas and her other authors may choose to stay in a hotel rather than attend Hemingway's rolling feast. Douglas tapes interviews with refugees while knowing the information won't be utilised in journalism because it can be easily labelled as propaganda.

As opposed to the other characters, Douglas goes to the refugee camp and witnesses the appalling conditions in which the refugees are living. She finds strength in the thought that she is the only journalist on the job which she repeats to herself often. There's hardly much purpose in socialising if nobody cares what you have to say.

Under our watchful care, orphaned children can go

about their days without fear. One can faintly hear a young person humming along to the tune of a song about a mother receiving a message from a bird.

Our worries about the future colour even the simplest, most happy moments of our existence. The field is now gone. Douglas has long looked up to a pair of Germans, Rita and Peter, who risk everything to be politically active. Though he would like to help, he has no idea how. Throughout history, many faiths' distinction and dignity suppliers have been forgotten. They were allowed to go about their daily lives unhindered until they were ultimately made to pay for their convictions out of their own pockets. Rita ignores warnings not to enter what she believes to be the Gestapo's headquarters in the basement. Plato's caveman analogy comes to mind when one thinks of how Rita reacts to the noises of Nazi torture: she can only perceive shadows.

An American journalist is useless in this situation. As a final resort, Rita decides to bury the written records of heroic deeds she fears will be lost forever if they are not preserved. Despite being fiction, *A Stricken Field* serves as a testament to the power of the written word.

In *A Stricken Field*, American journalist Mary Douglas convinces Adolf Hitler to attack the Sudetenland region of Czechoslovakia in 1938. People who escaped Nazi persecution and made it to Prague sometimes spent only a few weeks in the Czech capital before being sent to a concentration camp or executed. A reporter presents at the time wrote a fanciful recounting of real events that have been passed off as fiction. Various wars and conflicts, such as the Spanish Civil War, the Korean War, and the Vietnam War are covered in this book. Gellhorn thinks back most often on her valiant but ultimately fruitless efforts to persuade the UN High Commissioner for Refugees to provide a respite to the millions of refugees who had fled Germany, Austria, and the Sudetenland in search of safety in Prague. Gellhorn's first job in journalism wasn't exactly a success, despite the author's best efforts as chronicled in *What Mad Pursuit*. Depression and an STD loom large in this novel about three college friends' searches for meaning, fulfilment, and sexual experience. In *What Mad Pursuit*, three different young women are in a similar predicament.

Her compelling novel *Point of No Return* first published in 1948, is an account of World War II that takes place during and after the Battle of the Bulge as the Allies march into Germany and uncover Nazi murder camps. The atrocities of the Holocaust are exposed after Dachau is liberated, and a young soldier from St. Louis named Jacob Levy vows revenge. Questions of Jewish identity and individual moral responsibility that the author explored in the book, *Point of No Return*, continue to preoccupy him half a century after its publication. After a week of ignorance about Nazi concentration camps, she paid her first visit to Dachau which had been uncovered by American soldiers at the end of a village street. According to the publisher, *Point of No Return* by Martha Gellhorn first appeared in print in 1948.

Gellhorn was a war correspondent for many years, writing for publications all over the world. No other woman landed in Normandy on D-Day, June 6, 1944, but she did.

Soon after the camp's liberation in 1945, she was one of the first journalists to go there.

When portraying a US Army unit, it's essential to get inside the skin of the characters and feel what they're feeling as she feels.

Jacob Levy, who had been on the receiving end of hostile energy for a while, decided to make an extra effort to start the day because he was sick of feeling like a sitting duck. Throughout his service in the military, he served as a litter bearer and an ammunition carrier. Two blows had already been delivered, and he was ready for more. An unexpected opportunity arose for him when Lieutenant Colonel John Smithers needed a jeep driver.

The troops under John Smithers' command were weak and anxious. Amid the day, Smithers sprung to his feet and grabbed some orders. His facade cracked when he saw that subsequent battles would lead to more casualties. Smithers's unit was the first to include a Jew.

Having spent so much time together, they came to respect and admire one another. Lt. Col. Smithers was able to escape to the peaceful city of Luxembourg with the help of Levy. At the Officers Club, he met Dotty Brock, a nurse for the Red Cross. Dotty paid no attention to the comments made by the soldiers. She felt like she was being dragged down to the ground by the monotony of the tales. The Officer's Club allowed Jacob Levy to take a leave of absence for a set period, after which he could return whenever it suited him. A waitress named Kathe attended to Jacob in the Cafe Restaurant de la l'Etoile.

Whenever she tried to speak, she only managed to stutter nonsense.

In the end, it makes no difference what other people think. Jacob and Kathe kissed and hugged passionately in Kathe's bedroom. It took only a moment of silence and reassurance to know that everything would be okay. To fool her into thinking he was Jewish, Jacob pretended to be a different person when he met her: his name was John. None of the story's protagonists will be able to use time travel. Following the war, things will be different for them. Some of the victims may be hurt, while others will die from their wounds. The family of John would much value receiving letters from friends and admirers.

Many soldiers, despite their good names, engage in abnormal behaviour like the wilful destruction of property or the murder of unarmed civilians. The film *Point of No Return* captures the mental anguish of Europeans during the latter stages of World War II. After being out of print for some years, an imprint has reissued Gellhorn's important work.

Throughout her career, Gellhorn's writing demonstrated her vulnerability to her conscience as well as her ability to empathise with people of varying political beliefs. To prevent herself from losing track of the specific sights, sounds and words of her current environment, she frantically jotted down anything that came to mind. No matter where she moved, she never lost her resilience and determination. New York Times critics have called *The Face of War*, a collection of Gellhorn's best reporting on international wars, a superb anti-war book, and now it features an introduction by Lauren Elkin.

From the Spanish Civil War to the present day, Gellhorn covers events in Central America. Her determination to discover the truth shines through her photography whether she is documenting the smell of June grass on the Normandy beaches or the life of a disappeared Salvadoran mother. *The Face of War* is a collection of magazine articles by Martha Gellhorn which is her most famous work. She reported on numerous historical moments, including World War II, the Nuremberg trials, the Paris Peace Conference of 1946, the

Indonesian Revolution, the Six-Day War the Third Arab-Israeli War and the Vietnam War. Gellhorn spent 60 years of her working life as a journalist.

A new edition of the book, *Point of No Return* has been published, even though the original came out in 1959. The audiobook under evaluation includes both the original 1959 and the revised 1986 prologues. A lot of violence occurs throughout the narrative. It adds humanity to what could otherwise be an inhumane circumstance. It strives to put the spotlight on people who put their lives on the line daily rather than military leaders or those who plan wars to fulfil political goals. Dachau, a Nazi concentration camp freed in 1945, is visible to us.

When the camp was finally freed, we witnessed the same things that she had. We ride along with Gellhorn as he pilots a P61 Black Widow bomber at night over Europe and the Middle East. The plot of *Point of No Return* progresses inexorably. There wasn't just one war that happened; there were several. Few people can really appreciate the ugliness of war until they have experienced it themselves. To him, it is crucial to recognise war for what it is and stand united against it. When all else failed, Nadezhda Mandelstam advised Gellhorn to scream.

Even though she was married to the more well-known Russian poet Osip Mandelstam, Nadezhda Mandelstam was a major novelist in her own right. In a Vladivostok POW camp in 1938, he met his untimely end. According to Gellhorn, we all have responsibilities that must be met. Our chosen government must address all types of human wrongdoing. She needs us to make our voices heard for her.

Gellhorn is a hard worker who hopes to spark our interest with her writing. She hopes that her writing will motivate readers to take action. She uses sarcasm, irony, and sarcasm even when discussing tense situations in her work. In 1989, *The View from the Ground* was published, a collection of peacetime journalism. According to Martha Gellhorn, this collection comprises peace-time reporting spanning the past six decades. At the time this was written, the countries portrayed were peaceful, but obviously, the world was not at peace. Martha Gellhorn's over 60-year literary career is a testament to her elegance, fervour, and unyielding belief in right. They include her protests outside the White House, her narrative of home life in Africa, and her story of returning to Cuba after 41 years. Both books namely, *The View from the Ground* and *The Face of War* draw inspiration from fascism in Spain and Germany, as well as the courage of Central Americans who confront bullies from within and without the government.

The View from the Ground was first published in 1959 and is a compendium of Gellhorn's opinions on a wide range of political, social and civil matters after more than six decades of inquiry and writing. Gellhorn's writings will be around for a lot longer with this than in any other medium. The pieces in this collection, which spans sixty years, focus primarily on peacetime reporting. Her pieces about peaceful countries included paragraphs about places and times when things were anything but calm. She documented her observations of the horrific torture she witnessed daily in El Salvador, as well as the plight of orphans who had to start over in Rome. Those with a higher tolerance for such things should refrain from using torture and lynching.

Writings by journalist and author Gellhorn cover 60 years of our modern era.

Gellhorn had little more than a suitcase and $75

when she moved to Paris in 1930 to start her career as an international journalist. She lived through the lynching of African Americans in Mississippi, the fall of Czechoslovakia, the struggles of Italian war orphans in the 1940s, Israeli expansion and the Palestinian issue in the 1950s, and post-Franco Spain, to name a few.

The Great Depression serves as a unifying theme for the short stories in *The Trouble I've Seen* (1936). Through these interconnected tales, she relates her own experiences throughout the Great Depression. For those who refuse to believe that things in the United States can't get any worse, here is a superb depiction of that slide.

Greenham and Gellhorn chronicled the nuclear demonstrations by women in El Salvador and the abuse of El Salvadoran detainees during the McCarthy hearings and the Eichmann trial. Author and human rights activist James Mercer sees his work as recompense for the privilege of observation and comprehension. *The Trouble I Have Seen*, along with Gellhorn's companion piece, *The Face of War*, honours those who, like Gellhorn, have stood up for justice in the face of our century's unsavoury, polarising politics.

Only sixteen reporters, including Martha, were ever allowed to hear Roosevelt's unfiltered thoughts and feelings. Men's minds have been sucked in by this group and they no longer believe in man or God, let alone private industry. When Martha Gellhorn was hired in 1934, she had recently returned from a three-year sojourn in Paris, during which she had become deeply involved in an affair with the city's bohemian community.

Gellhorn, just 25 years old, was one of 16 journalists sent to report on the Great Depression.

While conducting her research on nameless dread, Gellhorn was stationed in the Carolina mill towns, where she witnessed the deterioration of hope and dignity as well as the moral decay. *The Trouble I've Seen*, was written during her tenure as First Lady. Male and female characters express sadness over their inability to find work and their weariness over the few sources of relief available to them. Here a young guy decided to turn to crime so that he and his future wife might get one final, spectacular glimpse of how their lives might have evolved had they not been destined to a life of crime. Despite their economic hardship, these people have managed to maintain their humanity. According to Gellhorn, she described the situation as a bird's eye view: a quick and frenetic flight of a bird.

With the same meticulous documentary precision, Gellhorn's work on this job occasionally reaches a level of imaginative understanding that goes beyond what she already knows and has observed. Martha Gellhorn's *The Heart of Another* is based on her personal experiences during World War II in Europe. These include time spent in Spain and France during the Civil War, the Mannerheim Line (air base), Corsica, and the Tyrol. These works are more attuned to the agonising emotions that this conflict tends to evoke. Two films that explore this theme are *Luigi's House*, which is about a vineyard hand in Corsica and *Portrait of a Lady* which depicts a woman reporter who exploits her sexuality to get her story.

During the early decades of the twentieth century, the number of female war correspondents in the English-speaking world was surprisingly low. Female journalists and editors were marginalised by English-speaking Allies throughout World War II. This is why academics have largely ignored women's reporting throughout the conflict. Women's and minorities' lives in the 21st century have been the subject of extensive research, but most of it has been done in the United States.

This book uses English-speaking Allied nation war correspondent Martha Gellhorn to argue that women journalists' coverage of World War II is vital to our understanding of the conflict. There are two main kinds of sources: primary and secondary. National biographies can also be found. We gain insight into the restrictions imposed on women by governments and military authorities throughout WWII, the media's treatment of female writers, and the challenges faced by women trying to gain access to combat zones and military institutions through her works. As a result, the contributions of women war correspondents were discounted, and they were denied equal access to the front lines as their male counterparts. Instead of focusing on the views of individual women, we will look at the experiences of women as a whole.

Martha Gellhorn was always up to date on the newest war developments because of her vivid, in-depth writing. Instead of only focusing on the specifics of military strategy and outcomes, she was able to convey the feelings of war in her writing. She paved the way for women in the field of war reporting far before anyone else. When her plane crashes, the main character in Gellhorn's *The Heart of Another* hands her a parachute and some basic instructions on how to deploy it. The troops led her out of the cockpit after dragging her there. She was exempt from serving in the military since she was a journalist.

The radar helped the night fighter pilots find their targets, but they wouldn't fire until they got a good look at them. The story of the pilots' selfless professionalism in Gellhorn's account will stay with me forever. War correspondents, to show the strength of the human spirit, would often recount heroic acts whenever possible. To get their jobs done, men frequently use tanks and jump out of planes.

Infantry could be mobilised whenever they are needed. There are both good and bad job opportunities out there. They care more about what else they can accomplish with their time than about the activity at hand. Gellhorn witnessed some of the fighting along the boots of Italy, where German forces were defending the Gothic Line, from Sicily.

Rather than being drawn to the Eighth Army because of its wartime significance, writer Martha Gellhorn was drawn to it because of the vast web of humanity that exists among its big tangle of races and civilizations.

The Germans used barbed wire, explosives, pillboxes, and slowing mechanisms on their tank turrets to protect their territory. The Canadian brigade leader described the conflict as spectacular to the *New York Times*. Her description of the dispute as small and crystal clear, splayed out in front of us, was completely unbelievable. No matter how many bombs and shells were fired, the men who drove the tanks and hid among the trees would always be able to survive. She, along with the other survivors, explored the battlefields once the fighting had ceased. An Italian teenager gave a hilarious account of the horrors she witnessed from the porch of her bombed-out home. The turret of a Sherman tank was covered with blood. The author keeps the reader engaged even though much of the story focuses on combat.

Despite their limited access, female reporters provided a wealth of knowledge. Women's stories must be included if journalists are to paint an accurate picture of life during WWII. The cultural status of female reporters in the United States remains high despite the many changes that have occurred in the area of journalism. Broadcasting has seen a rise in the number of female war reporters because of the industry's persistent need to spice up the drama of battle reporting in a market-driven profession. Despite the negative reviews, the story's portrayal of a woman in peril has nonetheless managed to captivate audiences.

Real-life female writers have left an everlasting mark on journalism and military letters, notwithstanding the pervasive promotion of stereotyped female reporters. Today's readers are more interested in first-person accounts from Bly and Gellhorn than in objective reporting from men. This is also true of stories about refugees and wounded soldiers.

There is a growing consensus of female reporters who play an important role in today's American literature and society. A lot of people have drawn parallels between Martha Ellis Gellhorn's writing and the journals kept by troops during the First and Second World Wars, the Spanish Civil War, and the Vietnam War.

Martha Gellhorn, a trailblazing combat correspondent, broke ground in a field dominated by males. Martha has been a journalist for nearly 60 years, during which she has reported on nearly every major conflict in the world.

The modernist ideal of an impartial and objective journalist is held back from the front lines by the romanticised and sentimentalised image of the woman reporter. Via story, passion, and a focus on the concrete repercussions of war on civilians—including the reporter herself—the young journalist demonstrates her dedication to social justice in this attempt rather than through physical conflict. One could say it's a win for modernity.

While female reporters covering conflicts may be normal today, it wasn't the case eight decades ago. During World War II, around one hundred women served as war correspondents. Very few people, like Martha Gellhorn, have achieved such widespread fame. She spent 50 years as a correspondent, witnessing and reporting on many crucial events throughout World War II and subsequent conflicts, and is best known as the third wife of journalist and literary genius Ernest Hemingway.

On November 8, 1908, Martha Gellhorn was born to George and Edna Gellhorn in St. Louis, Missouri. Edna was an outspoken advocate of women's suffrage and equality, and she carried her small daughter Martha to The Golden Lane rally at the Democratic Party's national convention in 1916. Martha first enrolled in Bryn-Mawr University, but she left after her freshman year to pursue a career in journalism, specifically as a foreign correspondent. It was during World War I, in Paris, with the United Press, that she first entered the workforce. She reported sexual harassment at United Press and was promptly fired then wrote for various European publications and covered fashion for *Vogue* while she travelled the continent.

Soon after her return to the United States in the early 1930s, Martha became close friends with First Lady Eleanor Roosevelt. She lived with the Roosevelts in the White House for two months, assisting Eleanor Roosevelt with night-time duties like mail sorting and contributing to Woman's Home Companion. Martha was hired by the Federal Emergency Relief Administration as a field investigator thanks to her connections inside the agency. Later, she worked alongside Dorothea Lange to record the Great Depression's effects on America's homeless and hungry. Martha was given an opportunity that very few women in the 1930s were granted, and she used it to her advantage by learning about taboo issues before landing a coveted foreign correspondent job.

When Martha met Ernest Hemingway in Key West while on vacation with her family in 1936, she had her second bit of good fortune. *Colliers's* called her shortly after that meeting to have her cover the Spanish Civil War for the publication. Since Hemingway had promised to meet her in Spain, she packed her last fifty bucks and a few canned supplies and bought a ticket. Everything that happened in the war was documented, from bombs to wounded soldiers to life in the trenches. In the 1930s, as the Nazi invasions of Czechoslovakia and Finland were becoming more imminent, Martha was dispatched to Europe to report on the situation. In her memoir, *A Stricken Field*, she detailed her experiences evading the Gestapo in Prague and the difficulties she faced. Martha's connections led to her getting a job as a federal field investigator with the Federal Emergency Relief Administration. Soon after, she teamed up with Dorothea Lange to document the plight of the homeless and hungry in America during the Great Depression. This was a rare possibility for women in the 1930s, and it gave Martha the ability to learn about controversial subjects before she landed a desired position as a foreign correspondent. The next stroke of luck in Martha's life came in 1936 when she met Ernest Hemingway on vacation in Key West. It wasn't long after that introduction until *Collier's* contacted her about covering the Spanish Civil War. Hemingway had told her that they would meet in Spain, so she took her last fifty dollars and some canned goods and boarded a plane. The Nazi conquests of Czechoslovakia and Finland in the late 1930s constituted a growing threat to European security and Martha was tasked with reporting on them. In 1968, she published *A Stricken Field*, a memoir about her time spent covering the atrocities of the Gestapo in Prague. It was in Wyoming in 1940 that Hemingway wed his third wife, Martha. *Collier's* hired her after the wedding to cover the fast-developing situation in China. She convinced her unwilling friend, as she called him in her book *Travels with Myself* and Another, to come along for the journey.

Although Hemingway disliked visiting China, the US government needed to do so to learn more about the connection between Communist and Nationalist troops during the Sino-Japanese War. The report from March 1941 stating that the Chinese would take calmly whatever might happen: hunger, exhaustion, cold, thirst, or danger caught Martha off guard. Although she likely expected muddy roads and unclean living conditions in war-torn countries, she was surprised by the reality.

Martha contracted China rot, a severe form of athlete's foot, from going barefoot for so long. She visited Madame Chiang Kai-shek after Stalin concluded a non-aggression deal with Japan on April 14. While Hemingway and Martha were in China, the United States imposed a trade embargo on Japan. While on vacation with her family in Key West in 1936, Martha was fortunate enough to meet Ernest Hemingway. It wasn't long after that introduction until *Collier's* contacted her about covering the Spanish Civil War. To spend her last $50 and get some food cans, she travelled to Spain, where Hemingway had agreed to meet her. In her role as a war correspondent, she covered stories as varied as the bombing of Barcelona and the care given to injured service members in military hospitals.

Since Hemingway now wrote for the *Collier's*, Martha had to struggle to get to the front lines on June 6, 1944, to cover the beginning of the Allied invasion of France. She hastened to the southern British coast in search of a hospital ship, which she eventually located. She deceived the military police into letting her on board by saying she had been invited to interview the ship's nurses. Once on board, she hid in a lavatory for the duration of the crossing of the English Channel. While the ship was docked near Omaha Beach, Martha made her way onto a landing craft that was being used as an emergency medical transport. As a result, on June 6, 1944, she was one of the few females and journalists to set foot on the ground. She waded into the water and helped the medics bring the injured soldiers back to the ship. After returning to the hospital ship, she recorded the conversations of the wounded soldiers as they waited to be evacuated from the shore on D-Day, once again showcasing the resilience of the human spirit in the face of adversity.

After the D-Day landings, British military police arrested Martha and took away her rank and credentials. This setback did not deter her, though. It took some time, but she was able to secure clearance from the military to report on the battle.

Amid World War II, *TIME* hailed Martha as one of *Collier's* top correspondents. Because of her perseverance and commitment to reporting on the experiences of ordinary people during the conflict, she gained widespread acclaim. She was quite resilient and determined. She used her writing skills to show how war affects everyday life.

Following WWII, Martha became a war correspondent, writing on conflicts such as the Arab-Israeli War, the Vietnam War, and the invasion of Panama. She wrote, "There has to be a better way of administering the world and we need to make sure we get it" just a few years before she passed away (Gellhorn, *Collier's*). We have here five of the most influential female war correspondents in history. There are certain similarities among the women who put their lives on the line to explain to the public how the United States military and government function during war and conflict, even if not every detail is included here. The first order of business was to demonstrate her competence to a male superior, be it a military officer or one of her editors.

Many people, including editors, commanders and soldiers, worry that female war correspondents won't be effective or safe in their roles. Margaret Bourke-White was permitted to photograph at the firm by Benjamin Moskowitz, an architect there. As she took photographs of steel mills, she was panned by many. Concerned for Dickey Chapelle's well-being, her husband and fellow service members took on extra duties during missions. Virginia Irwin, even though women were not allowed to serve as war journalists during WWII, did so nonetheless. She joined the American Red Cross so she could travel to London, and soon she was filing front-page stories for her paper.

As a bonus, Leslie Cockburn joined NBC's London bureau as the lone female correspondent. As her career progressed, she had to deal with the consequences. These women needed to carve out a path for themselves and demonstrate to the males that it could be done. There were no ominous threats, tense exchanges, or raucous displays of anger. Every day, they quietly went about their business, pushing the boundaries and succeeding when it counted most on the field.

There was no uniform system of education for all service members to follow to learn the ropes. Lisa Logan needed to question the military guys she saw on her mission as to why firearms were used in some areas but not others. The time Lisa Logan spent in Egypt is a perfect example of how important this is in the modern world. In today's dangerous and unpredictable environment, it is crucial to be self-aware and know how to protect oneself. NBC News is providing its journalists with training in self-defence techniques for use in conflict zones. The perils of conflict and how to handle dangerous situations are something that journalists should have more instruction on. Third, each of these women had to forego some aspect of her private life to pursue a career in this arena.

It seems like these women have an innate need to prove to the world that they are capable of anything. It's possible to be a mother and a war correspondent at the same time. Both Cockburn and Amanpour expressed regret for their absences, but they also seemed unable to detach themselves emotionally from their work. Cockburn went back to work just three weeks after giving birth to her first child. Amanpour takes only a short break from her career to care for her newborn. They both did a lot of travelling back in their day when they were famous war reporters. All these women faced perilous circumstances while working in war zones. Despite this, no one changed their ways (Staff, "Amanpour: A woman reporter with passion").

They found that it occasionally inspired acts of bravery and daring. Cockburn decided to wait out the onslaught on Tel Aviv from Iraqi Scud missiles on the hotel's rooftop, rather than in a bunker with the rest of the population. Chapelle ascended to the ship's upper deck while her medical ship was under attack from a Japanese bomber so that she could take pictures. Irwin travelled straight into Nazi-occupied Berlin after WWII ended to report the news. Every one of these ladies was in it for the long haul, and they would do everything to get their hands on the scoop. If breaking the rules was the only way to gain the best info or spot, they were willing to ask for forgiveness later. Their versatility and ability to spin a captivating tale out of any circumstance were remarkable.

After much deliberation, the military instituted its own censorship, applying it to all the ladies. There has been tension between the military and the media for decades if not centuries. Amid conflict, representatives from different institutions are certain to clash. Both the military and the media are motivated by a desire to end the conflict with minimal casualties. There is a struggle for control between the armed forces and the media. There is no way to rectify those fundamental inequalities. Amanpour saw first-hand the extreme level of military censorship during Desert Storm. Cockburn's 60 Minutes reporting on the Nicaragua Contra conflict led to her being criticised and maybe banned.

For weeks, SHAEF kept Irwin's incredible account of the city's deliverance from the Nazis under wraps because military leaders were so enraged by how she gained entry to Berlin.

It appears that censorship is more typically utilised as a mechanism of punishment than as a tool for managing content. Because of her position, Amanpour had to make concessions to gain access to some branches of the military.

The military may issue orders about what must be done or how a tale must be recorded at this time. During World War II, Chapelle ran into the same problem as Bourke-White experienced after gaining access in Vietnam. Journalists need to weigh how much access they need to the military for their stories against the risks involved in gaining that access. As soon as mainstream media outlets decide that embedded reporters are too obtrusive, they will stop employing them. This is called a unilateral action. Those who aren't scared to take chances can make it through a war zone. In 2003, during the Iraq War, Amanpour served as both an embedded journalist and an independent freelancer. Her personal experience was different from what she had read about which made for a fascinating comparison. The reporting practises of pools are governed and supervised by authorities. The term mass is used to indicate an extremely huge group of individuals. However, the constraints placed on their actions remain the same. Many news organisations have said that their interviews with the alleged victims were candid and in-depth, and I tend to believe them. However, they were given just a partial picture of the situation. No one can always see all that's happening. The question is, what did we see and learn? Though the coverage was riveting, little was reported from the other side. Unilateralism has the problem of being exceedingly hazardous, especially in high-tech, fast-paced wars like this one. Covering a crisis in a country where the United States military isn't involved requires specialised training for journalists. These journalists must get to where the action is without getting hurt. Censorship practises have adapted to the technological realities of the modern day. For processing, the film was typically transported to New York's Bourke-office White's or an impartial facility.

The Post-Dispatch received Irwin's reports via military channels.

In most cases, delays may be attributed to censors and technological progress. To put it simply, this was before the time when today's technology was widely available.

Reporters can submit their articles to any publication using only their mobile devices as computers, and the editor can then distribute the articles in whatever way they see fit.

People are also documenting the event with their own small phones, video cameras and laptops for use by journalists. The armed forces simply cannot avoid this situation. Many military secrets will inevitably be leaked due to the widespread dissemination of information made possible by social media platforms which allow users to communicate beyond national boundaries.

The military will need to rethink its approach to censorship in light of this change.

Since Bourke-White and Irwin shattered the glass ceiling and became television news' highest-paid foreign correspondents, much has changed. Therefore, this does not justify female indifference to global progress. There will always be battles to be fought in journalism, the military pools, and the media. Despite sexism, there are still plenty of strong, independent women who want to convey the truth as they see it. These women will face the same disadvantages as the aforementioned five women, including fewer chances for advancement, guilt at having to forsake loved ones, and lower wages throughout their lifetimes.

The book *Women Don't Ask* claims that since moms are afraid to rock the boat, there will be a $300,000 wage disparity between men and women throughout their lifetimes. 241 Women war correspondents of the future will find it just as challenging to break down barriers as their predecessors did. However, it's something they've always had. Female war reporters are driven by a deep conviction and an unwavering commitment to their craft, neither of which they will abandon until they have shown the world wrong.

Due to Russell's reporting on the state of the war and the conditions of the troops and artillery, the administration demanded that the *Times* denounce him. But his editor nonetheless told him to confine all his correspondents totally to the interpretation of past occurrences. This created a discussion between the administration and the media about how much detail about the war effort should be released to the public. They have been at odds with each other for generations, and it all started with the *Times* incident. In actuality, the army realised towards the conclusion of the war that it had made a mistake by allowing Russell to join them in the conflicts.

Russell's colleague Edwin Lawrence Godkind claimed that the presence of the special correspondent in Crimea led to a true awakening of the official attitude after the conflict ended. It was recently made clear to the War Office that wars do not simply fall under the purview of sovereigns and politicians. The field of war journalism was given a boost by technological developments during the Crimean War. After the telegraph was invented in the 1830s, Russell had a much easier time getting his writings to London.

However, with the advent of new media, came the beginning of a change in the way war correspondents gathered and submitted their reports to editors. The fact that the public was able to witness the combat for the first time thanks to photography which also lent a new reality to the event. Finally, technological developments permitted Russell and a small group of others to become the first war reporters.

Less than five years later, when the American Civil War broke out, approximately 500 war correspondents were covering just the Union side. Although the first war correspondents were primarily men, women soon began covering the war effort and reporting on what they had seen. Russell's early papers on wartime medical care led to the hiring of female nurses like Florence Nightingale. Some women war correspondents did exist in historical parallels, but they were often side-lined by their male counterparts.

In his writings, Coleman focused primarily on the human impact of the war's conclusion. Despite being barred from covering the news from the front lines, her articles were extensively read. As of the year 2000, Barbara M. Freeman's biography of Catherine Ferguson, titled *Kit Coleman* can be found in the online version of the Dictionary of Canadian Biography. She got a perfect score of 10 when it came to reporting on victims of violence. The treatment she received from the United States military was even more amazing. They thought Coleman was playing a joke on them and did everything they could to prevent her from entering Cuba.

When it comes to covering wars, women journalists sometimes find themselves walking creative tightropes between what was regarded respectable behaviour for a woman journalist and what was judged too daring, as Coleman puts it (qtd. in Ness "Women War Correspondents and the Battles They Overcame to Succeed"). Especially at the outset of a war's coverage, it's tough to measure the contributions of male and female reporters on an equal footing. While male reporters were free to cover battles and discuss military strategy with high-ranking officials, female reporters were encouraged to write more human articles about the people, culture, and changes. Coleman wanted to get paid the same as men did for the same work, and she wanted to fight like them. As late as the 1970s, discrimination against women in the workplace was still commonplace due to the lack of equality for women in pre-suffragist workplaces. Women had traditionally been expected to stay at home and care for their families rather than go internationally to observe how governments dealt with problems in other countries. Men couldn't see things from the same angle that they could. Their motivation was to learn something new and share an untold story.

After the women's suffrage movement, there was a surge of female reporters covering conflicts. When Martha Gellman wrote about Kathleen Blake Coleman for the 19 March 2008 and 18 April 2012 issues of Library and Archives Canada, The United States Army enlisted Kathleen Blake Coleman to serve during the Spanish Civil War (1936– 1939). Male co-workers praised her efforts to help civilian victims and those attempting to live during wartime. Nonetheless, Gellman herself wrote about her discontent with the gender gap in business and life. She felt like she was sinking into a pit of despair. She believed that is unfair to terrify people about life just because they are women, she stated in 1931, referring to the emotional makeup that women and men share. Nonetheless, she kept looking for the story (Ness, "Women War Correspondents and the Battles They Overcame to Succeed").

After the French government denied her entry documents, she went to the Spanish border and crossed on her own. Because of her and Coleman's work, women like Margaret Burke-White, Virginia Irwin, and Dickey Chapelle were able to break into the male-dominated field of war reporting in the early 20th century. This was the case despite the wishes of some government officials and the prevailing gender norms of the time.

In the early days of modern war reporting, when women journalists were still in the minority, they were assigned the less difficult stories. However, journalists have long risked their lives covering wars. It has been reported that an enemy of the state is terrorising locals. Since they usually have expensive equipment and cash on them, journalists are prime targets for thieves. On the other hand, women may be disproportionately affected by violent crime due to gender stereotypes.

Assaults, rapes, and killings are recorded at varying rates by male and female reporters. In 2011, the Committee to Protect Journalists (CPJ) questioned reporters who had experienced sexual assault while reporting from other countries. More than fifty reporters were interviewed for the study, the purpose of which was to learn how assaults affect journalists and their work. Researchers found that even while many assaults remained unreported, those that were recorded were typically severe and retaliatory such as mob-related sexual violence against journalists covering public events, sexual abuse of journalists in detention or captivity, and targeted sexual violence against specific journalists, generally in reprisal for their job, according to Reporters Without Borders. It is deeply concerning that victims often do not report crimes like this for fear of retaliation from both the host country and the home office. New York-based correspondent Jenny Nordberg was assaulted in Karachi, Pakistan in October 2007 while covering Benazir Bhutto's comeback to politics. It wasn't until the investigation in 2011 that she told anyone about the attack.

Gellhorn kept it a secret because she didn't want to risk losing work and she didn't want to be mislabelled as a girl when vying for parity and superiority with men. So, she says:

I didn't tell the editors because I didn't want to risk losing work. That unquestionably played a role. Additionally, I didn't want to be misgendered as a female when I was competing head-to-head with men for parity and superiority. There will be an atmosphere of intimidation toward the correspondent as a result, which few will dare to dispute (qtd. in Hartley "Martha Gellhorn: Eyewitness to War").

Many women who took part in the study expressed concern that conflict could lead to the rise of mob mentality in large crowds. Lara Logan, the lead foreign correspondent for CBS News, was brutally beaten and raped in February 2011 while covering the Egyptian uprising in Tahrir Square in Cairo. After being separated from her companions, she found herself in a dangerous situation. There have been a small number of high-profile incidents involving foreign war correspondents recently. Logan went on to attribute her achievement to the fact-checking efforts of CBS News. The most important thing a company can do is to stand behind a journalist. In light of this and previous attacks, some media outlets are providing training and instituting new safety procedures for their correspondents working in hostile environments. Despite her efforts and her inspiration, most incidents are not brought to light. When women are intimidated, it doesn't always take the form of physical violence.

Sexual harassment is commonplace, even within a female correspondent's workplace. An Iranian woman journalist claimed that one of the many incidents she reported involved a government official. CBS News' Lisa De Moraes and Paul Farhi reported on 25 March that Lara Logan had been sexually assaulted and beaten by an Egyptian mob in Tahrir Square. The Committee to Protect Journalists (CPJ) presented a global study of attacks on the press in 2011 on April 18th, 2012. Being a journalist in this part of the world is challenging. Your gender provides them an advantage. You're especially vulnerable as a journalist and a woman for the same reason.

American policies have been put in place to make sure that men and women both feel safe and comfortable in the workplace. These regulations cannot be applied to employees of a U.S. firm who are stationed abroad. In some places, especially in areas of upheaval, this risk cannot be avoided or mitigated. Some women just accept it as a fact of life in their profession. Furthermore, since the turn of the twentieth century, the risk of dying has risen. Women make for 6.7% of the 905 journalists slain since 1992, according to the Committee to Protect Journalists (CPJ). These women were doing the same work as males. As Colvin covered the revolt and increasing horrors in Homs for the British newspaper *The London Sunday Times*, she was assassinated in Syria in February 2012. She was a fan of risk-taking, so in *The Guardians*, she writes:

We are here, to tell the truth to those in authority. We provide a first draught of history to our students. We live in an era of constant news updates, blogs, and tweets, and we're always on call. Reporting on war, on the other hand, hasn't changed much through the years—someone still needs to go to the combat zone and document what's going on there. You will need to go to locations where individuals are being shot at and where other people will shoot at you in order to obtain this information (Colvin, "Our mission is to report these horrors of war with accuracy and without prejudice").

After everything was said and done, her lifelong purpose of educating the world about the atrocities of war came to an end with her passing. She had spent her entire life working toward this goal. However, this is not the case for the vast majority of women who are employed in this industry. They want to be the first to communicate these horrible stories, no matter the risks, so that everyone can know what is happening and so that these people are not brushed to the side and forgotten, even though doing so may be harmful to the journalist. Perhaps this is because they are women. When more women enter the job and compete for the same dangerous occupations, the number of fatalities will continue to rise, even though there are currently more men working in the field.

According to recent findings published by the Center for Public Integrity (CPI), technology and reporting are putting journalists in potentially hazardous situations. The body of Mexican journalist Maria Elisabeth Macias Castro was discovered in September 2011, along with her keyboard and a place card bearing the handle she used on various social networking sites. Even though she did much of her reporting via social media, Castro was nonetheless put in danger and was ultimately taken out as a result of the drug lord war that was going on in Mexico. Journalists who have just returned from perilous assignments overseas have a significantly increased risk of developing mental health problems. For instance, those who work in journalism are more likely to suffer from post-traumatic stress disorder (Walt, "Syria: War Reporter Marie Colvin and Photographer Rémi Ochlik Are Killed"). This is according to the Neiman Report. Vivienne Walt was responsible for her death, as reported by TIME on 18 April 2012 and 22 February 2012. Swearing authors Anthony Feinstein and Mark Sinyor discuss the topic of women war correspondents in their article titled Women War Correspondents: They Are Different in So Many Ways. According to Nieman Reports, Winter 2009, 18 April 2012 15, data collected from 218 frontline journalists who spent an average of 15 years reporting from war zones found a rate of post-traumatic stress disorder (PTSD) five times higher than the average rate in the general population.

As a direct consequence of this, returning foreign correspondents are now confronted with a completely different set of issues. Memories are never lost, regardless of how many times the narrative is revised. Kim Barker in the article observed that the women who choose to work in international journalism are aggressive; forceful; and strong; with a constant need to prove themselves ("Female Foreign Correspondents Code of Silence Finally Broken"). These women don't appear to be held back by anything. To put it another way, they are searching for stories that no one else can or will investigate further. In the memoir, Margaret states, "Nothing attracts me like a closed door. I cannot let my camera rest until I have pried it open, and I wanted to be first" (Bourke-White *Portrait of Myself* 302). The Neiman Report looked through its database of female journalists who have covered wars over the past half-century or thereabouts and found that many of them shared similar experiences and perspectives.

To begin, there was a significantly higher percentage of unmarried women. This may be because they keep switching from one story to the next throughout the show. Being in a situation where one's own life is constantly in jeopardy might make it difficult to think about the well-being of others, especially youngsters. Second, there are significantly more female journalists working now than there are male journalists.

It's possible to have the preconceived notion that a woman needs extra education before embarking on a professional career, regardless of how true or false this assumption actually is. Again, there was no correlation between the genders about the prevalence of post-traumatic stress disorder (PTSD). This puts an end to the debate of whether or not women can withstand the stresses and risks of war. The notion that women are more likely to suffer from issues related to their mental health in the aftermath of a war is no longer relevant.

Gellhorn woke up on D-Day feeling nauseous and hung over, but she was determined to make it to the Normandy beaches in time to witness the incredible spectacle. The sky was a frenzied mirror as airborne divisions dropped thousands of bombs simultaneously while the fleet consisted of thousands of destroyers, battleships, attack vessels, and transport ships.

Gellhorn realised in the middle of this unearthly disorder that her hands, or any hands, were needed regardless of the consequences to herself or her career. She had lucked out when the medical aid ship she had stowed away on was the first to arrive at the battleground. After the landing craft had arrived, she fetched food, water, and medical supplies like bandages and rations, and did what little interpreting she could. At night, she joined a small team of medics and surgeons on Omaha Beach, not as a reporter but as a stretcher bearer, diving into the icy sea full of bodies and following closely behind the minesweepers to pull out the injured.

Her mind and heart were wounded by the sight of pain and death, and her hands were blistered from working all night. The hundreds of credentialed journalists who were waiting in the Channel behind her with binoculars included her husband, as she would learn later. A short time later, Hemingway's story appeared in *Collier's* alongside hers, albeit with more prominence and glitz, but the truth had already been set in stone. Out of an estimated 160 men, there was only one woman on the beach. Gellhorn.

In 1946, Gellhorn was newly single after her divorce from Ernest Hemingway.

Sometimes, when she considers leaving the town, she pictures her doing the same. It's easy for her to picture her squinting against the sun as she ascended the hill, taking in the crepe myrtle and bougainvillaea in the air, and trying to read the future from there. Due to its long period of abandonment, the house's plaster was peeling, the pool was partially buried, and the surrounding jungle had grown over it. But there was a gigantic ceiba tree planted right next to the front steps, its twisted, hide-like trunk covered in orchids. She would later write about how this voice seemed to represent the farm's soul, and how it promised her safety, love, and a place in the community if only she would have the guts to ask for it (Mclain, "The

Extraordinary Life of Martha Gellhorn, the Woman Ernest Hemingway Tried to Erase").

Gellhorn's specific brand of nerve was as rare as radium in her 60-year journalism career. In fact, it appeared that her worries helped to galvanise rather than paralyse her, and to implant in her a sense of fearlessness rather than helplessness in the face of persecution. Her anger honed her voice, which she then used to aid others and ultimately turned into a weapon. She still can't say for sure if anything else comes close to it. It would be very useful if a large number of people made their voices heard.

Gellhorn covered practically every major combat of the 20th century, beginning at the age of 28 with her first war and ending in her early 80s with the U.S. invasion of Panama. As a war correspondent, she wrote about the Japanese invasion of China, the Czech Crisis, the Winter War between the Soviet Union and Finland, and every other major theatre of World War II after the Spanish Civil War including the liberation of Dachau.

From the beginning, Martha's work was imbued with humanism and activism. One of her early novels was titled *What Mad Pursuit* and it scared her parents and accomplished nothing. But in 1931, she met social worker Harry Hopkins at a party in Washington DC, and soon after, she began working as a writer for him and his small team of reporters at the Federal Emergency Relief Administration. It was Hopkins' job to relay a narrative portrait of what Americans were enduring during the Great Depression to President Roosevelt, and his group's mission was to visit hard-hit areas of the country and report back. This depiction wouldn't be based on numbers but on people's experiences and observations.

Her stories are vivid and moving because they show people on the brink of despair, teetering without hope of a better future, and yet too proud to ask for help. While her own body shook with rage, she was inspired by their resolve. Hopkins's letters to FDR and Eleanor Roosevelt, sent in secret and against Gellhorn's wishes, provide all of this information. She was invited to dinner at the White House so that she could share her story with the president. The two struck into a conversation when Eleanor encouraged Franklin to talk to the girl, and Franklin accepted Eleanor's open offer to drop by whenever he wanted to fill them in. Gellhorn was fired after nearly a year on the job for inciting unemployed people in rural Idaho to riot, and Eleanor wrote to invite her to remain at the White House until she could get back on her feet. Over two months, Gellhorn helped Eleanor respond to thousands of letters from people in need while living in what became known as the Lincoln Bedroom.

During Gellhorn's stay at the White House, she was inspired by Eleanor and grew to see her as a personal hero. Because of this, she decided to use her celebrity to draw attention to the plight of those less fortunate. She often based her fictitious stories on genuine events. *The Trouble I've Seen*, a collection of four novellas, was the result of a hectic few months of writing and has gained significant recognition. For this book, which looked to be woven not out of words but out of the tissues of actual individuals, Gellhorn was praised as the literary find of 1936 by *The Saturday Review of Literature*.

Only by coincidence did she and Hemingway both write books that year. She was on vacation with her mother and brother in Florida when they nearly collided with the author as he checked his mail at a tavern in Key West. After the publication of *The Sun Also Rises* in 1926 which served as both a bible and a lifestyle manual for an entire generation and *A Farewell to Arms* in 1929, he was arguably the most famous writer in the world, while she was only 28 which further raised the standard for American literature.

Gellhorn urged her readers to keep in mind that love fades. It's still just you and your job.

Hemingway's life was likewise fairly vibrant and prominent. He can't image her saying no to going with him to Madrid to cover the Spanish Civil War for the North American Newspaper Alliance. Without a question, her life path would have been substantially different if she had chosen that option. Despite Hemingway's best efforts to wreck her, his fostering of her as a correspondent is what is most often remembered.

The summer of 1944 marked the tipping point. Hemingway offered his by-line to *Collier's* after he became infuriated with Gellhorn for selecting her work once again. Hemingway was chosen by *Collier's* because each publication could only send one correspondent to the front. Neither Gellhorn's credentials nor her marriage status were relevant anymore. Hatred had replaced love. The atmosphere of paradise was heavy and oppressive.

It was on a munitions barge carrying amphibious transport craft and dynamite bound for England that Gellhorn finally made it back to Europe. She was meant to watch from the shore while Hemingway rode in on an attack transport, the Dorothea L. Dix, for the D-Day invasion. Instead, she shivered and improvised as she slunk along a dock in the rain. Operation Neptune had officially begun. In the greatest amphibious assault ever attempted, the Allies were preparing to cross the Channel and invade Normandy with over 160,000 troops aboard nearly 5,000 warships. She showed an expired press badge to the military personnel, pointed to the largest object in the area (a massive white hospital barge with a red cross on its side), and claimed she was there to interview nurses, even though she had no such intention. Unexpectedly, she was allowed to pass.

She boarded the plane trembling, certain that she would be promptly detained if anyone spotted her. She sat down on the floor of a restroom with a locked door, drew some strength from the flask in her bag, and said thanks. After midnight, when the barge finally started to move, she drank more quickly as she considered the many horrible possibilities that lay ahead of her capture and expulsion, the barge being blown up, or finally reaching her goal.

She awoke on D-Day, inebriated and seasick, but determined to watch the incredible spectacle unfolding on the Normandy cliffs. The fleet consisted of thousands of destroyers, battleships, attack vessels, and transport ships; the sky was a furious mirror as airborne divisions dropped thousands of bombs at once (McClain, "The Extraordinary Life of Martha Gellhorn, the Woman Ernest Hemingway Tried to Erase").

Leaving Hemingway and the Finca behind, Gellhorn may have effectively erased all trace of herself the only one of his four wives to do so. She remained in Europe after D-Day and was among the first reporters there in April 1945, when the Dachau concentration camp was freed. Mary Welsh, an attractive young journalist who had written for Time and the Daily Express, was one of the reasons Hemingway decided to stay. At the end of the war, he secretly brought

Welsh back to Cuba, where he lived with his family. He had the Finca's workers prepare the home by telegraph.

After Welsh had moved in, the house manager, René Villarreal, allegedly discovered some graffiti on the property. The vandalism was allegedly the work of a disgruntled employee or a local. In July of 1960, when Hemingway was expelled from Cuba, Welsh was still there with him. By that time, he was a shattered man who was fighting physical illness, mental illness, drunkenness, and memory loss. He appears to be much older than 60 in the photographs from that time. He planned to end his own life within a year. In 1986, on her way to do real work in Nicaragua, Gellhorn made a rare return to Cuba. On the island, she planned to do some nostalgic things for her before doing the usual vacation things like swimming, tanning, drinking rum and watching suspenseful movies. She drove to the Finca and picked up Gregorio Fuentes, the captain of Hemingway's prized cabin cruiser Pilar. It's unclear why the Ceiba was cut up. Gellhorn wrote in an envelope marked for Fuentes. In response to the roots pushing up the floor of the house, he explained the problem. The museum had to prune it.

Gellhorn committed suicide at the age of 89 on Valentine's Day. Her eyesight had been deteriorating, and she was battling cancers of the liver and ovaries. Glendinning and her husband found Gellhorn in the apartment. A plaque reads, that Martha Gellhorn, war correspondent and author, 1908-1998, called the apartment home. When Simpson pulled a cord on the velvet curtain, the plaque was uncovered, and the young men posed for photos without a hitch.

She toiled until exhaustion set in, fought until her health broke, and wrote until blindness threatened to cut off her creativity. When things became hopeless, she made the same decision Hemingway did and took her own life. The disease had spread throughout her body, and doctors had told her that she had just months to live. Her decision to discontinue swimming and snorkelling was relatively recent. She had been making preparations to visit Egypt to get a better look at the pyramids right up until she passed away.

She desires a life with people that is virtually explosive in its delight; a life that is fierce and rough and laughing and loud and gay as all hell let loose, and she believes she found it. To be an afterthought in someone else's narrative is an affront to her dignity, she had questioned once. It may be our responsibility now to make sure that doesn't happen.

Martha Gellhorn defied the norm. Gellhorn was the only woman to arrive in Normandy on D-Day after stowing away on a hospital ship. She spent the next 60 years covering practically every major conflict of the 20th century. Eleanor Roosevelt provided Gellhorn temporary housing in the White House after she was fired from her government job for inciting a riot in Idaho by aiding a group of employees in rising against a corrupt boss. Gellhorn, a woman of glitz and glamour, had a close relationship with the French novelist Colette and had done film tests for Hollywood. There, she made contact with Winston Churchill. H.G. Wells had feelings for her. In retrospect, it appears that Gellhorn's status as Ernest Hemingway's third wife was the only thing keeping her from becoming a household name.

Author Janet Somerville writes in her new book, Yours, for Probably Always: Martha Gellhorn's Letters of Love & War, 1930-1949, that despite being married to Ernest for five of her 89 years, she stayed in the shadow of his fame and influence. It's not that she didn't write consistently throughout her life or generate remarkable work while doing so. The lack of talent plays no role in this. The fact that she was his wife during a time when women were considered property explains everything, in my opinion. Somerville, a former educator and frequent literary tweeter, writes that she wrote the book to alter the course of Gellhorn's reputation. The thick volume contains letters sent and received by Gellhorn during the war years, with Somerville providing historical context (Doucet, "Yours, for Probably Always: Martha Gellhorn's Letters of Love and War 1930-1949 – Review").

Somerville is so enthralled by Gellhorn that she could talk about her for hours. Somerville enjoys the act of writing letters herself. Somerville made it a New Year's resolution in 2014 to write a handwritten letter every day. She didn't limit herself to writing to friends and family but instead reached out to about seventy people from all over the world who responded to her open Twitter appeal. Somerville was referred to a collection of letters between authors Eudora Welty and William Maxwell in May 2015 during a trip to Faulkner House Books in New Orleans. As a result of Somerville's tweeting her adoration, a Scottish bookseller that Somerville read the collected writings of Martha Gellhorn.

There was no turning back for Somerville. She devoured Caroline Moorehead's *Selected Letters of Martha Gellhorn* (2006) and *Martha Gellhorn: A Life* (2004) to learn as much as she could about Gellhorn. However, after Paula McLain published *Love and Ruin*, a novel about the relationship between Gellhorn and Hemingway, Somerville decided to write the story in a fictional format instead.

Somerville abandoned the plan to write a novel because she didn't want to risk his reputation by going head-to-head with a famous writer.

In addition, Somerville's project didn't seem to be going anywhere because Moorehead appeared to have the non-fiction aspect of Gellhorn's life all tied up. Then, though, a fascinating development occurred. Including the ones in this book, Somerville read previously unpublished works by Gellhorn.

This is how it went down. Somerville found Gellhorn's documents at the Howard Gotlieb Archival Research Centre in Boston after a series of fortunate meetings and emails. Sandy Matthews, Gellhorn's stepson, is in charge of the archive, and Somerville is one of only a select few who have ever been granted access. The fact that Matthews, who is known for fiercely guarding Gellhorn's honour, penned the foreword to *Yours, for Probably Always* is significant.

A lifetime of writings, jottings, clippings, photographs, and audio recordings are all stored in the archive. Letters from and to prominent figures such as Eleanor Roosevelt,

H.G. Wells, Lauren Bacall, Leonard Bernstein, and Jacqueline Kennedy Onassis were the most valuable items. It's as if the reader is seeing into someone's private life with some letters. In others, Gellhorn reveals an activist's compassion for the voiceless she encountered in the course of her reporting. She didn't think anyone but the intended recipients would read these messages.

Somerville assumed falsely that Gellhorn had destroyed all of her letters to and from Hemingway. Numerous letters written by Gellhorn to Hemingway are included in the book, but none of Hemingway's replies. The executors of his estate refused to provide authorization. Somerville does quote briefly from a letter in which Hemingway lauds Gellhorn's prose, stating that one of her short stories is excellent. Somerville was extremely cognizant of the fact that she didn't want Ernest to take over, explaining why she didn't share the full letter.

When she turned 87, Gellhorn retired from journalism. For the last time, she threw on a backpack and headed out to discover the truth about the dead Salvadoran and Brazilian street kids. After reading it over, she decided it was the worst thing she'd ever written, especially considering how difficult it would have been to revise with her declining eyesight. Nonetheless, Gellhorn never stopped penning letters, doing so right up until her untimely passing in 1998. Somerville plans to reveal more in subsequent volumes of *Yours for Probably Always* is well received. Somerville recalls up until the last, she wrote letters full of fury, but there was also love and charity.

She had connections with two presidents, Franklin D. Roosevelt and John F. Kennedy, in addition to her marriage to Ernest Hemingway and relationships with well-known lovers like H. G. Wells. Her battles against oppression and poverty, as well as her wrath at the brutality and corruption of the current governments, are symbolised by these partnerships. Her existence was mostly described over more than 60 years by leaping between trenches, shielding herself from explosions, and recounting sights of starvation and death. Gellhorn resisted the objectivity that her profession expected, driven by her rebelliousness and intellectual firm convictions. Her direct and empathetic memoirs covered dozens of battles in the twentieth century, making them the most important of the time.

Martha Gellhorn strove for creative fulfilment and literary acclaim during her lifetime and is now better renowned for being a trailblazing war correspondent. Gellhorn was born in St. Louis, Missouri, in 1908. She opted to become a journalist after a year of study at Bryn Mawr College in Pennsylvania, and therefore, she never received a diploma. She temporarily worked for the New Republic and the Times Union in New York before departing the country in 1930 on a speculative mission to conduct research in Europe. She paid for her transatlantic journey by penning an article about the service of the shipping line. She worked in Paris for several publications, including *Vogue* and the St. Louis Post-Dispatch, and had a contentious relationship with married novelist and writer Bertrand de Jouvenal. Between 1934 and 1967, she published a total of six novels. In 1937–1938, Gellhorn began her career as a war correspondent by contributing articles from the Spanish Civil War to the American publication *Collier's Weekly*. She collaborated with renowned American author Ernest Hemingway, whom she married on November 21, 1940, while reporting from Madrid. *For Whom the Bell Tolls*, Hemingway's 1940 novel on the Spanish Civil War, is dedicated to Gellhorn; yet, the union would only last for five years.

Thereafter, Gellhorn covered World War II, covering the liberation of the Dachau concentration camp as well as the D-Day landings.

She later reported for the *Guardian* from Vietnam in 1966 and the Arab/Israeli Six-Day War in 1967. Her final war mission, at the age of 81, was the United States invasion of Panama in 1989. *The Face of War* and *The View from the Ground* were collections of Gellhorn's journalism. *Travels*

With Myself and Another, her lone explicitly autobiographical work and the only piece in which she wrote in the first person, includes a description of a trip to China in 1941, with Hemingway referred to throughout as 'UC' – Gellhorn's Unwilling Companion. She died on February 15, 1998, at the age of 89.

WORKS CITED

Primary Sources

- Gellhorn, Martha. *The Face of War: Writings from the Frontline, 1937-1985*. Eland, 2016.
- *A Stricken Field*. The University of Chicago Press, 2011.
- *The Trouble I've Seen*. Eland, 2012.
- *The View from the Ground: Peacetime Dispatches, 1936-87*. Eland, 2016.
- *Travels with Myself and Another*. Eland, 2007.
- *Point of No Return*. University of Nebraska Press, 1995.
- *The Heart of Another*. Home & Van Thal, 1946.
- *The Wine of Astonishment*. Bantam Books, 1949.
- *What Mad Pursuit: A Novel*. Frederick A. Stokes Co., 1934.
- *Vietnam - a New Kind of War*. Manchester Guardian and Evening News., 1966.
- *Weather in Africa*. Eland Publishing Ltd, 2006.
- *The Novellas of Martha Gellhorn*. Picador, 1994.
- *Two by Two*. Simon & Schuster, 1958.
- *The Lowest Trees Have Tops*. Doss, Mead, 1969.

- *The Lowest Trees Have Tops.* Library of Congress, NLS/BPH, 1980.
- *Pretty Tales for Tired People.* 1965
- *The Short Novels of Martha Gellhorn.* Sinclair-Stevenson, 1991.
- *Travels with Myself and Another: A Memoir.* Jeremy P. Tarcher/Putnam, 2001.
- *The Face of War*, Grove Press, New York, 2018.
- "There is a point where you feel so small and helpless in an enormous, insane nightmare of a world that you cease to give a hoot and start laughing." *The Guardian, Collier's,* 28 May. 2004. Web. 10 Jan. 2021.
- https://www.theguardian.com/world/2004/may/28/secondworldwar.features116 >.
- "Reporting America at War: The Reporters." PBS, Web. 7 Aug. 2022.
- https://www.pbs.org/weta/reportingamericaatwar/reporters/gellhorn/ > .
- "MADRID TO MORATA." *The New Yorker*, 16 July. 1937. Web. 30 June. 2021.
- https://www.newyorker.com/magazine/1937/07/24/madrid-to-morata>.
- "Night Life in the Sky." *Collier's Weekly* 17 March.1945: pp. 18-19.
- "Obituary of a Democracy." *Collier's Weekly* 10 Dec.1938: pp. 12-13.
- **Secondary Sources:**
- Aguirre, Mercedes. "The Spanish Civil War in the

Works of Nancy Cunard, Martha Gellhorn, and Sylvia Townsend Warner." UCL (University College London), 28 Mar. 2015.Web. 7 June 2021. < https://discovery.ucl.ac.uk/1463625/>.

- "Martha Gellhorn: The Reporter as a Young Poet." Americas and Oceania Collections Blog, 24 Nov. 2017. Web. 30 Oct. 2020.
- https://blogs.bl.uk/americas/2017/11/martha-gellhorn-the-reporter-as-a-young-poet.html.
- Arons, Rachel. "Chronicling Poverty with Compassion and Rage." *The New Yorker*, 17 Jan. 2013. Web. 29 June. 2021. < https://www.newyorker.com/books/page-
- turner/chronicling-poverty-with-compassion-and-rage >.
- Atlas, Nava. "Martha Gellhorn, War Correspondent, Novelist, & Memoirist." Literary LadiesGuide, 17 Aug. 2022. Web. 13 Feb. 2023.
- https://www.literaryladiesguide.com/author-biography/martha-gellhorn/ >.
- "What Mad Pursuit: Martha Gellhorn's Lost 1934 Novel." Literary Ladies Guide, 18Nov. 2022. Web. 6 Jan. 2023.
- https://www.literaryladiesguide.com/book-reviews/mad-pursuit-martha-gellhorns- lost-1934-novel/ >.
- Aucoin, James L. "The Evolution of American Investigative Journalism." University of Missouri Press, 2005. Web. 21 Jan. 2023.
- https://books.google.co.in/books/about/The_Evolution_of_American_Investigati ve.html/>.

- Bak, Hans. *Uneasy Alliance: Twentieth-Century American Literature, Culture and Biography*. Rodopi, 2004.
- Barker, Kim. "Female Foreign Correspondents' Code of Silence, Finally Broken." Pro Publica, 19 Feb. 2011. Web. 22 Jan. 2021.
- https://www.propublica.org/article/breaking-the-code-of-silence >.
- Baym, Nina. *Woman's Fiction: A Guide to Novels by and about Women in America, 1820- 1870*. University of Illinois Press, 1993.
- Becker, Elizabeth. *You Don't Belong Here: How Three Women Rewrote the Story of War*. Public Affairs, 2022.
- Berlant, Lauren. "The Female Complaint and the Unfinished Business of Sentimentality in American Culture." Duke University Press, 2008. Web. 23 June. 2022.
- https://read.dukeupress.edu/books/book/2120/The-Female-ComplaintThe- Unfinished-Business-of>.
- "The Female Woman: Fanny Fern and the Form of Sentiment." *American Literary History*, 1991. Web. 12 Jan 2021. < https://academic.oup.com/alh/article-abstract/3/3/429/169925>.
- Bourke-White, Margaret. *Portrait of Myself*, Andesite Press, 2017.
- Carolyn Martindale, Edy. "Conditions of Acceptance: The United States Military, the Press, and the Woman War Correspondent, 1846-1945." *Carolina Digital Repository*, 22 March. 2019. Web. 16 Oct. 2020.
- https://cdr.lib.unc.edu/concern/dissertations/5t34sk269

- Chambers, Deborah, Linda Steiner, and Carole Fleming. *Women and Journalism.*
- *London and New York*, Routledge, 2004.
- Child, Lydia Maria. "Woman in the Nineteenth Century." *Norton Critical Edition*, 15, Feb. 1845. Web. 3 Jan. 2020. <
- https://wwnorton.com/books/9780393971576>.
- Clark, Suzanne. *Sentimental Modernism: Women Writers and the Revolution of the Word.* Bloomington: Indiana University Press, 1991.
- Clayton, Meg Waite. *Beautiful Exiles.* Lake Union Publishing, 2018.
- Colvin, Marie. "Courage Knows No Gender." Marie Colvin Memorial Foundation, *The Sunday Times*, 10 Oct. 1999. Web. 20 Nov. 2021. < https://mariecolvin.org/courage-knows-no-gender-marie-colvin >.
- "Our mission is to report these horrors of war with accuracy and without prejudice." The Guardian, 22 Feb. 2012. Web. 7 Oct. 2022.
- https://www.theguardian.com/commentisfree/2012/feb/22/marie-colvin-our- mission-is-to-speak-truth >.
- Doucet, Lyse. "Yours, for Probably Always: Martha Gellhorn's Letters of Love and War 1930-1949 – review." The Guardian, 3 Dec. 2019. Web. 15 June. 2021.
- https://www.theguardian.com/books/2019/dec/03/yours-for-probably-always- matha-gellhorn-letters-love-war-1930-1949-janet-somerville-review >.
- Elber, Lynn. "In Ukraine, female war reporters build on legacy of pioneers." AP News, 15 March. 2022. Web. 7 Aug. 2022.

- https://apnews.com/article/russia-ukraine-europe-clarissa-ward-newspapers- media- 681cc59e7b7999b78 38f39bb16d60e36>.
- Elizalde. "Enough with 'All That Objectivity Shit'." Lenny, 27 April. 2018. Web. 13 Sept. 2020. < https://www.lennyletter.com/story/martha-gellhorn-changed-war-reporting-forever >.
- Fergusson, Patsy. "Are You a War Correspondent, or a Wife in My Bed." Fourth Wave, 17 May. 2021. Web. 30 June. 2022. < https://medium.com/fourth-
- wave/are-you-a-war-correspondent-or-a-wife-in-my-bed-add9cf90f1ff >.
- Ellison, Julie. *Delicate Subjects: Romanticism, Gender, and the Ethics of Understanding.* Ithaca and London: Cornell University Press, 1990.
- Fern, Fanny, "Amiable Creatures." In Ruth Hall and Other Writings. American Women Writers Series, edited by Joyce W. Warren, 310-11. New Brunswick, NJ and London: Rutgers University Press, 1990. Originally published in New York Ledger, March 12, 1859.
- "Male Criticism on Ladies Books." In Ruth Hall and Other Writings. American Women Writers Series, edited by Joyce W. Warren, 285-6. New Brunswick, NJ and London: Rutgers University Press, 1990. Originally published in New York Ledger, May 23, 1857.
- "Mrs. Adolphus Smith Sporting the 'Blue Stocking,'" In Ruth Hall and Other Writings. *American Women Writers Series*, edited by Joyce W. Warren, 265-66. New Brunswick, NJ and London: Rutgers University Press, 1990. Originally published in Fern Leaves, 1854.

- "A Practical Blue Stocking." In Ruth Hall and Other Writings. *American Women Writers Series*, edited by Joyce W. Warren, 232-35. New Brunswick, NJ and London: Rutgers University Press, 1990. Originally published in Olive Branch, August 2, 1852.

- Ruth Hall and Other Writings. Edited by Joyce W. Warren. New Brunswick and London: Rutgers University Press, 1986.

- "Tom Pax's Conjugal Soliloquy." In Ruth Hall and Other Writings. *American Women Writers Series*, edited by Joyce W. Warren, 268-69. New Brunswick, NJ and London: Rutgers University Press, 1990. Originally published in New York Ledger February 9, 1856.

- Fine, Lisa M. "Women's Movement." *The Oxford Companion to Women's Writing in the United States*, edited by Cathy N. Davidson and Linda Wagner-Martin, 933-9. New York: Oxford University Press, 1995.

- Fraser, Nancy. "Rethinking the Public Sphere: A Contribution to the Critique of Actually Existing Democracy." *Postmodernism and the Re-Reading of Modernity*, edited by Francis Barker and Margaret Iverson, 197-231.

- Manchester: The Essex Symposia: Literature/Politics/Theory, 1992.

- Fuller, Margaret. Woman in the Nineteenth Century. Edited by Larry J. Reynolds.

- New York: Norton Critical Editions, 1998.

- "The Wrongs of American Women. The Duty of American Women." In Margaret Fuller, Critic: Writings from the New-York Tribune, 1844-1846, edited by Judith

Mattson Bean and Joel Myerson, 233-39. New York: Columbia University Press, 2000. Originally published in the New York Daily Tribune, September 30, 1845.
- Fyrth, Jim and Sally Alexander, eds. Women's Voices from the Spanish Civil War.
- London: Lawrence & Wishart Ltd., 2008.Gallagher, Jean. The World Wars through the Female Gaze. Carbondale: Southern Illinois University Press, 1998. Print.
- Gallagher, Jean. *The World Wars Through the Female Gaze.* Carbondale and Edwardsville: Southern Illinois UP, 1998.
- Gutjahr, Paul. "Sentimental Men: Masculinity and the Politics of Affect in American Culture (review)." Duke University Press, 3 Sept. 2000. Web. 5 Nov. 2020.
- https://muse.jhu.edu/article/1558/pdf>.
- Hardy Dorman, Angelia. *Martha Gellhorn: Myth, Motif and Remembrance*, JettDrivePublications, Charleston, SC, 2015.
- Hartley, Maggie. "Martha Gellhorn: Eyewitness to War." WWI THE NATIONAL WWII MUSEUM NEW ORLEANS, 9 March. 2022. Web. 30 March. 2022.
- https://www.nationalww2museum.org/war/articles/martha-gellhorn-eyewitness-war>.
- Hoiby, Marte. "Sexual violence against journalists in conflict zones, and gendered practices and cultures in the newsroom." Academia, 2016. Web. 24 July. 2022.
- https://www.academia.edu/33497537/Sexual_violence_against_journalists_in_conflit_zones_and_gendered_practices_and_cultures_in_the_newsroom >.

- Karsten, Brian. "The Church of Craiglockhart: Wilfred Owen and Siegfried Sassoon Sassoon's Critique and Use of Religion in their Critique and Use of Religion in their World War I Poetry." Grand Valley State University, Dec. 2012. Web. March. 2021.<https:// scholarworks.gvsu.edu/cgi/viewcontent.cgi?article=1037&context=theses>.

- Knight, Sam. "A Memorial for the Remarkable Martha Gellhorn." *The New Yorker*, 18 Sept. 2019. Web. 11 Sept. 2022. < https://www.newyorker.com/news/letter-from-the-uk/a-memorial-for-the-remarkable-martha-gellhorn >.

- Lancaster, Marc. "D-DAY: MARTHA GELLHORN GOES ROGUE TO GET HER

- STORY." World War II on Deadline, *Collier's*, 7 June. 2020. Web. 19 Jan. 2022.< https://ww2ondeadline.com/2020/06/07/d-day-martha-gellhorn-ernest-hemingway-colliers/ >.

- Lippe, Berit von der. "Gendering War and Peace Reporting." Nordicom, 5 Dec. 2016.

- Web.15 Sept. 2022. < https://www.nordicom.gu.se/en/publications/gendering-war-and-peace-reporting >.

- Lyman, Rick. "Martha Gellhorn, Daring Writer, Dies at 89." The New York Times, 17 Feb. 1998. Web. 28 March. 2021.

- https://www.nytimes.com/1998/02/17/arts/martha-gellhorn-daring-writer-dies-at-89. html>.

- Mackrell, Judith. *The Correspondents: Six Women Writers on the Front Lines of World War II*, Vintage Books, New York, 2023.

- McEuen, Mellisa A. Seeing America: Women Photographers Between the Wars.
- University Press of Kentucky, 2004.
- McLain, Paula. *Love and Ruin: A Novel*. Ballantine Books, 2019.
- "The Extraordinary Life of Martha Gellhorn, the Woman Ernest Hemingway Tried toErase." Town & Country, 13 July. 2018. Web. 22 Oct. 2021.
- https://www.townandcountrymag.com/society/tradition/a22109842/martha-gellhorn-career-ernest-hemingway/ >.
- McLoughlin, Kate. *Martha Gellhorn: The War Writer in the Field and in the Text*, Manchester University Press, Manchester (GB), 2007.
- Moore, Charles., "Virginia Cowles: The American who Saw Britain at its Best" Rev.
- Looking for Trouble by Virginia Cowles. 15 Aug 2011. The Telegraph. Web. 20 Feb. 2014.
- Moorehead, Caroline. *Martha Gellhorn: A Life*, Vintage Digital, London, 2011.
- *Selected Letters of Martha Gellhorn*. Picador, 2013.
- Afterword. *The Face of War*, Gellhorn, Martha, London, 2016, pp. 317-319.
- Foreword. The Stricken Field, Gellhorn, Martha, The University of Chicago Press, 2011, pp. vi-ix.
- Afterword. *The Stricken Field*, Gellhorn, Martha, Virago press,1986, pp. 304-314.
- Introduction. *The Trouble I Have Seen*, Gellhorn, Martha,

Eland, 2012, pp. 2-19. Moreira, Peter. *Hemingway on the China Front: His WWII Spy Mission with Martha Gellhorn.* Potomac, 2007.

- Mundsh, Heike. "The liberation of Dachau, 75 years ago." DW, 29 April. 2020. Web. 20Dec. 2021. < https://www.dw.com/en/the-liberation-of-dachau-75-years-ago/a- 53270700 >.

- Ness, Angela. "Women War Correspondents and the Battles The Correspondents and the Battles They Overcame to Succeed." Washington University in St. Louis, 1 Jan. 2012.Web. 17 Feb. 2021.

- https://openscholarship.wustl.edu/cgi/viewcontent.cgi?article=1741&context=etd

- Orsagh, Jacqueline Elizabeth. *A Critical Biography of Martha Gellhorn. Ph.D. Dissertation.* Michigan State University. 1977.

- Olson, Liesl. *Modernism and Ordinary.* New York: Oxford University Press,2009.

- O'Toole, Fintan. "A Moral Witness: Fintan O'Toole." The New York Review of Books, 26 Oct. 2022. Web. 12 Nov. 2023.

- <https://www.nybooks.com/articles/2020/10/08/martha-gellhorn- moral-witness/>.

- Packard, Elizabeth Parsons Ware. *Modern Persecution or Insane Asylums Unveiled.*

- 1873. Reprint, New York: Arno Press, 1973.

- Pattee, Fred Lewis. *The Feminine Fifties.* New York: D. Appleton-Century Company, 1940.

- Pinder, Rodney, Judith Matloff, et al. "Women Reporting War Survey."

- Transcript of International News Safety Institute Debate at the Frontline Club, 20 Jan. 2005. Web. 12 Feb. 2021.
- http://www.newssafety.org/index.php?view=article&id=6214%3Awomen-war-reporters-air-safety concerns&option=com_content&Itemid=100081>.
- Ransley, Lattie. "The Trouble I've Seen by Martha Gellhorn – review." *The Guardian*, 24 March. 2013. Web. 15 Nov. 2020.
- https://www.theguardian.com/books/2013/mar/24/trouble-seen-martha-gellhorn- review >.
- Ray, Isaac. "A Treatise on the Medical Jurisprudence of Insanity." 1836. Harvard University Press, 01 Jan. 1962. Web. 09 Feb. 2022.
- https://www.hup.harvard.edu/catalog.php?isbn=9780674863682>.
- Reiss, Benjamin. *Theatres of Madness: Insane Asylums and Nineteenth-Century American Culture*. Chicago and London: The University of Chicago Press, 2008.
- Reynolds, Larry J. *Woman in the Nineteenth Century*, New York: Norton Critical Edition, 1998.
- Richards, Thomas. *The Commodity Culture of Victorian England 1851-1914*. London: Verso, 1991.
- Roggenkamp, Karen. *Narrating the News. Kent, OH and London: The Kent* State University Press, 2005.
- Rollyson, Carl E. *Nothing Ever Happens to the Brave: The Story of Martha Gellhorn*, Vermilion Bks., New York, 1990.
- *Beautiful Exile: The Life of Martha Gellhorn.* OPEN ROAD

DISTRIBUTION, 2016. Ross, Ishbel. *Ladies of the Press: The Story of Women in Journalism by an Insider.* New York and London: Harper & Brothers, 1936.

- Roosevelt, Eleanor. "My Day." The George Washington University, 26 Sept. 1962.
- Web. 8Jan. 2021. < https://erpapers.columbian.gwu.edu/my-day >.
- Rosen, Gerald. *Cold Eye, Warm Heart: A Novelist's Search for Meaning, CGA Winter 2016 Magazine,* Calm Unity Press,2009.
- Senstius, Bas. "Martha Gellhorn: A Furious Footnote in History." *Rozenberg Quartertly,* 1991. Web. 2021. < https://rozenbergquarterly.com/martha-gellhorn-a-furious- footnote-in-history/>.
- Seul, Stephanie. "Women War Reporters." *International Encyclopaedia,* 22 July. 2019. Web. 18 March. 2022.
- https://www.academia.edu/39951176/Women_War_Reporters>.
- Schudson, Michael. *Discovering the News: A Social History of American Newspapers.* New York: Basic Books, 1978.
- Showalter, Elaine. *The Female Malady: Women, Madness and English Culture 1830- 1980.* New York: Pantheon Books, 1985.
- Shute, Nancy. "MARTHA GELLHORN: A WOMAN AT WAR." Historynet, 26 April. 2018. Web. 25 Aug. 2021.
- https://www.historynet.com/martha-gellhorn-woman-war/ > .
- Smith, Susan Belasco and Kenneth M. Price. *Introduction*

to *Periodical Literature in Nineteenth-Century America,* Charlottesville and London: University of Virginia Press, 1995.

- Smith-Rosenberg, Carroll. *Disorderly Conduct: Visions of Gender in Victorian America.*
- Oxford: Oxford University Press, 1985.
- Smith, Wilda M. and Eleanor A. Bogart. *The Wars of Peggy Hull: The Life and Times of a War Correspondent.* El Paso: Texas Western Press, 1991.
- Somerville, Janet. *Yours, for Probably Always: Martha Gellhorn's Letters of Love & War, 1930-1949.* Firefly Books, 2022.
- "The Only Woman at D-Day: What Martha Gellhorn's
- Letters Reveal about the Trailblazing War Correspondent | CBC
  Radio." CBC news, CBC/Radio Canada, 6 Dec. 2019, https://www.cbc.ca/radio/day6/king- tides-impeach-o-meter-frosty-at-50-lindy-west-k-pop-deaths-and-mental- health-martha-gellhorn-more-1.5384775/the-only-woman-at-d-day-what- martha-gellhorn-s-letters-reveal-about-the-trailblazing-war-correspondent- 1.5384779.
- Staff, Impact. "Christiane Amanpour: A woman reporter with passion." *Impactonnet,* Web. 24 May. 2017. < https://www.impactonnet.com/amp/spotlight/christiane-amanpour-a-woman- reporter-with-passion-1849.html
- Stern, Julia. *The Plight of Feeling: Sympathy and Dissent in the Early American Novel.* Chicago and London: The University of Chicago Press, 1997.
- Stradling, Robert. *Your Children Will Be Next: Bombing*

and *Propaganda in the Spanish Civil War 1936-1939.* Cardiff: University of Wales Press, 2008.

- Stokes, Frederick A. "Three Modern Girls: What Mad Pursuit", *The New York Times,* 18 Nov. 1934. Web. 15 Oct. 2022.

- https://www.nytimes.com/1934/11/18/archives/three-modern-girls- what-mad-pursuit-by-martha-gellhorn-278-pp-new.html>

- Syeda, Seema. "War Reporters: Martha Gellhorn." Military History Matters, 1 Oct. 2019. Web. 3 Nov. 2020. <https://www.military-history.org/feature/world-war-2/war-reporters-martha-gellhorn.htm>.

- Szanton, Andrew. "Martha Gellhorn, a Great War Reporter." Medium, 24 Aug. 2022. Web. 12 Nov. 2022. < https://medium.com/@andrewszanton/martha-gellhorn- a-great-war-reporter-1a8beec5524e >.

- Taylor, Jasmine. "Martha Gellhorn: Quotes by a Courageous Woman." *Literary Ladies Guide,* 9 May. 2023. Web. 16 May. 2023.

- https://www.literaryladiesguide.com/author-quotes/martha-gellhorn-quotes-courageous-woman/>.

- Vaill, Amanda. *Hotel Florida: Truth, Love, and Death in the Spanish Civil War.* Picador,2015.

- Valis, Noel. "From the Face of My Memory': How American Women Journalists Covered the Spanish Civil War." *Springer,* 18 Oct. 2017. Web. 21 Sept. 2020.

- https://link.springer.com/article/10.1007/s12115-017-0189-7

- Walt, Vivienne. "Syria: War Reporter Marie Colvin and Photographer Rémi Ochlik

- AreKilled." TIME, 22 Feb. 2012. Web. 13 March. 2022.
- https://content.time.com/time/world/article/0,8599,2107394,00.html >.
- Wood, Robin. *Howard Hawks*. Detroit: Wayne State UP, 2006.
- Woolsey, Gamel. *Malaga Burning: An American Woman's Eyewitness Account of the Spanish Civil War*. U.S.: Pythia Press, 1998.
- Writer, Steve Newman. "Martha Gellhorn-Profile of a Writer." Medium, Medium, 27 Jan.2022. Web. 3 Jan. 2023. <https://stevenewmanwriter.medium.com/martha-gellhorn-portrait-of-a-writer- 82ad136ac16b>.
- Woolf, Christopher. "Remembering Clare Hollingworth, a reporter who broke the news of World War II." USA Today, 11 Jan. 2017. Web. 21 Aug. 2019.
- https://www.usatoday.com/story/news/world/2017/01/11/remembering-
- clare- hollingworth-reporter-who-broke-news-world-war-ii/96435238/>.

Black Eagle Books

www.blackeaglebooks.org
info@blackeaglebooks.org

Black Eagle Books, an independent publisher, was founded as a nonprofit organization in April, 2019. It is our mission to connect and engage the Indian diaspora and the world at large with the best of works of world literature published on a collaborative platform, with special emphasis on foregrounding Contemporary Classics and New Writing.

www.ingramcontent.com/pod-product-compliance
Lightning Source LLC
Chambersburg PA
CBHW060554080526
44585CB00013B/556